Ian Allan

abc
LOCOMOTIVES
1944

SOUTHERN RAILWAY
GREAT WESTERN RAILWAY
LONDON MIDLAND & SCOTTISH RAILWAY
LONDON & NORTH EASTERN RAILWAY

BCA

LONDON   NEW YORK   SYDNEY   TORONTO

This edition published 1993 by BCA by
arrangement with Ian Allan Ltd

CN 2108

First published 1944
First reprinted 1992
Second reprint 1993

Published by Ian Allan Ltd, Shepperton, Surrey;
and printed in Great Britain by
Ian Allan Printing Ltd, Coombelands House,
Addlestone, Surrey KT15 1HY

THE A B C OF
SOUTHERN
LOCOMOTIVES

Awaiting their duties—top link engines at Nine Elms.

THE A B C OF SOUTHERN LOCOMOTIVES

AT the time of the amalgamation there were 2,275 locomotives in service; but owing to suburban electrification on a vast scale many of the smaller engines were scrapped, while the introduction of newer and better types for express services made obsolete many of the former "crack" locos, which found themselves used for local and freight services, even though not really suitable. At present there are about 1,850 steam locos on the active list (including 5 service engines), 3 electric locos (including 2 service), and 3 Diesel engines.

The classes built between 1922 and 1937 include L 1, 4–4–0; S 15, 4–6–0; N, N 1, U, U 1, 2–6–0; W, 2–6–4 T; Z, 0–8–0 T; Q, 0–6–0; and, of course, "King Arthur," "Lord Nelson" and "Schools" classes. All these were built under the supervision of Mr. R. E. L. Maunsell, and have great similarity of detail.

After 1938, no further engines were built until 1941, when an entirely fresh type was seen—the "Merchant Navy" class, the first 4–6–2 tender engine to be used on the S.R. Hardly had these air-smoothed and unusually designed mixed traffic engines come into service when the Q 1 class followed. Built to cope with increasingly heavy war-time freight traffic, and presenting a most austere exterior, they have proved their worth, and are often to be seen working loads formerly hauled by H 15 and S 15 4–6–0s.

Another war-time innovation is the electric locomotive of Mr. A. Raworth's design. Mounted on two six-wheel motor bogies, it takes current from the third rail, but is fitted with pantagraphs for overhead wires, which have been installed in certain goods yards. It is capable of hauling loads up to 1,000 tons and speeds up to 75 m.p.h. (Full details of this locomotive appear in the "A B C of Southern Electrics.")

Classification.—The classification of Southern locomotives follows no hard and fast rule. The L.B. & S.C.R. appears to have been more methodical than the other lines in attempting a classification. Each class at first was lettered A, B, C, etc. Slight modifications of the design of the prototype were shown by the addition of a figure after the letter for the new type, and also a "1" after the letter of the original: thus, an alteration from E type is classed E 2, and all the E's become E 1, and so on. A rebuild is signified by an X following the class letter and number.

With the Eastern Section the termination of a figure 1 to a class designation letter shows that the original design has been modified and a new class produced or that the class has been rebuilt. This practice has been perpetuated by the Southern—N, N 1 ; Q, Q 1 ; etc.

" Dignity and Impudence."   G 16 and C 14 Class Locos at Feltham.

The duplication of classes " R " and " R 1 " is due to the fact that the " R " class, 0–4–4T, were London, Chatham and Dover Railway engines and still bear their original L.C. & D.R. class letter, while the " R 1," 0–4–4 T, although built for the S.E. & C.R. after the amalgamation of the L.C.D.R. and S.E.R., were a modification of the " R " class 0–4–4T. The " R " and " R 1 " classes of 0–6–0T were South Eastern Railway engines and retain their S.E.R. class letter.

The Western Section engine system of classes is based on the Works Order number for the first engine of the class to be built. These Order numbers run in a series from A 1, B 1 and C 1, etc., to Z 1, followed by A 2, B 2 to Z 2, and so on, the highest reached being C 17. They do not cover locomotives only, so that only a very few of them actually apply to new classes of engines. The system was slightly different at the beginning, so that the earliest class in the system, class A 12, does not follow the general rule. All classes of engines not built by the L.S.W.R., but bought from locomotive builders, were classified by the number of the first engine of the class to be delivered, for example, " 700 " class, although where both the L.S.W.R. and contractors built engines of the same class, the L.S.W.R. Order Number was used for the whole class, e.g., T 9 class.

Numbering.—After the grouping, engines belonging to the L.S.W.R., which formed the Western Section of the S.R., had an " E " added to their numbers, while engines of the L.B.S.C.R. and

4

S.E. & C.R. (the Central and Eastern Sections) had " B " and " A " added respectively. Engines built by the S.R. were allocated to the sections from which the designs originated, and were repaired at the Works for their respective sections. It should be mentioned that the fact that a locomotive belongs to a particular section does not mean that it is used in that section, particularly with classes of engines built since the grouping, which are generally used on all sections.

In 1931 the system of section letters was altered and Eastern Section engines had 1000 added to their numbers, Central Section engines, 2000, and Western Section engines retained their numbers with the " E " deleted. The only exception to this rule was that the " Z " class 0–8–0Ts (which were originally A 950–95) became 950–95, and were transferred to Eastleigh for repairs.

In 1931 all engine repairs at Brighton ceased and the work was divided between Ashford and Eastleigh. Ashford Works now repair all 0–6–0 and 0–6–2 T classes, with the exception of the E 1 R class, while Eastleigh deals with all the remaining classes. A small plate with either "A" or " E " on the cab side by the drivers' look-out on Brighton engines shows at which Works they are repaired.

The new style, introduced by Mr. Bulleid to the Southern, gives, in shorthand, the wheel-arrangement of the locomotive and its wheel-arrangement. Thus in 21C3 the 2 signifies the number of axles in front of the coupled wheels ; the 1 gives the number of axles behind the coupled wheels ; the letter, the number of coupled wheel axles (A:1, B:2, etc.) ; and the last figure is the engine's number. So that 21C3 means 4–6–2, No. 3.

Service engines do not conform to either of these systems. Numbers are all below 1,000, and each number is followed immediately by the letter S, *e.g.*, 680S.

*   *   *

Much has been written on the virtues of the popular locomotive types—the " Nelsons," the " Schools " and the " Arthurs "—but there are several most interesting engines tucked away in various parts of the system which one never hears about and rarely sees.

" Ironside " and " Clausentum " are two of these, the only representatives of the 0458 class. They were taken over by the L.S.W.R. in 1895 from the Southampton Docks Company. " Ironside " is now stationed at Guildford, and " Clausentum " at Eastleigh.

Four more interesting engines are 756, 757, 758 and 949, all built by Hawthorn Leslie in 1904–7. Very much alike in exterior appearance, they are named "A. S. Harris" (0–6–0 T), "Earl of Mount Edgcumbe" (0–6–2 T), "Lord St. Levan" (0–6–2 T) and "Hecate" (0–8–0 T). The first three were taken over from the Plymouth, Devonport and South Western. "A. S. Harris" is now domiciled at Fratton, while the other two are still shedded at Plymouth for working the Callington line service. "Hecate" came to the Southern from the Kent and East Sussex and is now well known at Clapham Junction, marshalling empty carriages.

Crane engine 1302, which is now at Stewarts Lane, has an interesting history. Built in 1881 by Neilson's as one of two works shunters for Ashford Works, it was transferred to Service stock as 234 S at the grouping. It was sent to Lancing Works in 1933, and was fitted with Westinghouse Brake pipes for working electric stock in the Works Yard. In 1938 it was returned to the Running Stock and received its original number.

The oldest S.R. engine now running is A1 X Class No. 2636, built in 1872. This also has had an interesting history. It was sold by the L.B.S.C.R. to the Newhaven Dock Company, and was absorbed into S.R. stock when the Dock Company was taken over at the time of the grouping. Before the present all-black livery was adopted for locomotives, 2636 had the doubtful honour of being the only "Terrier" to be painted black.

[A.B.M.

The Royal Engine, No. 119 (T9 Class).

ACKNOWLEDGMENTS

For kind assistance in the production of this book, and for the loan of photographs, sincere thanks are extended to the Southern Railway Company, and Messrs. B. W. Anwell, F. E. Box, A. B. MacLeod, O. J. Morris, A. R. Nicholls, S. Oborne and N. Wakeman.

LOCOMOTIVE RUNNING SHEDS

For the purposes of locomotive running, the Southern system is divided into two main sections—Eastern and Western—with a third division comprising the Isle of Wight. Below is a list of sheds and sub-sheds :—

Eastern Division.

STEWARTS LANE
BRICKLAYERS ARMS.
NEW CROSS GATE
   Norwood Junction
HITHER GREEN
TONBRIDGE
TUN. WELLS WEST
ASHFORD
   Canterbury West
DOVER MARINE
   Folkestone Jc.
REDHILL
GILLINGHAM
   Faversham
ST. LEONARDS
   (W. Marina)
   Bexhill
   Eastbourne
RAMSGATE
BRIGHTON
   Newhaven

Western Division.

NINE ELMS
FELTHAM
GUILDFORD
   Bordon
BASINGSTOKE
FRATTON
   Gosport
   Midhurst
HORSHAM
   Three Bridges
READING
SALISBURY
EASTLEIGH
   Winchester
   Southampton
   Lymington
   Andover Jc.

BOURNEMOUTH CTL.
   Swanage
   Hamworthy Junctn.
   Dorchester
YEOVIL
   Templecombe
EXMOUTH JUNCTION
   Seaton
   Lyme Regis
   Exmouth
   Okehampton
   Bude
   Launceston
   Plymouth Friary
   Callington
   Wadebridge
   Barnstaple
   Torrington
   Ilfracombe

Isle of Wight. RYDE Newport

The word "Southern" showing correct spacing.

Below: Some specimen numbers, also spaced correctly.

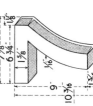

In these Diagrams

Black = **Black**

Tone = Green

White = **Yellow or Old Gold**

6" figure as used on buffer beam.

Specimen 9" letter and figure showing exact measurements

SOUTHERN RAILWAY STANDARD
LOCOMOTIVE LETTERING

It has become necessary for the Southern Railway during the war, owing to shortage of paint, to abandon its well-known green livery, and 1,234 steam locomotives have, therefore, on passing through the workshops, been repainted black. In order to retain a little of the bright green which previously adorned the passenger locomotives, lettering and numbering have been evolved, which, although dispensing with the gilt (for the purpose of economy), have, with an old gold (or yellow) colour, been shaded in the bright green already referred to. As the Railway in the past has been known as the " Sunshine Line," a yellow highlight has been added to the shading which represents the sunshine striking the block figures and letters.

For the especial benefit of model makers, particulars of the 9-in. standard lettering and numbering for cab, tank or tender sides are shown on the opposite page. Engines which bear this size of lettering have numbers of 6 in. height on the front buffer beam, the shape and body colour of these figures being the same as on the side sheeting, and black shading is used instead of the bright green, although the yellow highlight remains the same.

On the sheeting of some of the smaller tank engines space has been inadequate to take the 9-in. lettering, and a smaller size of 4-in. has been used, and in these cases the buffer beam figures have been reduced to 4½ in. The classes of engines in this latter category are as follow :—

A1X, B.4 (0-4-0 Tank), C 14, D1 (0-4-2 Tank), E 1 (0-6-0 Tank), E 1/R, E 2, G 6, 02, P, T, 756, 757, 1302, 0298, 0458, 0415, Diesel.

Q Class.

0395 Class. [A.B.M.

C 2X Class.

O I Class. [A.B.M.

FREIGHT LOCOMOTIVES

700 Class. [B.W.A.

C 3 Class. [O. J. Morris.

C Class.

WESTERN SECTION.	9 T 1	22 M 7	32 M 7	42 M 7
1 T 1	10 T 1	23 M 7	33 M 7	43 M 7
2 T 1	13 T 1	24 M 7	34 M 7	44 M 7
3 T 1	15 T 1	25 M 7	35 M 7	45 M 7
4 T 1	16 T 1	26 M 7	36 M 7	46 M 7
5 T 1	17 T 1	27 M 7†	37 M 7	47 M 7
6 T 1	20 T 1	28 M 7†	38 M 7	48 M 7
7 T 1		29 M 7†	39 M 7	49 M 7
8 T 1	21 M 7†	30 M 7	40 M 7	50 M 7
		31 M 7	41 M 7	51 M 7

T I Class.

52 M 7†	86 B 4	101 B 4	115 T 9	130 M 7
53 M 7†	87 B 4	102 B 4	116 T 9	131 M 7
54 M 7†	88 B 4	103 B 4	117 T 9	132 M 7
55 M 7†	89 B 4	104 M 7†	118 T 9	133 M 7
56 M 7†	90 B 4	105 M 7†	119 T 9	
57 M 7†	91 B 4	106 M 7†	120 T 9	134 L 11
58 M 7†	92 B 4	107 M 7†	121 T 9	
59 M 7†	93 B 4	108 M 7†	122 T 9	135 K 10
60 M 7†	94 B 4	109 M 7†		136 K 10
	95 B 4	110 M 7†	123 M 7	137 K 10
81 B 4	96 B 4	111 M 7†	124 M 7	138 K 10
82 B 4	97 B 4	112 M 7	125 M 7†	139 K 10
83 B 4	98 B 4		127 M 7	140 K 10
84 B 4	99 B 4	113 T 9	128 M 7†	141 K 10
85 B 4	100 B 4	114 T 9	129 M 7†	142 K 10

143 K 10
144 K 10
145 K 10
146 K 10

147 B 4

148 L 11

149 K 10
150 K 10
151 K 10
152 K 10
153 K 10

B 4 Class.   [A.B.M.

154	L 11	162	G 6	170	L 11	177	O 2	198	O 2
155	L 11			171	L 11	179	O 2	199	O 2
156	L 11	163	L 11	172	L 11	181	O 2	200	O 2
157	L 11	164	L 11	173	L 11	182	O 2†	201	O 2
158	L 11	165	L 11	174	L 11	183	O 2†	203	O 2
159	L 11	166	L 11	175	L 11	187	O 2†	204	O 2
160	G 6	167	L 11			192	O 2	207	O 2†
		168	L 11	176	B 4	193	O 2	212	O 2
161	L 11	169	L 11			197	O 2		

L II Class   [B.W.A.

L.S.W.R. DESIGN 4-6-0 TYPES

Express Passenger Locomotives.

T 14 Class.

Express Freight Locomotives.

H 15 Class. [B.W.A.

S 15 Class (1927-36 batch). [A. B. M

213	O	2	254	M	7	300	T	9	329	K 10		355		700
216	O	2	255	M	7	301	T	9	330	H 15		356	M	7
221	O	2	256	M	7	302	T	9	331	H 15		357	M	7
223	O	2	257	G	6	303	T	9	332	H 15		358	T	1
224	O	2	258	G	6	304	T	9	333	H 15		359	T	1
225	O	2†	259	G	6	305	T	9	334	H 15		360	T	1
228	O	2	260	G	6				335	H 15		361	T	1
229	O	2	261	G	6	306		700				363	T	1
230	O	2	262	G	6				336	T	9	364	T	1
231	O	2	263	G	6	307	T	9	337	T	9	366	T	1
232	O	2	264	G	6				338	T	9	367	T	1
233	O	2	265	G	6	308		700						
236	O	2	266	G	6	309		700	339		700	368		700
			267	G	6									
237	G	6	268	G	6	310	T	9	340	K 10		374	M	7
238	G	6	269	G	6	311	T	9	341	K 10		375	M	7
239	G	6	270	G	6	312	T	9	342	K 10		376	M	7
240	G	6	271	G	6	313	T	9	343	K 10		377	M	7
			272	G	6	314	T	9	344	K 10		378	M	7
			273	G	6				345	K 10		379	M	7†
241	M	7	274	G	6	315		700						
242	M	7	275	G	6	316		700	346		700	380	K 10	
243	M	7	276	G	6	317		700				381	K 10	
244	M	7	277	G	6				347	K 10		382	K 10	
245	M	7	278	G	6	318	M	7				383	K 10	
246	M	7	279	G	6	319	M	7	348	G	6	384	K 10	
247	M	7				320	M	7	349	G	6	385	K 10	
248	M	7	280	T	9	321	M	7				386	K 10	
249	M	7	281	T	9	322	M	7	350		700	387	K 10	
250	M	7	282	T	9	323	M	7				388	K 10	
251	M	7	283	T	9	324	M	7	351	G	6	389	K 10	
252	M	7	284	T	9							390	K 10	
253	M	7	285	T	9	325		700	352		700	391	K 10	
			286	T	9	326		700				392	K 10	
			287	T	9	327		700	353	G	6	393	K 10	
			288	T	9				354	G	6	394	K 10	
			289	T	9	328	M	7†						

No.	Class	No.	Class	No.	Class	No.	Class	No.	Class
		418	L 12	444	T 14	471	D 15	494	G 16
		419	L 12	445	T 14	472	D 15	495	G 16
		420	L 12	446	T 14			496	S 15
395	S 11	421	L 12	447	T 14	473	H 15	497	S 15
396	S 11	422	L 12			474	H 15	498	S 15
397	S 11	423	L 12	448	N 15	475	H 15	499	S 15
398	S 11	424	L 12	449	N 15	476	H 15	500	S 15
399	S 11	425	L 12	450	N 15	477	H 15	501	S 15
400	S 11	426	L 12	451	N 15	478	H 15	502	S 15
401	S 11	427	L 12	452	N 15			503	S 15
402	S 11	428	L 12	453	N 15			504	S 15
403	S 11	429	L 12	454	N 15	479	M 7	505	S 15
404	S 11	430	L 12	455	N 15	480	M 7†	506	S 15
		431	L 12	456	N 15	481	M 7†	507	S 15
405	L 11	432	L 12	457	N 15			508	S 15
406	L 11	433	L 12			482	H 15	509	S 15
407	L 11	434	L 12	459	T 14	483	H 15	510	S 15
408	L 11			460	T 14	484	H 15	511	S 15
409	L 11	435	L 11	461	T 14	485	H 15	512	S 15
410	L 11	436	L 11	462	T 14	486	H 15	513	S 15
411	L 11	437	L 11	463	D 15	487	H 15	514	S 15
412	L 11	438	L 11	464	D 15	488	H 15	515	S 15
413	L 11	439	L 11	465	D 15	489	H 15		
414	L 11	440	L 11	466	D 15	490	H 15		
		441	L 11	467	D 15	491	H 15	516	H 16
415	L 12	442	L 11	468	D 15			517	H 16
416	L 12			469	D 15	492	G 16	518	H 16
417	L 12	443	T 14	470	D 15	493	G 16	519	H 16

A 12 Class. [A. B. M.

This locomotive, seen above at Guildford, is now
withdrawn from service.

M 7 Class.

Western	546	Q	630	A 12	676	M 7	709	T 9
Section—	547	Q	634	A 12			710	T 9
continued.	548	Q	636	A 12			711	T 9
520	H 16	549	Q	637	A 12	687	700	712	T 9
				638	A 12	688	700	713	T 9
521	H 15			641	A 12	689	700	714	T 9
522	H 15	563	T 3	642	A 12	690	700	715	T 9
523	H 15			643	A 12	691	700	716	T 9
524	H 15			644	A 12	692	700	717	T 9
		597	A 12	648	A 12	693	700	718	T 9
530	Q	598	A 12	649	A 12	694	700	719	T 9
531	Q	599	A 12	652	A 12	695	700	721	T 9
532	Q	600	A 12	654	A 12	696	700	722	T 9
533	Q	606	A 12			697	700	723	T 9
534	Q	609	A 12			698	700	724	T 9
535	Q	612	A 12	658	X 6	699	700	725	T 9
536	Q	613	A 12			700	700	726	T 9
537	Q	614	A 12			701	700	727	T 9
538	Q	615	A 12	667	M 7			728	T 9
539	Q	618	A 12	668	M 7			729	T 9
540	Q	620	A 12	669	M 7	702	T 9	730	T 9
541	Q	623	A 12	670	M 7	703	T 9	731	T 9
542	Q	624	A 12	671	M 7	704	T 9	732	T 9
543	Q	625	A 12	672	M 7	705	T 9	733	T 9
544	Q	627	A 12	673	M 7	706	T 9		
545	Q	629	A 12	674	M 7	707	T 9		
				675	M 7	708	T 9	734	0458

"Schools" class No. 930, "Radley" with new large diameter chimney.

736 N 15	763 N 15	791 N 15	834 S 15	863 L.N.
737 N 15	764 N 15	792 N 15	835 S 15	864 L.N.
738 N 15	765 N 15	793 N 15	836 S 15	865 L.N.
739 N 15	766 N 15	794 N 15	837 S 15	
740 N 15	767 N 15	795 N 15	838 S 15	
741 N 15	768 N 15	796 N 15	839 S 15	900 V
742 N 15	769 N 15	797 N 15	840 S 15	901 V
743 N 15	770 N 15	798 N 15	841 S 15	902 V
744 N 15	771 N 15	799 N 15	842 S 15	903 V
745 N 15	772 N 15	800 N 15	843 S 15	904 V
746 N 15	773 N 15	801 N 15	844 S 15	905 V
747 N 15	774 N 15	802 N 15	845 S 15	906 V
748 N 15	775 N 15	803 N 15	846 S 15	907 V
749 N 15	776 N 15	804 N 15	847 S 15	908 V
750 N 15	777 N 15	805 N 15		909 V
751 N 15	778 N 15	806 N 15	850 L.N.*	910 V
752 N 15	779 N 15		851 L.N.	911 V
753 N 15	780 N 15	823 S 15	852 L.N.	912 V
754 N 15	781 N 15	824 S 15	853 L.N.	913 V
755 N 15	782 N 15	825 S 15	854 L.N.	914 V
	783 N 15	826 S 15	855 L.N.	915 V
	784 N 15	827 S 15	856 L.N.	916 V
	785 N 15	828 S 15	857 L.N.	917 V
	786 N 15	829 S 15	858 L.N.	918 V
	787 N 15	830 S 15	859 L.N.	919 V
756 0.6.0T	788 N 15	831 S 15	860 L.N.	920 V
757 0.6.2T	789 N 15	832 S 15	861 L.N.	921 V
758 0.6.2T	790 N 15	833 S 15	862 L.N.	922 V

* L.N.: "Lord Nelson" class.

949 "Hecate." ⌈A.B.M.

Z Class.

923	V	**EASTERN**		1046	O 1	1101	B 1	1164	H	
924	V	**SECTION.**		1047	R 1	1102	C	1165	E 1	
925	V			1048	O 1	1105	F 1	1166	E	
926	V	1002	F 1	1051	O 1	1106	O 1	1174	R 1	
927	V	1003	O 1	1054	C	1107	R 1	1175	E	
928	V	1004	C	1057	D	1108	O 1	1176	E	
929	V	1005	H	1059	C	1109	O 1	1177	H	
930	V	1007	O 1	1060	F 1	1110	F 1	1178	P	
931	V	1010	R 1	1061	C	1112	C	1179	E 1	
932	V	1013	B 1	1062	F 1	1113	C	1182	H	
933	V	1014	O 1	1063	C	1123	O 1	1183	F 1	
934	V	1016	H	1064	O 1	1127	R 1	1184	H	
935	V	1018	C	1065	O 1	1128	R 1	1188	F 1	
936	V	1019	E 1	1066	O 1	1140	F 1	1191	C	
937	V	1021	B 1	1067	E 1	1145	D 1	1193	H	
938	V	1027	P	1068	C	1147	R 1	1195	F 1	
939	V	1028	F 1	1069	R 1	1150	C	1205	F 1	
949 K.E.S.		1031	F 1	1071	C	1151	F 1	1215	F 1	
		1033	C	1075	D	1154	R 1	1217	B 1	
950	Z	1036	E	1078	F 1	1156	F 1	1218	C	
951	Z	1037	C	1079	F 1	1157	E	1219	C	
952	Z	1038	C	1080	O 1	1158	H	1221	C	
953	Z	1039	O 1	1084	F 1	1159	E	1223	C	
954	Z	1041	O 1	1086	C	1160	E 1	1225	C	
955	Z	1042	F 1	1090	C	1161	H	1227	C	
956	Z	1043	F 1	1092	D	1162	H	1229	C	
957	Z	1044	O 1	1093	O 1	1163	E 1	1231	F 1	

1234	C	1262	C	1297	C	1326	H	1388	O 1
1238	O 1	1263	H	1298	C	1327	H	1389	O 1
1239	H	1264	H			1328	H	1390	O 1
1242	C	1265	H	1302		1329	H	1391	O 1
1243	C	1266	H		0.4.0 CT			1395	O 1
1244	C	1267	C					1396	O 1
1245	C	1268	C	1305	H	1335	R 1	1397	O 1
1246	D 1	1269	H	1306	H	1337	R 1	1398	O 1
1247	D 1	1270	C	1307	H	1339	R 1		
1248	O 1	1271	C	1308	H	1340	R 1		
1251	O 1	1272	C	1309	H			1400	N
1252	C	1273	E	1310	H			1401	N
1253	C	1274	H	1311	H	1369	O 1	1402	N
1255	C	1275	E	1312	H	1370	O 1	1403	N
1256	C	1276	H	1315	E	1373	O 1	1404	N
1257	C	1277	C	1316	O 1	1374	O 1	1405	N
1258	O 1	1278	H	1317	C	1377	O 1	1406	N
1259	H	1279	H	1319	H	1378	O 1	1407	N
1260	C	1280	C	1320	H	1379	O 1	1408	N
1261	H	1287	C	1321	H	1380	O 1	1409	N
		1291	C	1322	H	1381	O 1	1410	N
		1293	C	1323	P	1384	O 1	1411	N
		1294	C	1324	H	1385	O 1	1412	N
		1295	H	1325	P	1386	O 1	1413	N

R 1 Class.

Eastern			1449	B	1	1492	D	1	1514	E		1547	E
Section—			1450	B	1	1493	D		1515	E		1548	H
continued.			1451	B	1	1494	D	1	1516	E		1549	D
1414	N		1452	B	1	1495	C		1517	H			
			1453	B	1	1496	D		1518	H		1550	H
1425	O	1	1454	B	1	1497	E	1	1519	H		1551	H
1426	O	1	1455	B	1	1498	C		1520	H		1552	H
1428	O	1	1457	B	1	1499	C		1521	H		1553	H
1429	O	1	1459	B	1	1500	H		1522	H		1554	H
1430	O	1				1501	D		1523	H			
1432	O	1	1460	C		1502	D	1	1530	H		1555	P
1434	O	1	1461	C		1503	H		1531	H		1556	P
1437	O	1	1470	D	1	1504	E	1	1532	H		1557	P
1438	O	1	1477	D		1505	D	1	1533	H		1558	P
1439	O	1	1480	C		1506	E	1	1540	H			
			1481	C		1507	E	1	1541	H		1572	C
1440	B	1	1486	C		1508	C		1542	H		1573	C
1441	B	1	1487	D	1	1509	D	1	1543	H			
1443	B	1	1488	D		1510	C		1544	H		1574	D
1445	B	1	1489	D	1	1511	E	1				1575	C
1446	B	1	1490	D		1512	H		1545	D	1	1576	C
1448	B	1	1491	E		1513	C		1546	H			

N Class.

Next to the loco is a self-propelled break-down crane.

1577 D

1578 C
1579 C
1580 C
1581 C
1582 C
1583 C
1584 C
1585 C

T Class.   [S.O.

1586	D	1595	J	1613	U	1624	U
		1596	J	1614	U	1625	U
1587	E	1597	J	1615	U	1626	U
1588	C	1598	J	1616	U	1627	U
1589	C	1599	J	1617	U	1628	U
1590	C			1618	U	1629	U
		1602	T	1619	U	1630	U
1591	D	1604	T	1620	U	1631	U
		1610	U	1621	U	1632	U
1592	C	1611	U	1622	U	1633	U
1593	C	1612	U	1623	U	1634	U

1635	U
1636	U
1637	U
1638	U
1639	U
1658	R†
1659	R†
1660	R†
1661	R
1662	R†

J Class.

23

Eastern Section—continued.									
1663	R†	1703	R 1†	1739	D 1	1776	L	1811	N
1665	R†	1704	R 1†	1740	D	1777	L	1812	N
1666	R†	1705	R 1	1741	D 1	1778	L	1813	N
1667	R	1706	R 1†	1742	D	1779	L	1814	N
1670	R†	1707	R 1†	1743	D 1	1780	L	1815	N
1671	R†	1708	R 1	1744	D	1781	L	1816	N
1672	R†	1709	R 1	1745	D 1			1817	N
1673	R	1710	R 1†	1746	D	1782	L 1	1818	N
1674	R			1747	D 1	1783	L 1	1819	N
1675	R†	1711	C	1748	D	1784	L 1	1820	N
		1712	C	1749	D 1	1785	L 1	1821	N
1681	C	1713	C	1750	D	1786	L 1		
1682	C	1714	C			1787	L 1		
1683	C	1715	C	1753	L 1	1788	L 1	1822	N 1
1684	C	1716	C	1754	L 1	1789	L 1		
		1717	C	1755	L 1			1823	N
1685	S	1718	C	1756	L 1	1790	U	1824	N
		1719	C	1757	L 1	1791	U	1825	N
		1720	C	1758	L 1	1792	U	1826	N
		1721	C	1759	L 1	1793	U	1827	N
		1722	C			1794	U	1828	N
1686	C	1723	C	1760	L	1795	U	1829	N
1687	C	1724	C	1761	L	1796	U	1830	N
1688	C	1725	C	1762	L	1797	U	1831	N
1689	C	1726	D	1763	L	1798	U	1832	N
1690	C	1727	D 1	1764	L	1799	U	1833	N
1691	C	1728	D	1765	L	1800	U	1834	N
1692	C	1729	D	1766	L	1801	U	1835	N
1693	C	1730	D	1767	L	1802	U	1836	N
1694	C	1731	D	1768	L	1803	U	1837	N
1695	C	1732	D	1769	L	1804	U	1838	N
		1733	D	1770	L	1805	U	1839	N
1696	R 1	1734	D	1771	L	1806	U	1840	N
1697	R 1†	1735	D 1	1772	L	1807	U	1841	N
1698	R 1	1736	D 1	1773	L	1808	U	1842	N
1699	R 1	1737	D	1774	L	1809	U	1843	N
1700	R 1†	1738	D	1775	L	1810	N	1844	N

1845	N	1860	N	1875	N	1898	U 1	1912	W
1846	N	1861	N	1876	N 1	1899	U 1	1913	W
1847	N	1862	N	1877	N 1	1900	U 1	1914	W
1848	N	1863	N	1878	N 1	1901	U 1	1915	W
1849	N	1864	N	1879	N 1	1902	U 1	1916	W
1850	N	1865	N	1880	N 1	1903	U 1	1917	W
1851	N	1866	N			1904	U 1	1918	W
1852	N	1867	N	1890	U 1	1905	U 1	1919	W
1853	N	1868	N	1891	U 1	1906	U 1	1920	W
1854	N	1869	N	1892	U 1	1907	U 1	1921	W
1855	N	1870	N	1893	U 1	1908	U 1	1922	W
1856	N	1871	N	1894	U 1	1909	U 1	1923	W
1857	N	1872	N	1895	U 1	1910	U 1	1924	W
1858	N	1873	N	1896	U 1			1925	W
1859	N	1874	N	1897	U 1	1911	W		

U I Class.

W Class.

25

	2054 B 4	2101 E 2	2215 D 1§	2330 N 15X
	2055 B 4X	2102 E 2	2220 D 1§	2331 N 15X
	2056 B 4X	2103 E 2	2229 D 1†	2332 N 15X
2001 I 1X	2060 B 4X	2104 E 2	2232 D 1†	2333 N 15X
2002 I 1X	2062 B 4	2105 E 2	2233 D 1	
2003 I 1X	2063 B 4	2106 E 2	2234 D 1†	2337 K
2004 I 1X	2067 B 4X	2107 E 2	2235 D 1†	2338 K
2005 I 1X	2068 B 4	2108 E 2	2239 D 1§	2339 K
2006 I 1X	2070 B 4X	2109 E 2	2240 D 1	2340 K
2007 I 1X	2071 B 4X		2244 D 1§	2341 K
2008 I 1X	2072 B 4X	2112 E 1	2252 D 1§	2342 K
2009 I 1X	2073 B 4X	2113 E 1	2253 D 1§	2343 K
2010 I 1X	2074 B 4	2122 E 1	2255 D 1§	2344 K
		2124 E 1/R	2259 D 1†	2345 K
	2075 I 3	2127 E 1	2260 D 1	2346 K
2021 I 3	2076 I 3	2128 E 1	2269 D 1†	2347 K
2022 I 3	2077 I 3	2129 E 1	2274 D 1†	2348 K
2023 I 3	2078 I 3	2133 E 1	2283 D 1†	2349 K
2024 I 3	2079 I 3	2135 E 1/R	2284 D 1†	2350 K
2025 1 3	2080 I 3	2138 E 1	2286 D 1	2351 K
2026 I 3	2081 I 3	2139 E 1	2289 D 1†	2352 K
2027 I 3	2082 I 3	2141 E 1	2299 D 1†	2353 K
2028 I 3	2083 I 3	2142 E 1	2300 C 3	2355 D 1†
2029 I 3	2084 I 3	2145 E 1	2301 C 3	2357 D 1§
2030 I 3	2085 I 3	2147 E 1	2302 C 3	2358 D 1†
	2086 I 3	2151 E 1	2303 C 3	2359 D 1
2037 H 1	2087 I 3	2153 E 1	2306 C 3	2361 D 1†
2038 H 1	2088 I 3	2156 E 1	2307 C 3	
2039 H 1	2089 I 3	2160 E 1	2308 C 3	2363 D 3†
	2090 I 3	2162 E 1	2309 C 3	2364 D 3†
	2091 I 3	2164 E 1		2365 D 3†
2042 B 4		2165 E 3	2325 J 1	2366 D 3†
2043 B 4X	2094 E 1/R	2166 E 3	2326 J 2	2367 D 3†
2044 B 4	2095 E 1/R	2167 E 3	2327 N 15X	2368 D 3†
2045 B 4X	2096 E 1/R	2168 E 3	2328 N 15X	2370 D 3†
2050 B 4X	2097 E 1	2169 E 3	2329 N 15X	2371 D 3†
2051 B 4		2170 E 3		2372 D 3†
2052 B 4X	2100 E 2			2373 D 3†

B 4X Class.

I 3 Class.   [B.W.A.

K Class.

27

No.	Code	No.	Code	No.	Code	No.	Code	No.	Code
		2412	E 6	2458	E 3	2495	E 4	2534	C 2X
		2413	E 6	2459	E 3	2496	E 4	2535	C 2X
		2414	E 6	2460	E 3	2497	E 4	2536	C 2X
2374	D 3†	2415	E 6	2461	E 3	2498	E 4	2537	C 2X
2376	D 3†	2416	E 6	2462	E 3	2499	E 4	2538	C 2X
2377	D 3†	2417	E 6			2500	E 4	2539	C 2X
2378	D 3†	2418	E 6	2463	E 4	2501	E 4	2540	C 2X
2379	D 3†			2464	E 4	2502	E 4	2541	C 2X
2380	D 3†	2421	H 2	2465	E 4	2503	E 4	2543	C 2X
2383	D 3†	2422	H 2	2466	E 4X	2504	E 4	2544	C 2X
2384	D 3†	2423	H 2	2467	E 4	2505	E 4	2545	C 2X
2385	D 3†	2424	H 2	2468	E 4	2506	E 4	2546	C 2X
2386	D 3†	2425	H 2	2469	E 4	2507	E 4	2547	C 2X
2387	D 3†	2426	H 2	2470	E 4	2508	E 4	2548	C 2X
2388	D 3†			2471	E 4	2509	E 4	2549	C 2X
2389	D 3†	2434	C 2X	2472	E 4	2510	E 4	2550	C 2X
2390	D 3†	2435	C 2	2473	E 4	2511	E 4	2551	C 2X
2391	D 3†	2436	C 2	2474	E 4	2512	E 4	2552	C 2X
2393	D 3†	2437	C 2X	2475	E 4	2513	E 4	2553	C 2X
2394	D 3†	2438	C 2X	2476	E 4	2514	E 4	2554	C 2X
2395	D 3†	2440	C 2X	2477	E 4X	2515	E 4	2556	E 4
2397	D 3X	2441	C 2X	2478	E 4X	2516	E 4	2557	E 4
2398	D 3†	2442	C 2 X	2479	E 4	2517	E 4	2558	E 4
		2443	C 2 X	2480	E 4	2518	E 4	2559	E 4
2399	E 5	2444	C 2 X	2481	E 4	2519	E 4	2560	E 4
2400	E 5	2445	C 2 X	2482	E 4	2520	E 4	2561	E 4
2401	E 5X	2446	C 2 X	2483	E 4			2562	E 4
2402	E 5	2447	C 2 X	2484	E 4	2521	C 2X	2563	E 4
2403	E 5	2448	C 2 X	2485	E 4	2522	C 2X	2564	E 4
2404	E 5	2449	C 2 X	2486	E 4	2523	C 2X	2565	E 4
2405	E 5	2450	C 2 X	2487	E 4	2524	C 2X	2566	E 4
2406	E 5	2451	C 2 X	2488	E 4	2525	C 2X		
				2489	E 4X	2526	C 2X	2567	E 5
2407	E 6X	2453	E 3	2490	E 4	2527	C 2X	2568	E 5
2408	E 6	2454	E 3	2491	E 4	2528	C 2X	2570	E 5X
2409	E 6	2455	E 3	2492	E 4	2529	C 2X	2571	E 5
2410	E 6	2456	E 3	2493	E 4	2532	C 2X	2572	E 5
2411	E 6X	2457	E 3	2494	E 4	2533	C 2	2573	E 5

E 4 Class. [A.B.M.

Central Section—*continued.*									
		2581	E 4	2591	E 5	2602	I 1X	2635	A 1X
		2582	E 4	2592	E 5	2603	I 1X	2636	A 1X
				2593	E 5	2604	I 1X	2644	A 1X
2574	E 5	2583	E 5	2594	E 5			2647	A 1X
2575	E 5	2584	E 5	2595	I 1X	2605	D 1†	2655	A 1X
2576	E 5X	2585	E 5	2596	I 1X	2606	E 1	2659	A 1X
		2586	E 5X	2597	I 1X	2608	E 1/R	2661	A 1X
2577	E 4	2587	E 5	2598	I 1X	2609	E 1	2662	A 1X
2578	E 4	2588	E 5	2599	I 1X	2610	E 1/R	2678	A 1X
2579	E 4	2589	E 5	2600	I 1X				
2580	E 4	2590	E 5	2601	I 1X	2627	D 1†	2689	E 1

E 5 Class. [O. J. Morris

29

Central Section— continued.		Western Section— continued.							
2690	E 1	3496	0395	26	O 2	C 11	Q 1		
2691	E 1	3506	0395	27	O 2	C 12	Q 1		
2694	E 1	3509	0395	28	O 2	C 13	Q 1		
2695	E 1/R	3520	0415	29	O 2	C 14	Q 1	**DIESEL**	
2696	E 1/R	3741	C 14	30	O 2	C 15	Q 1	**LOCOS.**	
2697	E 1/R	3744	C 14	31	O 2	C 16	Q 1		
2699	D 1†			32	O 2	C 17	Q 1	1	0.6.0
				33	O 2	C 18	Q 1	2	0.6.0
						C 19	Q 1	3	0.6.0
						C 20	Q 1		
						C 21	Q 1		
						C 22	Q 1		
Western Section— continued.		ISLE OF WIGHT LOCOS.		NEW STYLE NUMBER- ING.		C 23	Q 1	**SERVICE**	
						C 24	Q 1	**LOCOS.**	
						C 25	Q 1		
						C 26	Q 1	74S	Bo+Bo
3029	0395	1	E 1	21C1	MN	C 27	Q 1	75S	Bo
3083	0395	2	E 1	21C2	MN	C 28	Q 1	77S	C14
3101	0395	3	E 1	21C3	MN	C 29	Q 1	380S	A1
3125	0415	4	E 1	21C4	MN	C 30	Q 1	500S	T
3154	0395			21C5	MN	C 31	Q 1	515S	A1X
3155	0395	8	A1X†	21C6	MN	C 32	Q 1	680S	A
3163	0395	11	A1X†	21C7	MN	C 33	Q 1		
3167	0395	13	A1X†	21C8	MN	C 34	Q 1	Petrol Shunt-	
3298	0298			21C9	MN	C 35	Q 1	ing Loco.	
3314	0298	14	O 2	21C10	MN	C 36	Q 1		
3329	0298	15	O 2			C 37	Q 1		
3397	0395	16	O 2	C 1	Q 1	C 38	Q 1		
3400	0395	17	O 2	C 2	Q 1	C 39	Q 1		
3433	0395	18	O 2	C 3	Q 1	C 40	Q 1		
3436	0395	19	O 2	C 4	Q 1				
3439	0395	20	O 2	C 5	Q 1			† Fitted for	
3440	0395	21	O 2	C 6	Q 1			Motor	
3441	0395	22	O 2	C 7	Q 1			Working.	
3442	0395	23	O 2	C 8	Q 1	**ELECTRIC**			
3458	0458	24	O 2	C 9	Q 1	**LOCO.**		§ Fitted for	
		25	O 2	C 10	Q 1	CC1	CC	Fire-fighting	

T Class (**5005 in original S.R. numbering A555**).

Q I Class.

EASTERN SECTION 4-4-0 TYPES

L Class.

D Class.

L I Class.

D I Class.

B I Class.

33

"Lord Nelson" Class Loco. 852 "Sir Walter Raleigh"

NAMED ENGINES

"Merchant Navy" Class (21C).

21C1	Channel Packet	21C6	Peninsular & Oriental
21C2	Union Castle	21C7	Aberdeen [S. N. Co.
21C3	Royal Mail		Commonwealth
21C4	Cunard White Star	21C8	Orient Line
21C5	Canadian Pacific	21C9	Shaw Savill
		21C10	Blue Star

"Lord Nelson" Class.

850	Lord Nelson	858	Lord Duncan
851	Sir Francis Drake	859	Lord Hood
852	Sir Walter Raleigh	860	Lord Hawke
853	Sir Richard Grenville	861	Lord Anson
854	Howard of Effingham	862	Lord Collingwood
855	Robert Blake	863	Lord Rodney
856	Lord St. Vincent	864	Sir Martin Frobisher
857	Lord Howe	865	Sir John Hawkins

"King Arthur" Class (N 15).

448	Sir Tristram	457	Sir Bedivere
449	Sir Torre		
450	Sir Kay	736	Excalibur
451	Sir Lamorak	737	King Uther
452	Sir Meliagrance	738	King Pellinore
453	King Arthur	739	King Leodegrance
454	Queen Guinevere	740	Merlin
455	Sir Launcelot	741	Joyous Gard
456	Sir Galahad	742	Camelot
		743	Lyonnesse

"King Arthur" Class Loco. 755, "The Red Knight"
(as now fitted with large diameter chimney).

36

"King Arthur" Class (N 15).

—continued.

744	Maid of Astolat	779	Sir Colgrevance
745	Tintagel	780	Sir Persant
746	Pendragon	781	Sir Aglovale
747	Elaine	782	Sir Brian
748	Vivien	783	Sir Gillemere
749	Iseult	784	Sir Nerovens
750	Morgan le Fay	785	Sir Mador de la Porte
751	Etarre	786	Sir Lionel
752	Linette	787	Sir Menadeuke
753	Melisande	788	Sir Urre of the Mount
754	The Green Knight	789	Sir Guy
755	The Red Knight	790	Sir Villiars
		791	Sir Uwaine
763	Sir Bors de Ganis	792	Sir Hervis de Revel
764	Sir Gawain	793	Sir Ontzlake
765	Sir Gareth	794	Sir Ector de Maris
766	Sir Geraint	795	Sir Dinadan
767	Sir Valence	796	Sir Dodinas le Savage
768	Sir Balin	797	Sir Blamor de Ganis
769	Sir Balan	798	Sir Hectimere
770	Sir Prianius	799	Sir Ironside
771	Sir Sagramore	800	Sir Meleaus de Lile
772	Sir Percivale	801	Sir Meliot de Logres
773	Sir Lavaine	802	Sir Durnore
774	Sir Gaheris	803	Sir Harry le Fise Lake
775	Sir Agravaine	804	Sir Cador of Cornwall
776	Sir Galagars	805	Sir Constantine
777	Sir Lamiel	806	Sir Galleron
778	Sir Pelleas		

Miscellaneous Locos.

756	A. S. Harris	758	Lord St. Levan
757	Earl of Mount Edgcombe	949	Hecate

"Schools" Class (V).

900	Eton	920	Rugby
901	Winchester	921	Shrewsbury
902	Wellington	922	Marlborough
903	Charterhouse	923	Bradfield
904	Lancing	924	Haileybury
905	Tonbridge	925	Cheltenham
906	Sherborne	926	Repton
907	Dulwich	927	Clifton
908	Westminster	928	Stowe
909	St. Paul's	929	Malvern
910	Merchant Taylors	930	Radley
911	Dover	931	King's Wimbledon
912	Downside	932	Blundells
913	Christ's Hospital	933	King's Canterbury
914	Eastbourne	934	St. Lawrence
915	Brighton	935	Sevenoaks
916	Whitgift	936	Cranleigh
917	Ardingly	937	Epsom
918	Hurstpierpoint	938	St. Olave's
919	Harrow	939	Leatherhead

B 4 Class ("Dock Engines").

81	Jersey	93	St. Malo	101	Dinan
85	Alderney	95	Honfleur	102	Granville
86	Havre	96	Normandy	147	Dinard
89	Trouville	97	Brittany	176	Guernsey
90	Caen	98	Cherbourg		

"Remembrance" Class (N 15X).

2327	Trevithick	2330	Cudworth
2328	Hackworth	2331	Beattie
2329	Stephenson	2332	Stroudley

2333   Remembrance

"Brighton Atlantic" Type.

H I Class.

2037	Selsey Bill
2038	Portland Bill
2039	Hartland Point

H 2 Class.

2421	South Foreland
2422	North Foreland
2423	The Needles
2424	Beachy Head
2425	Trevose Head
2426	St. Alban's Head

734　Clausentum　　　　　　3458　Ironside

2-4-0 " BEATTIE WELL TANKS "

" 0298 " Class.

　　The Well tanks, one of which is shown above, are the oldest engines now working on the Southern. They were introduced in 1863 and 83 put into service. They proved most successful on sub-urban services but gradually increasingly heavy loads proved too much for them and they were all scrapped except three, which are now shedded at Wadebridge for working the Wenford china clay branch.

ISLE OF WIGHT ENGINES

O 2 Class. [B. W. Anwell.

E I Class

1 Medina
2 Yarmouth
3 Ryde
4 Wroxall

A IX Class

8 Freshwater
11 Newport
13 Carisbrooke

O 2 Class

14 Fishbourne
15 Cowes
16 Ventnor
17 Seaview
18 Ningwood
19 Osborne
20 Shanklin
21 Sandown
22 Brading

23 Totland
24 Calbourne
25 Godshill
26 Whitwell
27 Merstone
28 Ashey
29 Alverstone
30 Shorwell
31 Chale
32 Bonchurch
33 Bembridge

E I Class.

41

PRINCIPAL DIMENSIONS OF S.R. LOCOMOTIVES

Where a rebuild class appears in the following list (except D 15, T 9 and 700 classes) the man who designed the rebuild is shown as the designer, and the "building date" is the date the rebuild took place. (All locomotives have two cylinders unless another number is in parentheses in the cylinders column).

CLASS	WHEELS	DESIGNER	BUILDING DATE	WEIGHT OF LOCO. tons. cwt.	BOILER PRESSURE LB. PER SQ. IN.	CYLINDERS ins.	DRIVING WHEELS	TRACTIVE EFFORT at 85 % B.P. LB.	No. OF LOCOS	
A 1 X	0.6.0 T	Marsh ¶¶	1911–32	28 5	150	12 × 20	4' 0"	7,600	13	"Terriers," "Rooters," "Jubilees," "Flying Bedsteads"
A 12	0.4.2	Adams	1887–95	43 8	160	18 × 26	6' 0"	15,900	30	
B 1	0.4.0	Wainwright †	1911–27	45 2	170	18 × 26	7' 0"	14,500	19	
B 4	0.4.0 T	Adams	1891–93	33 9	140	16 × 22	3' 9¼"	14,660	25	—
B 4	4.4.0	Drummond	1908	32 18	180	19 × 26¼‡	6' 9"	17,700‡	8	"Scotchmen,"
B 4 X	4.4.0	L. Billinton *	1899–02 1922–24	51 1	180	20 × 26	6' 9"	19,645	12	"Greybacks,"
C	0.6.0	Wainwright	1900–08	43 16	160	18½ × 26	5' 2"	19,519	108	
CC	Co + Co	Raworth	1942	99 2	—	—	—	18,050	1	Electric loco
C 2	0.6.0	R. Billinton	1893–02	39 10	160	17½ × 26	5' 0"	18,050	3	"Small Vulcans,"
C 2 X	0.6.0	Marsh *	1908–40	45 5	170	17½ × 26	5' 0"	19,180	45	"Vulcans,"
C 3	0.6.0	Marsh	1906	47 10	170	17½ × 26	5' 0"	19,200	8	"Marsh Goods,"
C 14	0.4.0 T	Drummond	1906–07	25 15	150	14 × 14	3' 0"	9,700	3	"Rockets," "Potato Cans"
D	4.4.0	Wainwright	1901–07	50 0	175	19 × 26	6' 8"	17,453	30	"Coppertops,"
D 1	4.4.0	Maunsell	1921–27	52 2	180	19 × 26	6' 8"	17,950	21	—
D 1	0.4.2 T	Stroudley	1873–87	43 10	160	17 × 24	5' 6"	14,300	30	"D Tanks,"
					170			15,200		—
D 3	0.4.4 T	R. Billinton	1892–96	52 0	170	17½ × 26	5' 6"	17,430	29	"Bogie Tanks,"

Class	Type	Builder & Nos.	Date		Loco Nos.	Press. (lb.)	Cylinders	Driving Wheels	Tractive Effort	No.	
	4.4.0	Wainwright	1907-09	5	52	180	19 × 26	6′ 6″	18,411	15	
E 1	4.4.0	Maunsell	1919-20	9	53	180	19 × 26	6′ 6″	18,411	11	"Black Tanks,"
E 1	0.6.0 T	Stroudley	1874-91	3	44	170	17 × 24	4′ 6″	18,600	30	"E1 Radials"
E 1/R	0.6.2 T	Maunsell *	1927-29	5	50, 52, 53	170	17½ × 24	4′ 6″	18,600	10	
E 2	0.6.2 T	L. Billinton	1913-16 *	15 / 10**	56	170	17½ × 26	4′ 6″	21,300	10	
E 3	0.6.2 T	R. Billinton	1894-95	10	57	160 / 170	17½ × 26	4′ 6″	20,050 / 21,300	16	"Small Radials,"
E 4	0.6.2 T	R. Billinton	1897-03	10	59	160 / 170	17½ × 26	5′ 0″	18,050 / 19,180	71	"Radials,"
E 4 X	0.6.2 T	Marsh	1909-11	5	60	160 / 170	17½ × 26	5′ 0″	19,180	4	
E 5	0.6.2 T	R. Billinton	1902-04	0	64	160 / 170	17½ × 26	5′ 0″	16,400 / 17,400	25	"Large Radials,"
E 5 X	0.6.2 T	Marsh *	1911	5	61	160 / 170	17½ × 26	5′ 0″	17,400	4	
E 6	0.C.2 T	R. Billinton	1904-05	0	63	160 / 170	18 × 26	4′ 6″	21,200 / 22,500	10	
E 6 X	0.6.2 T	Marsh *	1911	0	45	170	18 × 26	4′ 6″	22,500	2	"Jumbos,"
F 1	4.4.0	Wainwright ††	1903-19	2	45	170	18 × 26	4′ 7″	14,491	22	
G 6	0.6.0 T	Adams	1894-00	4	95	160	17½ × 24	4′ 10″	17,230	34	
G 16	4.8.0 T	Urie	1921	2		180	22 × 28	5′ 1″	34,000	4	"Hump Engines."
H	0.4.4 T	Wainwright	1904-15	8	54	160	18 × 26	5′ 6″	17,358	66	
H 1	4.4.2	Marsh	1905-06	5	68	200	18½ × 26	6′ 7½″	19,028	3	"Atlantics,"
H 2	4.4.2	Marsh	1911-12	5	68	170	21 × 26	7½″	20,841	6	"Atlantics."
H 15	4.6.0	Urie 330-335 §§	1914-25	12	79	175	21 × 28	6′ 0″	25,500	26	
		Urie 482-490	1914	5	81	180	21 × 28	6′ 0″	26,200		
		Maunsell 473-8, 491 & 521-4	1923-24	19	79	180	21 × 28	6′ 0″	26,200		

NOTES.—(*) Rebuilt from preceding class.
(†) Rebuilt from Stirling "B" Class, built 1898-9.
(‡) Loco. 2044 : Cyls. 20 × 26 tractive effort 19,650.
(§) Rebuilt with superheater 1915 (No. 464) onwards.
(¶) E Super cyls. 20¼ × 26

(**) Nos. 2105-9 with 1,256 gall. tanks.
(††) Rebuilt with dome boilers from Stirling "F" Class, built 1883-98.
(§§) Nos. 330-335 rebuilt from Drummond 4-cyl. 4.6.0s.
(¶¶) Rebuilt from Stroudley "A" Class, built 1872-80

43

CLASS	WHEELS	DESIGNER	BUILDING DATE	WEIGHT OF LOCO. tons cwt.	BOILER PRESSURE LB. PER SQ. IN.	CYLINDER ins.	DRIVING WHEELS	TRACTIVE EFFORT at 85% B.P. LB.	No. of Locos	
H 16	4.6.2 T	Urie	1921–22	96 8	180	21 × 28	5' 7"	28,200	5	"Green Tanks."
I 1X	4.4.2 T	Maunsell	1925–32	71 18	180	17½ × 26	5' 6"	18,450	20	"Wankers."
I 3	4.4.2 T	Marsh (2021)	1907	75 10	180	19 × 26	6' 9"	16,700	27	"Marsh Tanks."
		(2028/9 & 2076)	1909–10	76 0	180	19 × 26	6' 7½"	18,063		
		(2027)	1909	76 0	180	20 × 26	6' 7½"	20,015		
		(Others)	1908–13	76 0	180	21 × 26	6' 7½"	22,100		
J 1	0.6.4 T	Wainwright	1913	70 14	160	19½ × 26	5' 6"	20,400	5	"Pacific Tanks."
J 2	4.6.2 T	Marsh	1910	89 0	170	21 × 26	6' 7½"	20,800	1	
	4.6.2 T	Marsh	1912	89 0	170	21 × 26	6' 7½"	20,800		
K	2.6.0	L. Billinton	1913–21	63 15	170 / 180	21 × 26	5' 6"	25,100	17	"Moguls."
K 10	4.4.0	Drummond	1901–02	46 14	175	18½ × 26	5' 7"	19,760	40	"Small Hoppers."
KES	0.8.0 T	H'th'rn L'slie	1904	43 10	160	16 × 24	4' 3"	16,384	1	"He-gate."
L	4.4.0	Wainwright	1914	57 9	160	20½ × 26	6' 8"	18,600	22	"German Engines."
L 1	4.4.0	Maunsell	1926	57 16	180	19½ × 26	6' 8"	18,910	15	"Large Hoppers."
L 11	4.4.0	Drummond	1903–07	50 11	175	18½ × 26	5' 7"	19,760	40	
L 12	4.4.0	Drummond	1904–05	55 5	175	19 × 26	6' 7"	17,670	20	"Bulldogs."
L N	4.6.0	Maunsell	1926–29	83 10	220	(4) 16¼ × 26	6' 7"*	33,500	16	"Nelsons."
M 7	0.4.4 T	Drummond	1897–11	60 3	175	18½ × 26	5' 7"	19,750	104	"Motor Tanks."
MN	4.6.2	Bulleid	1941–42	92 10	280	(3) 18 × 24	6' 2"	37,500	10	"Flannel Jackets."
N	2.6.0	Maunsell	1917–34	61 4	200	19 × 28	5' 6"	26,000	80	"Mongolipers." "Woolworths" (1826–75).
N 1	2.6.0	Maunsell	1919–30	64 5½	200†	(3) 16 × 28	5' 6"	27,700	6	

44

Class	Wheels	Built by	Date	Weight (tons · cwt)		B.P.	Cylinders	Driving Wheels		T.E.	No. in Class	Name
N 15X	4.6.0	Urie	1918–23	77	5	180	21 × 28	6′	7″	23,900	74	"Urie Arthurs."
		Maunsell (736–55) ‡‡ §§	1925	80	1	200	20½ × 28	6′	7″	25,320	7	} "Scotch Arthurs."
		Maunsell (763–92)	1926–27	80	19	200	20½ × 28	6′	7″	25,320		
		Maunsell (793–806) ‡‡ §§	1934–36	73	2	180	21 × 28	6′	9″	23,300		"Remembrance."
O 1	0.6.0	Wainwright ‖‖	1903–	41	1	150	18 × 26	5′	2″	17,300	53	—
O 2	0.4.4 T	Adams	1889–95	46	18§	160	17½ × 24	4′	10″	17,245	50	—
P	0.6.0 T	Wainwright	1909–10	28	10	160	12 × 18	3′	9¾″	7,830	8	—
Q	0.6.0	Maunsell	1938–39	49	10	200	19 × 26	5′	1″	26,157	20	—
Q 1	0.6.0	Bulleid	1942	51	5	230	19 × 26	5′	1″	30,000	40	"Austerity Engines."
R	0.6.0 T	Stirling	1888–98	42	10	140	18 × 26	5′	2″	16,400	1	"R Goods."
R	0.4.4 T	Kirtley (L.C.D.R.)	1891–92	49	15	160	17½ × 24	5′	6″	15,150	15	"Bob tails."
R 1	0.6.0 T	Wainwright ¶	1900	46	9	160	18 × 26	5′	2″	18,478	13	—
R 1	0.4.4 T	Kirtley **	1917	51	10	160	17½ × 24	5′	6″	15,150	13	"Bob tails."
S 11	4.4.0	Drummond	1903	53	15	160	18½ × 26	6′	0″	19,519	1	—
S 11	4.4.0	Drummond	1903	53	15	175	19 × 26	5′	7″	19,400	10	—
S 15	4.6.0	Urie (496–515)	1920–21	77	8	180	21 × 28	5′	7″	28,200	} 45	—
S 15	4.6.0	Maunsell (823–847)	1927–36	79	5	200	20½ × 28	5′	7″	29,860		—
T 1	0.6.0 T	Kirtley	1879–91	40	13	160	17½ × 24	5′	6″	18,509	3	—
T 3	0.4.4 T	Adams	1888–96	53	0	160	18 × 26	5′	7″	17,100	23	—
T 6	4.4.0	Adams	1892–93	48	11	175	19 × 26	6′	7″	17,670	1	—
T 9	4.4.0	Drummond ‡‡	1899–01	51	16	175	19 × 26	6′	7″	17,670	66	"Greyhounds"
T 14	4.6.0	Maunsell ‡‡	1930–31	76	10	175	(4) 15 × 26	6′	7″	22,030	9	"Paddleboxes"

NOTES.—(*) No. 859 has 6′ 3″ driving wheels.
(†) No. 1822: B.P. 190; weight 62 tons 15 cwt. T.E. 26,200.
(‡) These locos. fitted with 6-wheel tenders. All others in class have 8-wheelers.
(§) Engines working in Isle of Wight slightly heavier owing to larger bunkers.

(¶) Modified by Wainwright.
(**) No. 1685 rebuilt from C Class.
(††) Rebuilt.
(‡‡) Rebuilt from Drummond 4.6.0, 1911–12.
(§§) Rebuilt from L. Billinton's "L" class 4.6.4 T, built 1914–22.
(‖‖) Rebuilt from Stirling "O" Class, built 1891–8.

CLASS	WHEELS	DESIGNER	BUILDING DATE	WEIGHT OF LOCO. tons cwt.	BOILER PRESSURE LB. PER SQ. IN.	CYLINDERS ins.	DRIVING WHEELS	TRACTIVE EFFORT AT 85 % B.P. LB.	NO. OF LOCOS	
U*	2.6.0	Maunsell	1917–31	62 6	200	19 × 28	6' 0"	23,866	50	⎱ "U Boats"
U 1†	2.6.0	Maunsell	1925–31	65 6	200	(3) 16 × 28	6' 0"	25,387	21	⎰
V	4.4.0	Maunsell	1930–35	67 2	220	(3) 16¼ × 26	6' 7"	25,130	40	"Schools."
W	2.6.4 T	Maunsell	1931–36	90 14	200	(3) 16½ × 28	5' 6"	29,452	15	—
X 6	4.4.0 T	Adams	1895–96	49 13	175	19 × 26	6' 7"	17,670	1	—
Z	0.8.0 T	Maunsell	1929	71 12	180	(3) 16 × 28	4' 8"	29,376	8	"Black
700	0.6.0	Drummond	1897¶	46 14	180	19 × 26	5' 1"	23,500	30	Motors."
756‡	0.6.0 T	H'th'rm L'slie	1907	35 15	170	14 × 22	3' 10"	13,550	1	Crane.
757‡	0.6.2 T	H'th'rm L'slie	1907	49 17	170	16 × 24	4' 0"	18,500	2	"Beattie
1302	0.4.0CT	Neilson	1881	17 17	160	11 × 20	3' 3"	6,330	1	Tanks."
0298	2.4.0 WT	Beattie	1874–75	37 16	160	16½ × 20	5' 7"	11,053	3	"Jumbos."
0395	0.6.0	Adams	1881–86	38 14	⎱ 140 ⎰ 150	17½ × 26	5' 1"	⎱ 15,500 ⎰ 16,640	⎱ 18	
0458	0.4.0 ST	H'th'rm L'slie	1890	21 2	120	12 × 20	3' 2"	7,730	2	"Dock Engines."
0415	4.4.2 T	Adams	1885	55 2	160	17½ × 24	5' 7"	14,919	2	"Radial Tanks."
Diesel	0.6.0	English Electric Co.	1938	55 5	—	(6)	4' 6"	30,000§	3	—

NOTES.—(*) Including 20 rebuilt "River" (K) Class 2.6.4 T.
(†) Including one rebuilt "River" (K 1) Class (No. 1890).
(‡) Ex P.D. & S.W.R.
(§) Maximum T.E.
(‖) Ex K. & E.S.R.
(¶) Rebuilt with superheater 1921 (No. 316) onwards.

POWER CLASSIFICATION

Some types of locomotives on the Western Section (only) have a " haulage classification " mark, consisting of a single letter painted on the side of the framing near the front buffer beam. The letters indicate the powers of haulage, A being the most powerful, and the other classifications graded down to K, the lowest.

A :—G 16, H 15, H 16, Lord Nelson, N 15, Q 1, S 15, V

B :—Q, T 14

C :—700

D :—D 15, L 12

E :— S 11

F :—K 10, L 11

G :—0395

H :—T 9

I :— T 3, X 6

J :—A 12

K :—All tank locos (except G 16, H 16).

LOCOMOTIVE SUPERINTENDENTS
AND CHIEF MECHANICAL ENGINEERS.*

L.S.W.R.

J. Woods	1835
J. V. Gooch	1841
J. Beattie	1850
W. G. Beattie	1871
W. Adams	1878
D. Drummond	1895
R. W. Urie	1912

L.B.S.C.R.

J. Gray	1845
S. Kirtley	1847
J. C. Craven	1847
W. Stroudley	1870
R. J. Billinton	1890
D. Earle Marsh	1905
L. B. Billinton	1911

S.E.R.

B. Cubitt	1842
J. I. Cudworth	1845
A. M. Watkin	1876
R. C. Mansell	1877
J. Stirling	1878

L.C.D.R.

W. Cubitt	1853
W. Martley	1860
W. Kirtley	1874

S.E.C.R.

H. S. Wainwright	1898
R. E. L. Maunsell	1913

S.R.

R. E. L. Maunsell	1923
O. V. Bulleid	1937

* The title ''Locomotive Superintendent'' changed to "Chief Mechanical Engineer" about the beginning of the century.

21 C 10 " Blue Star " (of the " Merchant Navy " Class).

THE ABC OF
GREAT WESTERN
LOCOMOTIVES

No. 5101 standing in Birmingham (Snow Hill)

Compiled by
IAN ALLAN

4th Edition
July 1944

"King George V" in original colours and shewing the old style of tender lettering and coat of arms.

(Photo : Locomotive Publishing Co.

2

PREFACE

NOTES ON NUMBERING AND CLASSIFICATION

Originally the G.W.R. numbered their engines consecutively from 1 upwards, using numbers previously carried by withdrawn engines for new engines, but in 1911, when the first engines of some of the present standard types were beginning to appear, a new system was started in which each class of standard engine was allocated a batch, or a number of batches, of one hundred consecutive numbers, the number of the first engine in the batch ending in 00.

The following table shows the blocks of numbers allocated to the various wheel types :

4-6-0 (4 cyl.)	...	...	...	4000, 5000, 6000
2-6-2T large	...	...	...	3100, 4100, 5100, 6100, 8100
2-8-0T	...	...	...	4200, 5200
2-8-2T	...	...	...	7200
2-6-0	...	...	...	4300, 5300, 6300 7300, 8300, 9300
0-6-0T (passenger)		...	...	5400, 6400, 7400
2-6-2T (small)	...		...	4500, 5500
0-6-2T	...	...	...	5600, 6600
0-6-0T (goods)		...	...	3600, 4600
0-6-0T (goods)		...	...	2700, 3700, 5700 6700, 7700, 8700, 9700
2-8-0 (goods)	...	...	...	2800, 3800
0-4-2T	...	...	...	4800, 5800
4-6-0 (2 cyl. mixed traffic)			6800, 7800
4-6-0 (2 Cyl.)	...	...	2900, 4900, 5900, 6900

There are, in addition, a number of small classes of generally standard design which do not come within this system, such as the 2251 class, 0-6-0 ; 2600 class, 2-6-0 ; 3000 class R.O.D., 2-8-0, 3200 class, 4-4-0 ; 4400 class, 2-6-2T and 4700 class, 2-8-0 ; while the 2300 class, 0-6-0 and "Bulldog" and "Duke" class 4-4-0's retain the original series of numbers allocated to them when they were built.

Most of the G.W.R. locomotives carrying low numbers have been scrapped and these spare numbers were used for the engines belonging to the various smaller Companies which were grouped with the G.W.R. in 1923. It is of interest to note that these engines, which were taken over at the grouping have the initials G.W.R. above the number on the number plates, while engines built for the G.W.R. proper, or taken over before the grouping, do not bear these initials on the number plates.

3

A system of locomotive power classification and route restriction is used on the G.W.R. and the group to which a locomotive belongs can be seen on the cabside in the form of a letter superimposed on a coloured disc. The most powerful locomotives are classed " E " and the remainder are graded down to " A ", the lowest, although many of the smaller classes are unclassified. The route restriction colours, which form the background to the power classification are—red, blue, yellow and uncoloured according to the locomotives' weights and general dimensions. The red coloured engines are the most restricted, while the uncoloured locomotives can, owing to their weights, run anywhere on the system without restriction.

The " King " class is very restricted and carries a special colouring of two red discs without any power classification letter.

The route restriction colours and power class group letters of each class can be found included in the tables on pages 40 and 41.

The approximate limits of the power classification are :—

Class		Tractive Effort lb.	Class		Tractive Effort lb.
E	...	31,000—35,380	B	...	18,950—20,499
D	...	23,500—30,999	A	...	14,000—18,949
C	...	20,500—23,499			

*   *   *

Thanks for the use of photographs and for help in the compilation of this booklet are extended to Messrs. B. W. Anwell, G. H. Cannon, H. Hall and B. F. B. Tatford, and to the Great Western Railway Company who have also kindly checked the details contained herein.

No. 942, ex Powesland and Mason.

Note

This book contains a complete list of all G.W.R. engines in service and has been checked by the Company up to January 1st, 1944.

Throughout the book the dimensions shewn at the head of each class are only typical examples and should not be taken as applying to every engine.

The following is a list of abbreviations :—

AD	Alexandra (Newport and South Wales) Docks & Railway	NB	Neath and Brecon Railway
BR	Barry Railway	PM	Powesland & Mason (Contractor)
BM	Brecon and Merthyr Railway	PT	Port Talbot Rly.
BPGV	Burry Port & Gwendraeth Valley Rly.	RSB	Rhondda & Swansea Bay Railway
Cam.R	Cambrian Railways	RR	Rhymney Railway
Car.R	Cardiff Railway	SHT	Swansea Harbour Trust
CMDP	Cleobury, Mortimer and Ditton Priors Light Railway	TV	Taff Vale Railway
		WCPR	Weston, Clevedon & Portishead Rly.
Cor.R	Corris Railway	V of R	Cambrian Railways (Vale of Rheidol)
LMM	Llanelly & Mynydd Mawr Railway		
MSWJ	Midland and South Western Junction Railway	W & L	Cambrian Railways (Welshpool and Llanfair)

Locomotive Superintendents and Chief Mechanical Engineers

Sir Daniel Gooch	...	...	1837—1864
Joseph Armstrong	...	...	1864—1877
William Dean ...	...	...	1877—1902
G. J. Churchward	...	...	1902—1921
Charles B. Collett	...	...	1921—1941
F. W. Hawksworth	...	...	1941—

NUMERICAL LIST OF LOCOMOTIVES

The tables on these pages shew engine number, wheel arrangement and pre-grouping owner or G.W. Class. For abbreviations see page 5. Where no initials are shown, the loco is of G.W.R. Origin.

2	0-6-0	Diesel Electric	47	0-6-2T	RR	77	0-6-2T	RR
3	0-4-2T*	Cor. R.	48	0-6-2T	RR	78	0-6-2T	RR
4	0-4-2T*	Cor. R.	51	0-6-2T	RR	79	0-6-2T	RR
5	0-6-0T	W.C.&P.R.	52	0-6-2T	RR	80	0-6-2T	RR
6	0-6-0T	W.C.&P.R.*	53	0-6-2T	RR	81	0-6-2T	RR
7	2-6-2T*	V. of R. †	54	0-6-2T	RR	82	0-6-2T	RR
8	2-6-2T*	V. of R. †	55	0-6-2T	RR	83	0-6-2T	RR
11	0-6-2T	BM	56	0-6-2T	RR	100 A1	4-6-0	4073 Class
13	0-4-0T	Sentinel	57	0-6-2T	RR	111	4-6-0	4073 Class
21	0-6-2T	BM	58	0-6-2T	RR	155	0-6-2T	Car.R.
28	0-6-0T	CMDP	59	0-6-2T	RR	184	0-6-2T	PT
29	0-6-0T	CMDP	60	0-6-2T	RR	188	0-6-2T	PT
30	0-6-2T	RR	61	0-6-2T	RR	190	0-6-2T	AD
31	0-6-2T	RR	62	0-6-2T	RR	192	0-6-2T	AD
32	0-6-2T	RR	63	0-6-2T	RR	198	0-6-2T	BR
33	0-6-2T	RR	64	0-6-2T	RR	200	0-6-2T	BR
34	0-6-2T	RR	65	0-6-2T	RR	207	0-6-2T	BR
35	0-6-2T	RR	66	0-6-2T	RR	212	0-6-2T	BR
36	0-6-2T	RR	67	0-6-2T	RR	213	0-6-2T	BR
37	0-6-2T	RR	68	0-6-2T	RR	214	0-6-2T	BR
38	0-6-2T	RR	69	0-6-2T	RR	224	0-6-2T	BR
39	0-6-2T	RR	70	0-6-2T	RR	231	0-6-2T	BR
40	0-6-2T	RR	71	0-6-2T	RR	236	0-6-2T	TV
41	0-6-2T	RR	72	0-6-2T	RR	238	0-6-2T	BR
42	0-6-2T	RR	73	0-6-2T	RR	240	0-6-2T	BR
43	0-6-2T	RR	74	0-6-2T	RR	242	0-6-2T	BR
44	0-6-2T	RR	75	0-6-2T	RR	246	0-6-2T	BR
46	0-6-2T	RR	76	0-6-2T	RR			

* Narrow Gauge   † Built to V. of R. design by G.W.R., 1923

The complete locomotive stock of the former Corris Railway.
Nos. 3 and 4

0-6-2 tank, No. 441, ex-Taff Vale Railway

247	0-6-2T	BR	294	0-6-2T	TV	362	0-6-2T	TV
248	0-6-2T	BR	295	0-6-2T	TV	364	0-6-2T	TV
250	0-6-2T	BR	296	0-6-2T	TV	365	0-6-2T	TV
257	0-6-2T	BR	297	0-6-2T	TV	366	0-6-2T	TV
258	0-6-2T	BR	298	0-6-2T	TV	367	0-6-2T	TV
259	0-6-2T	BR	299	0-6-2T	TV	368	0-6-2T	TV
261	0-6-2T	BR	300	0-6-2T	TV	370	0-6-2T	TV
262	0-6-2T	BR	301	0-6-2T	TV	371	0-6-2T	TV
263	0-6-2T	BR	302	0-6-2T	TV	372	0-6-2T	TV
265	0-6-2T	BR	310	0-6-2T	TV	373	0-6-2T	TV
266	0-6-2T	BR	311	0-6-2T	TV	374	0-6-2T	TV
267	0-6-2T	BR	313	0-6-2T	TV	375	0-6-2T	TV
268	0-6-2T	BR	314	0-6-2T	TV	376	0-6-2T	TV
269	0-6-2T	BR	315	0-6-2T	TV	377	0-6-2T	TV
270	0-6-2T	BR	317	0-6-2T	TV	378	0-6-2T	TV
271	0-6-2T	BR	318	0-6-2T	TV	379	0-6-2T	TV
272	0-6-2T	BR	319	0-6-2T	TV	380	0-6-2T	TV
273	0-6-2T	BR	320	0-6-2T	TV	381	0-6-2T	TV
274	0-6-2T	BR	321	0-6-2T	TV	382	0-6-2T	TV
275	0-6-2T	BR	324	0-6-2T	TV	383	0-6-2T	TV
276	0-6-2T	BR	332	0-6-2T	BM	384	0-6-2T	TV
277	0 6-2T	BR	333	0-6-2T	TV	385	0-6-2T	TV
278	0-6-2T	TV	335	0-6-2T	TV	386	0-6-2T	TV
279	0-6-2T	TV	337	0-6-2T	TV	387	0-6-2T	TV
280	0-6-2T	TV	343	0-6-2T	TV	388	0-6-2T	TV
281	0-6-2T	TV	344	0-6-2T	TV	389	0-6-2T	TV
282	0-6-2T	TV	345	0-6-2T	TV	390	0-6-2T	TV
283	0-6-2T	TV	346	0-6-2T	TV	391	0-6-2T	TV
284	0-6-2T	TV	347	0-6-2T	TV	393	0-6-2T	TV
285	0-6-2T	TV	348	0-6-2T	TV	394	0 6-2T	TV
286	0-6-2T	TV	349	0-6-2T	TV	397	0-6-2T	TV
287	0-6-2T	TV	351	0-6-2T	TV	398	0-6-2T	TV
288	0-6-2T	TV	352	0-6-2T	TV	399	0-6-2T	TV
289	0-6-2T	TV	356	0-6-2T	TV	401	0-6-2T	TV
290	0-6-2T	TV	357	0-6-2T	TV	402	0-6-2T	TV
291	0-6-2T	TV	359	0-6-0T	LMM	403	0-6-2T	TV
292	0-6-2T	TV	360	0-6-2T	TV	404	0-6-2T	TV
293	0-6-2T	TV	361	0-6-2T	TV			

No. 855, ex-Cambrian Railways

406 0-6-2T	TV	823 0-6-0T*	W. & L.	1106 0-4-0T	110, Class
408 0-6-2T	TV	844 0-6-0	Cam. R.	1113 0-6-2T	BM
409 0-6-2T	TV	848 0-4-2T	517 Class	1159 0-4-2T	517 Class
410 0-6-2T	TV	849 0-6-0	Cam. R.	1161 0-4-2T	517 Class
411 0-6-2T	TV	855 0-6-0	Cam. R.	1163 0-4-2T	517 Class
414 0-6-2T	TV	864 0-6-0	Cam. R.	1196 2-4-0T	Cam. R.
420 0-6-2T	TV	873 0-6-0	Cam. R.	1197 2-4-0T	Cam. R.
438 0-6-2T	TV	876 0-6-0	Cam. R.	1205 2-6-2T	AD
439 0-6-2T	TV	884 0-6-0	Cam. R.	1206 2-6-2T	AD
440 0-6-2T	TV	885 0-6-0	Cam. R.	1213 2-6-2T*	V. of R.
441 0-6-2T	TV	887 0-6-0	Cam. R.	1287 0-6-0T	"Sir Dan."
504 0-6-0T	BM	888 0-6-2T	BM	1308 2-4-0T	[Class
604 0-6-0T	RR	892 0-6-0	Cam. R.	1331 0-6-0T	
605 0-6-0T	RR	893 0-6-0	Cam. R.	1334 2-4-0	MSWJ
606 0-6-0T	RR	894 0-6-0	Cam. R.	1335 2-4-0	MSWJ
608 0-6-0T	RR	895 0-6-0	Cam. R.	1336 2-4-0	MSWJ
609 0-6-0T	RR	896 0-6-0	Cam. R.	1338 0-4-0T	Car. R.
610 0-6-0T	RR	898 0-6-0	Cam. R.	1341 0-4-0T	AD
611 0-6-0T	RR	900 0-6-0	Cam. R.	1358 0-8-2T	PT
666 0-6-0T	AD	905 0-6-0T	1701 Class	1361 0-6-0T	1361 Class
667 0-6-0T	AD	906 0-6-0T	1701 Class	1362 0-6-0T	1361 Class
680 0-6-0T	AD	907 0-6-0T	1701 Class	1363 0-6-0T	1361 Class
681 0-6-0T	Car. R.	929 0-4-0T	SHT	1364 0-6-0T	1361 Class
682 0-6-0T	Car. R.	935 0-4-0T	PM	1365 0-6-0T	1361 Class
683 0-6-0T	Car. R.	942 0-4-0T	PM	1366 0-6-0T	1366 Class
684 0-6-0T	Car. R.	943 0-4-0T	SHT	1367 0-6-0T	1366 Class
696 0-4-0T	PM	968 0-4-0T	SHT	1368 0-6-0T	1366 Class
698 0-6-2T	BM	974 0-4-0T	SHT	1369 0-6-0T	1366 Class
701 0-4-0T	SHT	992 0-6-0T	1901 Class	1370 0-6-0T	1366 Class
779 0-4-0T	PM	1084 0-6-2T	BM	1371 0-6-0T	1366 Class
783 0-6-0T	BR	1085 0-6-0T	SHT	1372 0-6-2T	BM
784 0-6-0T	BR	1086 0-6-0T	SHT	1373 0-6-2T	BM
792 0-6-0T	TV	1098 0-6-0T	SHT	1374 0-6-2T	BM
793 0-6-0T	TV	1101 0-4-0T	1101 Class	1375 0-6-2T	BM
794 0-6-0T	TV	1102 0-4-0T	1101 Class	1436 0-4-2T	517 Class
803 0-6-0T	LMM	1103 0-4-0T	1101 Class	1442 0-4-2T	517 Class
819 0-6-0T	Cam. R.	1104 0-4-0T	1101 Class	1498 2-4-0T	3500 Class
822 0-6-0T*	W. & L.	1105 0-4-0T	1101 Class	1499 2-4-0T	3500 Class

* Narrow Gauge.

8

0-6-0T	1501 Class	1799	0-6-0T	2012
1501 Class	1742	1800	**1901 Class**	2013
1527	1743	**1501 Class**		2014
1531	1745	1803	1903	2015
1532	1746	1808	1907	2016
1538	1747	1810	1909	2017
1542	1748	**1813 Class**	1910	2018
1554	1749	1823	1912	2019
" Sir	1750	1831	1917	
Daniel "	**1701 Class**	1835	1919	**0-6-0T**
Class	1751	1838	1925	**2021 Class**
1585	1752	1846	1930	
1624	1753	1847	1935	2021
	1754	**1701 Class**	1941	2022
0-6-2T	1756 RSB	1854	1943	2023
BM	1758	1855	1945	2025
1668	1759	1856	1949	2026
1670	1760	1858	1954	2027
	1761	1859	1957	2029
0-6-0T	1762	1861	1964	2030
1701 Class	1763	1862	1965	2031
1703	1764	1863	1967	2032
1705	1767	1866	1968	2033
1706	1768	1867	1969	2034
1707	1769	1870	1973	2035
1709	**1501 Class**	1873	1979	2037
1712	1773	1875	1988	2038
1713	1779	1878	1989	2039
1714	1780	1882 NB*	1990	2040
1715 NB*	1782	1883	1991	2041
1716	1784	1884	1993	2042
1719	1785	1886	1996	2043
1720	1786	1887	1999	2044
1721	1787	1888		2045
1722	1788	1889		2046
1725	1789	1890	2000	2047
1726	1790	1891	2001	2048
1730	**1701 Class**	1893	2002	2049
1731	1792	1894	2004	2050
1732	1793	1895	2005	2051
1734	1794	1896	2006	2052
1735	1795	1897	2007	2053
1736	1796	1898	2008	2054
1737	1797	1899	2009	2055
1740	1798	1900	2010	2056
			2011	

*Standard G.W. loco sold out of stock and later reinstated.

9

2058	2081	2103	2127	2153	2183
2059	2082	2104	2129	2154	2184
2060	2083	2106	2130	2155	2185
2061	2084	2107	2131	2156	2186
2063	2085	2108	2132	2158	2187
2064	2086	2109	2134	2159	2188
2065	2088	2110	2135	2160	2189
2066	2089	2111	2136		2190
2067	2090	2112	2137	**0-6-0T**	
2068	2091	2113	2138	**BPGV**	**0-6-0T**
2069	2092	2114	2139		**BPGV**
2070	2093	2115	2140	2162	
2071	2094	2116	2141	2165	2192
2072	2095	2117	2142	2166	2193
2073	2096	2119	2144	2167	2194
2075	2097	2120	2146	2168	2195
2076	2098	2121	2147	2176	2196
2077	2099	2122	2148		2197
2078	2100	2123	2150	**2181 Class**	2198
2079	2101	2124	2151	2181	
2080	2102	2126	2152	2182	

MISCELLANEOUS NAMED ENGINES
(Shewn in Tables above)

5 Portishead	1308 Lady Margaret	2195 Cwm Mawr
359 Hilda	2192 Ashburnham	2196 Gwendraeth
822 The Earl	2193 Burry Port	2197 Pioneer
823 Countess	2194 Kidwelly	

An 0-6-0 saddle tank of the former Cardiff Railway

Some 0-6-0 Pannier Tanks

7400 Class

2021 Class

No. 29, ex-C.M.D.P.

0-6-0   2251 Class

Introduced 1930.

Weights : Loco. 43 tons 8 cwt.

            Tender 36 tons 15 cwt.

Pressure : 200 lb.   Cyls. 17½″×24″

Driving Wheels : 5′ 2″   T.E.: 20155.

2200	2220	2260	2280
2201	2221	2261	2281
2202	2222	2262	2282
2203	2223	2263	2283
2204	2224	2264	2284
2205	2225	2265	2285
2206	2226	2266	2286
2207	2227	2267	2287
2208	2228	2268	2288
2209	2229	2269	2289
2210	2230	2270	2290
2211	2251	2271	2291
2212	2252	2272	2292
2213	2253	2273	2293
2214	2254	2274	2294
2215	2255	2275	2295
2216	2256	2276	2296
2217	2257	2277	2297
2218	2258	2278	2298
2219	2259	2279	2299

0-6-0   2301 Class

Introduced 1883.

Weights : Loco. 36 tons 16 cwt.

            Tender 36 tons 15 cwt.

Pressure : 180 lb.   Cyls. 17¼″×24″

Driving Wheels : 5′ 2″.   T.E.: 18140.

2315	2381	2449	2535
2320	2382	2452	2537
2322	2383	2458	2538
2323	2385	2460	2541
2325	2386	2462	2543
2327	2389	2464	2551
2339	2395	2468	2554
2340	2401	2474	2556
2343	2406	2482	2564
2345	2407	2483	2568
2348	2408	2484	2569
2349	2409	2513	2570
2350	2411	2515	2572
2351	2414	2516	2573
2354	2424	2523	2575
2356	2426	2525	2578
2360	2431	2530	2579
2362	2444	2532	
2378	2445	2534	

> Throughout this book the dimensions shewn at the head of each class are only typical examples, and should not be taken as applying to every engine.

2800 Class

2600("Aberdare") Class

"Aberdare" Class
2-6-0   2600 Class

Introduced 1900.
Weights : Loco. 56 tons 15 cwt.
          Tender 47 tons 14 cwt.
Pressure : 200 lb. Cyls. 18" × 26".
Driving Wheels : 4' 7½". T.E.: 25800.

2608	2635	2651	2667
2612	2636	2652	2669
2619	2637	2655	2673
2620	2638	2656	2676
2622	2639	2657	2677
2623	2640	2660	2679
2625	2643	2662	2680
2631	2649	2665	

0-6-0T   2700 Class

Introduced 1896.
Weight : 45 tons 13 cwt.
Pressure : 180 lb. Cyls. 17½" × 24"
Driving Wheels : 4' 7½". T.E.: 20260.

2700	2709	2718	2727
2701	2710	2719	2728
2702	2711	2720	2729
2703	2712	2721	2730
2704	2713	2722	2731
2705	2714	2723	2732
2706	2715	2724	2733
2707	2716	2725	2734
2708	2717	2726	2735

2736	2752	2768	2784
2737	2753	2769	2785
2738	2754	2770	2786
2739	2755	2771	2787
2740	2756	2772	2788
2741	2757	2773	2789
2742	2758	2774	2790
2743	2759	2775	2791
2744	2760	2776	2792
2745	2761	2777	2793
2746	2762	2778	2794
2747	2763	2779	2795
2748	2764	2780	2796
2749	2765	2781	2797
2750	2766	2782	2798
2751	2767	2783	2799

2-8-0   2800 Class

Introduced 1903.
Weights : Loco. 75 tons 10 cwt.
          Tender 40 tons 0 cwt.
Pressure : 225 lb. Cyls. 18½" × 30".
Driving Wheels : 4' 7½". T.E.: 35380

2800	2807	2814	2821
2801	2808	2815	2822
2802	2809	2816	2823
2803	2810	2817	2824
2804	2811	2818	2825
2805	2812	2819	2826
2806	2813	2820	2827

2800 Class—*continued*.

2828	2846	2864	2882
2829	2847	2865	2883
2830	2848	2866	2884
2831	2849	2867	2885
2832	2850	2868	2886
2833	2851	2869	2887
2834	2852	2870	2888
2835	2853	2871	2889
2836	2854	2872	2890
2837	2855	2873	2891
2838	2856	2874	2892
2839	2857	2875	2893
2840	2858	2876	2894
2841	2859	2877	2895
2842	2860	2878	2896
2843	2861	2879	2897
2844	2862	2880	2898
2845	2863	2881	2899

(Class continued 3800)

"Saint" Class
4-6-0   2900 Class

Introduced 1902.
Weights : Loco. 72 tons 0 cwt.
           Tender 40 tons 0 cwt.
Pressure : 225 lb. Cyls. $18\frac{1}{2}'' \times 30''$.
Driving Wheels : 6' $8\frac{1}{2}''$. T.E.: 24395.

2902 Lady of the Lake
2903 Lady of Lyons
2905 Lady Macbeth
2906 Lady of Lynn
2908 Lady of Quality
2912 Saint Ambrose
2913 Saint Andrew
2914 Saint Augustine
2915 Saint Bartholomew
2916 Saint Benedict
2920 Saint David
2921 Saint Dunstan
2922 Saint Gabriel
2924 Saint Helena
2926 Saint Nicholas
2927 Saint Patrick
2928 Saint Sebastian
2929 Saint Stephen
2930 Saint Vincent
2931 Arlington Court
2932 Ashton Court
2933 Bibury Court
2934 Butleigh Court
2935 Caynham Court
2936 Cefntilla Court
2937 Clevedon Court
2938 Corsham Court
2939 Croome Court
2940 Dorney Court
2941 Easton Court
2942 Fawley Court
2943 Hampton Court
2944 Highnam Court
2945 Hillingdon Court

"Saint" Class No. 2924, "Saint Helena"

R.O.D. Type 2–8–0

2900 Class—*continued.*

2946 Langford Court
2947 Madresfield Court
2948 Stackpole Court
2949 Stanford Court
2950 Taplow Court
2951 Tawstock Court
2952 Twineham Court
2953 Titley Court
2954 Tockenham Court
2955 Tortworth Court
2971 Albion
2975 Lord Palmer
2978 Charles J. Hambro
2979 Quentin Durward
2980 Cœur de Lion
2981 Ivanhoe
2983 Redgauntlet
2987 Bride of Lammermoor
2988 Rob Roy
2989 Talisman

3016	3025	3034	3042
3017	3026	3035	3043
3018	3027	3036	3044
3019	3028	3037	3045
3020	3029	3038	3046
3021	3030	3039	3047
3022	3031	3040	3048
3023	3032	3041	3049
3024	3033		

2-6-2T   3100 Class

Introduced 1938. Rebuilt from 3150 Class.
Weigh : 81 tons 9 cwt.
Pressure : 225 lb.   Cyls. : $18\frac{1}{2}'' \times 30''$
Driving Wheels : 5′ 3″   T.E.31170.

3100	3102	3103	3104
3101			

2-6-2T   3150 Class

Introduced 1907.
Weight : 81 tons 12 cwt.
Pressure : 200 lb.   Cyls. $18\frac{1}{2}'' \times 30''$.
Driving Wheels : 5′ 8″.   T.E.: 25670.

3150	3161	3170	3182
3151	3162	3171	3183
3152	3163	3172	3184
3153	3164	3174	3185
3154	3165	3175	3186
3157	3166	3176	3187
3158	3167	3177	3188
3159	3168	3178	3189
3160	3169	3180	3190

2-8-0   R.O.D. Class

Introduced 1919.
Weights : Loco. 73 tons 11 cwt.
         Tender 47 tons 14 cwt.
Pressure : 185 lb.   Cyls. $21'' \times 26''$
Driving Wheels : 4′ 8″   T.E.32200.

3000	3004	3008	3012
3001	3005	3009	3013
3002	3006	3010	3014
3003	3007	3011	3015

4-4-0   3200 Class

Introduced 1936.
Weights : Loco. 49 tons 0 cwt.
           Tender 40 tons 0 cwt.
Pressure : 180 lb. Cyls. 18″ × 26″.
Driving Wheels : 5′ 8″. T.E. : 18955.

3200	3202	3204	3206
3201	3203	3205	3207

3208	3214	3220	3226
3209	3215	3221	3227
3210	3216	3222	3228
3211	3217	3223	
3212	3218	3224	
3213	3219	3225	

" Duke " class loco No. 3259, " Merlin "
(now withdrawn from service)

No. 3448, " Kingfisher " of the " Bulldog " class

"Duke" Class

4-4-0　　　3252 Class

Introduced 1895.
Weights : Loco. 47 tons 6 cwt.
　　　　　Tender 34 tons 5 cwt.
Pressure : 180 lb.　Cyls. 18″×26″.
Driving Wheels : 5′ 8″.　T.E. : 18955.

3254 Cornubia
3264 Trevithick
3265 Tre Pol and Pen
3272
3273 Mounts Bay
3276
3283 Comet
3284 Isle of Jersey
3287 Mercury
3289
3291 Thames

"Bulldog" Class

4-4-0　　　3300 Class

ntroduced 1898.
Weights : Loco. 51 tons 16 cwt.
　　　　　Tender 40 tons 0 cwt.
Pressure : 200 lb.　Cyls. 18″ × 26″.
Driving Wheels : 5′ 8″.　T.E. : 21060.

3313 Jupiter
3335
3341 Blasius
3353 Pershore Plum
3358 Tremayne
3361
3363 Alfred Baldwin
3364 Frank Bibby
3366
3371 Sir Massey Lopes
3375 Sir Watkin Wynn
3376 River Plym
3377
3378
3379 River Fal
3382
3383

3386
3389
3391 Dominion of Canada
3393 Australia
3395 Tasmania
3396 Natal Colony
3399 Ottawa
3400 Winnipeg
3401 Vancouver
3406 Calcutta
3407 Madras
3408 Bombay
3417 Lord Mildmay of Flete
3418 Sir Arthur Yorke
3419
3421
3426
3430 Inchcape
3431
3432
3435
3438
3440
3441 Blackbird
3442 Bullfinch
3443 Chaffinch
3444 Cormorant
3445 Flamingo
3446 Goldfinch
3447 Jackdaw
3448 Kingfisher
3449 Nightingale
3450 Peacock
3451 Pelican
3452 Penguin
3453 Seagull
3454 Skylark
3455 Starling

2-4-0T   3500 Class

3561	3562	3563	3568

(Class continued 3581)

0-4-2T   517 Class

3573	3575	3578	3580
3574	3577		

2-4-0T   3500 Class

(Continued from 3568)

3581	3585	3589	3596
3582	3586	3592	3597
3583	3587	3594	3599
3584	3588	3595	

0-6-0T   5700 Class

Introduced 1929.
Weight : 49 tons 0 cwt.
Pressure : 200 lb. Cyls. $17\frac{1}{2}'' \times 24''$.
Driving Wheels : 4' $7\frac{1}{2}''$. T.E. : 22515.

3600	3624	3648	3672
3601	3625	3649	3673
3602	3626	3650	3674
3603	3627	3651	3675
3604	3628	3652	3676
3605	3629	3653	3677
3606	3630	3654	3678
3607	3631	3655	3679
3608	3632	3656	3680
3609	3633	3657	3681
3610	3634	3658	3682
3611	3635	3659	3683
3612	3636	3660	3684
3613	3637	3661	3685
3614	3638	3662	3686
3615	3639	3663	3687
3616	3640	3664	3688
3617	3641	3665	3689
3618	3642	3666	3690
3619	3643	3667	3691
3620	3644	3668	3692
3621	3645	3669	3693
3622	3646	3670	3694
3623	3647	3671	3695

3696	3722	3748	3774
3697	3723	3749	3775
3698	3724	3750	3776
3699	3725	3751	3777
3700	3726	3752	3778
3701	3727	3753	3779
3702	3728	3754	3780
3703	3729	3755	3781
3704	3730	3756	3782
3705	3731	3757	3783
3706	3732	3758	3784
3707	3733	3759	3785
3708	3734	3760	3786
3709	3735	3761	3787
3710	3736	3762	3788
3711	3737	3763	3789
3712	3738	3764	3790
3713	3739	3765	3791
3714	3740	3766	3792
3715	3741	3767	3793
3716	3742	3768	3794
3717	3743	3769	3795
3718	3744	3770	3796
3719	3745	3771	3797
3720	3746	3772	3798
3721	3747	3773	3799

(Class continued 4600)

2-8-0   2800 Class

Class continued from 2899

3800	3813	3826	3839
3801	3814	3827	3840
3802	3815	3828	3841
3803	3816	3829	3842
3804	3817	3830	3843
3805	3818	3831	3844
3806	3819	3832	3845
3807	3820	3833	3846
3808	3821	3834	3847
3809	3822	3835	3848
3810	3823	3836	3849
3811	3824	3837	3850
3812	3825	3838	3851

2800 Class—*continued*.

3852	3856	3860	3864
3853	3857	3861	3865
3854	3858	3862	3866
3855	3859	3863	

"Star" Class
4-6-0 (4 Cyl.) 4000 Class

Introduced 1906.
Weights : Loco. 75 tons 12 cwt.
　　　　　Tender 46 tons 14 cwt.
Pressure : 225 lb.　Cyls. 15″ × 26″.
Driving Wheels : 6′ 8½″.　T.E.: 27800.

4003 Lode Star
4004 Morning Star
4007 Swallowfield Park
4012 Knight of the Thistle
4013 Knight of St. Patrick
4014 Knight of the Bath
4015 Knight of St. John
4017 Knight of Liège
4018 Knight of the Grand
　　　　　　　　　　Cross
4019 Knight Templar
4020 Knight Commander
4021 British Monarch
4022
4023
4025
4026
4028

4030
4031 Queen Mary
4033 Queen Victoria
4034 Queen Adelaide
4035 Queen Charlotte
4036 Queen Elizabeth
4038 Queen Berengaria
4039 Queen Matilda
4040 Queen Boadicea
4041 Prince of Wales
4042 Prince Albert
4043 Prince Henry
4044 Prince George
4045 Prince John
4046 Princess Mary
4047 Princess Louise
4048 Princess Victoria
4049 Princess Maud
4050 Princess Alice
4051 Princess Helena
4052 Princess Beatrice
4053 Princess Alexandra
4054 Princess Charlotte
4055 Princess Sophia
4056 Princess Margaret
4057 Princess Elizabeth
4058 Princess Augusta
4059 Princess Patricia
4060 Princess Eugénie
4061 Glastonbury Abbey
4062 Malmesbury Abbey

NOTE : FOR LOCOS 4000, 4016, 4032 AND 4037 SEE " CASTLE " CLASS

" Star" Class, No. 4031, " Queen Mary "

"Castle" Class

No. 5071, "Spitfire"

" Castle " Class

4-6-0 (4 Cyl.)   4073 Class

Introduced 1923.
Weights : Loco. 79 tons 17 cwt.
                Tender 46 tons 14 cwt.
Pressure : 225 lb.   Cyls. 16″×26″.
Driving Wheels : 6′8½″. T.E. : 31625

100	A1 Lloyds
111	Viscount Churchill
4000	North Star
4016	The Somerset Light Infantry (Prince Albert's)
4032	Queen Alexandra
4037	The South Wales Borderers
4073	Caerphilly Castle
4074	Caldicot Castle
4075	Cardiff Castle
4076	Carmarthen Castle
4077	Chepstow Castle
4078	Pembroke Castle
4079	Pendennis Castle
4080	Powderham Castle
4081	Warwick Castle
4082	Windsor Castle
4083	Abbotsbury Castle
4084	Aberystwyth Castle
4085	Berkeley Castle
4086	Builth Castle
4087	Cardigan Castle
4088	Dartmouth Castle
4089	Donnington Castle
4090	Dorchester Castle
4091	Dudley Castle
4092	Dunraven Castle
4093	Dunster Castle
4094	Dynevor Castle
4095	Harlech Castle
4096	Highclere Castle
4097	Kenilworth Castle
4098	Kidwelly Castle
4099	Kilgerran Castle

(Class continued Locos 5000-5097)

2-6-2T   5100 Class

4100	4110	4120	4130
4101	4111	4121	4131
4102	4112	4122	4132
4103	4113	4123	4133
4104	4114	4124	4134
4105	4115	4125	4135
4106	4116	4126	4136
4107	4117	4127	4137
4108	4118	4128	4138
4109	4119	4129	4139

(Class continued 5100)

2-8-0T   4200 Class

Introduced 1910.
Weight : 82 tons 2 cwt.
Pressure : 200 lb.   Cyls. 19″ × 30″.
Driving Wheels : 4′7½″. T.E. : 33170.

4200	4230	4258	4279
4201	4231	4259	4280
4203	4232	4260	4281
4206	4233	4261	4282
4207	4235	4262	4283
4208	4236	4263	4284
4211	4237	4264	4285
4212	4238	4265	4286
4213	4241	4266	4287
4214	4242	4267	4288
4215	4243	4268	4289
4217	4246	4269	4290
4218	4247	4270	4291
4221	4248	4271	4292
4222	4250	4272	4293
4223	4251	4273	4294
4224	4252	4274	4295
4225	4253	4275	4296
4226	4254	4276	4297
4227	4255	4277	4298
4228	4256	4278	4299
4229	4257		

(Class continued 5200)

4300 Class

5600 Class

4500 Class

2-6-0　　　4300 Class

Introduced 1911.
Weights : Loco. 62 tons 0 cwt.
　　　　　Tender 40 tons 0 cwt.
Pressure : 200 lb. Cyls. 18½″×30″.
Driving Wheels : 5′ 8″. T.E. : 25670.

4303	4326	4358	4377
4318	4337	4365	4381
4320	4353	4375	4386

(Class continued 5303)

2-6-2T　　　4400 Class

Introduced 1904.
Weight : 56 tons 13 cwt.
Pressure : 180 lb Cyls. 17″×24″
Driving Wheels : 4′ 1½″ T.E. 21440.

4400	4403	4406	4409
4401	4404	4407	4410
4402	4405	4408	

2-6-2T　　　4500 Class

Introduced 1906.
Weight : 61 tons 0 cwt.
Pressure : 200 lb. Cyls. 17″ × 24″.
Driving Wheels : 4′ 7½″. T.E. : 21250.

4500	4517	4534	4551
4501	4518	4535	4552
4502	4519	4536	4553
4503	4520	4537	4554
4504	4521	4538	4555
4505	4522	4539	4556
4506	4523	4540	4557
4507	4524	4541	4558
4508	4525	4542	4559
4509	4526	4543	4560
4510	4527	4544	4561
4511	4528	4545	4562
4512	4529	4546	4563
4513	4530	4547	4564
4514	4531	4548	4565
4515	4532	4549	4566
4516	4533	4550	4567

4568	4576	4584	4592
4569	4577	4585	4593
4570	4578	4586	4594
4571	4579	4587	4595
4572	4580	4588	4596
4573	4581	4589	4597
4574	4582	4590	4598
4575	4583	4591	4599

(Class continued 5500)

0-6-0T　　　5700 Class

(Class continued from 3799)

4600	4620	4640	4660
4601	4621	4641	4661
4602	4622	4642	4662
4603	4623	4643	4663
4604	4624	4644	4664
4605	4625	4645	4665
4606	4626	4646	4666
4607	4627	4647	4667
4608	4628	4648	4668
4609	4629	4649	4669
4610	4630	4650	4670
4611	4631	4651	4671
4612	4632	4652	4672
4613	4633	4653	4673
4614	4634	4654	4674
4615	4635	4655	4675
4616	4636	4656	4676
4617	4637	4657	4678
4618	4638	4658	4679
4619	4639	4659	

(Class continued 5700)

2-8-0　　　4700 Class

Introduced 1919.
Weights : Loco. 82 tons 0 cwt.
　　　　　　Tender 46 tons 14 cwt.
Pressure : 225 lb. Cyls. 19″ × 30″.
Driving Wheels : 5′ 8″. T.E. : 30460.

4700	4703	4705	4707
4701	4704	4706	4708
4702			

" Hall " Class

No. 5916, "Trinity Hall"

4800 Class

0-4-2T   4800 Class

introduced 1932.
Weight : 41 tons 6 cwt.
Pressure : 165 lb. Cyls. 16″ × 24″.
Driving Wheels : 5′ 2″. T.E.: 13900.

FITTED FOR AUTO TRAIN WORKING

4800	4819	4838	4857
4801	4820	4839	4858
4802	4821	4840	4859
4803	4822	4841	4860
4804	4823	4842	4861
4805	4824	4843	4862
4806	4825	4844	4863
4807	4826	4845	4864
4808	4827	4846	4865
4809	4828	4847	4866
4810	4829	4848	4867
4811	4830	4849	4868
4812	4831	4850	4869
4813	4832	4851	4870
4814	4833	4852	4871
4815	4834	4853	4872
4816	4835	4854	4873
4817	4836	4855	4874
4818	4837	4856	

(Class continued 5800)

" Hall " Class

4-6-0   4900 Class

introduced 1928.
Weights : Loco. 75 tons 0 cwt.
          Tender 46 tons 14 cwt.
Pressure : 225 lb. Cyls. 18½″ × 30″.
Driving Wheels : 6′ 0″. T.E. : 27275.

4900 Saint Martin
4901 Adderley Hall
4902 Aldenham Hall
4903 Astley Hall
4904 Binnegar Hall
4905 Barton Hall
4906 Bradfield Hall
4907 Broughton Hall
4908 Broome Hall
4909 Blakesley Hall
4910 Blaisdon Hall
4912 Berrington Hall
4913 Baglan Hall
4914 Cranmore Hall
4915 Condover Hall
4916 Crumlin Hall
4917 Crosswood Hall
4918 Dartington Hall
4919 Donnington Hall
4920 Dumbleton Hall
4921 Eaton Hall
4922 Enville Hall
4923 Evenley Hall
4924 Eydon Hall

4900 Class—*continued.*
4925 Eynsham Hall
4926 Fairleigh Hall
4927 Farnborough Hall
4928 Gatacre Hall
4929 Goytrey Hall
4930 Hagley Hall
4931 Hanbury Hall
4932 Hatherton Hall
4933 Himley Hall
4934 Hindlip Hall
4935 Ketley Hall
4936 Kinlet Hall
4937 Lanelay Hall
4938 Liddington Hall
4939 Littleton Hall
4940 Ludford Hall
4941 Llangedwyn Hall
4942 Maindy Hall
4943 Marrington Hall
4944 Middleton Hall
4945 Milligan Hall
4946 Moseley Hall
4947 Nanhoran Hall
4948 Northwick Hall
4949 Packwood Hall
4950 Patshull Hall
4951 Pendeford Hall
4952 Peplow Hall
4953 Pitchford Hall
4954 Plaish Hall
4955 Plaspower Hall
4956 Plowden Hall
4957 Postlip Hall
4958 Priory Hall
4959 Purley Hall
4960 Pyle Hall
4961 Pyrland Hall
4962 Ragley Hall
4963 Rignall Hall
4964 Rodwell Hall
4965 Rood Ashton Hall
4966 Shakenhurst Hall
4967 Shirenewton Hall
4968 Shotton Hall
4969 Shrugborough Hall

4970 Sketty Hall
4971 Stanway Hall
4972 Saint Brides Hall
4973 Sweeney Hall
4974 Talgarth Hall
4975 Umberslade Hall
4976 Warfield Hall
4977 Watcombe Hall
4978 Westwood Hall
4979 Wootton Hall
4980 Wrottesley Hall
4981 Abberley Hall
4982 Acton Hall
4983 Albert Hall
4984 Albrighton Hall
4985 Allesley Hall
4986 Aston Hall
4987 Brockley Hall
4988 Bulwell Hall
4989 Cherwell Hall
4990 Clifton Hall
4991 Cobham Hall
4992 Crosby Hall
4993 Dalton Hall
4994 Downton Hall
4995 Easton Hall
4996 Eden Hall
4997 Elton Hall
4998 Eyton Hall
4999 Gopsal Hall
(Class continued: 5900–5999)

" Castle " Class
4-6-0 (4-Cyl.) 4073 Class
(Continued from 4099)
5000 Launceston Castle
5001 Llandovery Castle
5002 Ludlow Castle
5003 Lulworth Castle
5004 Llanstephan Castle
5005 Manorbier Castle
5006 Tregenna Castle
5007 Rougemont Castle
5008 Raglan Castle
5009 Shrewsbury Castle

4073 Class—*continued.*

5010 Restormel Castle
5011 Tintagel Castle
5012 Berry Pomeroy Castle
5013 Abergavenny Castle
5014 Goodrich Castle
5015 Kingswear Castle
5016 Montgomery Castle
5017 St. Donats Castle
5018 St. Mawes Castle
5019 Treago Castle
5020 Trematon Castle
5021 Whittington Castle
5022 Wigmore Castle
5023 Brecon Castle
5024 Carew Castle
5025 Chirk Castle
5026 Criccieth Castle
5027 Farleigh Castle
5028 Llantilio Castle
5029 Nunney Castle
5030 Shirburn Castle
5031 Totnes Castle
5032 Usk Castle
5033 Broughton Castle
5034 Corfe Castle
5035 Coity Castle
5036 Lyonshall Castle
5037 Monmouth Castle
5038 Morlais Castle
5039 Rhuddlan Castle
5040 Stokesay Castle
5041 Tiverton Castle
5042 Winchester Castle
5043 Earl of Mount Edgcumbe
5044 Earl of Dunraven
5045 Earl of Dudley
5046 Earl Cawdor
5047 Earl of Dartmouth
5048 Earl of Devon
5049 Earl of Plymouth
5050 Earl of St. Germans
5051 Earl Bathurst
5052 Earl of Radnor
5053 Earl Cairns
5054 Earl of Ducie
5055 Earl of Eldon
5056 Earl of Powis
5057 Earl Waldegrave
5058 Earl of Clancarty
5059 Earl St. Aldwyn
5060 Earl of Berkeley
5061 Earl of Birkenhead
5062 Earl of Shaftesbury
5063 Earl Baldwin
5064 Bishop's Castle
5065 Newport Castle
5066 Wardour Castle
5067 St. Fagans Castle
5068 Beverston Castle
5069 Isambard Kingdom
                    Brunel
5070 Sir Daniel Gooch
5071 Spitfire
5072 Hurricane
5073 Blenheim
5074 Hampden
5075 Wellington
5076 Gladiator
5077 Fairey Battle
5078 Beaufort
5079 Lysander
5080 Defiant
5081 Lockheed-Hudson
5082 Swordfish
5083 Bath Abbey
5084 Reading Abbey
5085 Evesham Abbey
5086 Viscount Horne
5087 Tintern Abbey
5088 Llanthony Abbey
5089 Westminster Abbey
5090 Neath Abbey
5091 Cleeve Abbey
5092 Tresco Abbey
5093 Upton Castle
5094 Tretower Castle
5095 Barbury Castle
5096 Bridgwater Castle
5097 Sarum Castle

2-6-2T 5100 Class

Introduced 1929.
Weight : 78 tons 9 cwt.
Pressure : 200 lb. Cyls. 18" × 30".
Driving Wheels: 5' 8".   T.E.: 24300·

(Continued from 4139)

5101	5131	5156	5178
5102	5132	5157	5179
5103	5134	5158	5180
5104	5135	5159	5181
5105	5136	5160	5182
5106	5137	5161	5183
5107	5138	5162	5184
5108	5139	5163	5185
5109	5140	5164	5186
5110	5141	5165	5187
5111	5142	5166	5188
5112	5143	5167	5189
5113	5144	5168	5190
5114	5146	5169	5191
5117	5147	5170	5192
5119	5148	5171	5193
5121	5149	5172	5194
5122	5150	5173	5195
5125	5151	5174	5196
5127	5152	5175	5197
5128	5153	5176	5198
5129	5154	5177	5199
5130	5155		

2-8-0T 4200 Class

(Continued from 4299)

5200	5217	5234	5251
5201	5218	5235	5252
5202	5219	5236	5253
5203	5220	5237	5254
5204	5221	5238	5255
5205	5222	5239	5256
5206	5223	5240	5257
5207	5224	5241	5258
5208	5225	5242	5259
5209	5226	5243	5260
5210	5227	5244	5261
5211	5228	5245	5262
5212	5229	5246	5263
5213	5230	5247	5264
5214	5231	5248	
5215	5232	5249	
5216	5233	5250	

2-6-0 4300 Class

(Continued from 4386)

5303	5323	5349	5385
5306	5324	5355	5392
5310	5330	5356	5394
5311	5336	5367	5395
5312	5339	5370	5396
5316	5345	5371	5397
5317	5346	5375	5398
5319	5347	5377	5399
5321	5348	5380	

(Class continued 6300)

4200 Class

28

0-6-0T   5400 Class

Introduced 1931.
Weight : 46 tons 12 cwt.
Pressure : 165 lb. Cyls. 16½″×24″.
Driving Wheels : 5′ 2″. T.E. : 14780.

FITTED FOR AUTO TRAIN WORKING.

5400	5407	5414	5421
5401	5408	5415	5422
5402	5409	5416	5423
5403	5410	5417	5424
5404	5411	5418	
5405	5412	5419	
5406	5413	5420	

2-6-2T   4500 Class

(Continued from 4599)

5500	5519	5538	5557
5501	5520	5539	5558
5502	5521	5540	5559
5503	5522	5541	5560
5504	5523	5542	5561
5505	5524	5543	5562
5506	5525	5544	5563
5507	5526	5545	5564
5508	5527	5546	5565
5509	5528	5547	5566
5510	5529	5548	5567
5511	5530	5549	5568
5512	5531	5550	5569
5513	5532	5551	5570
5514	5533	5552	5571
5515	5534	5553	5572
5516	5535	5554	5573
5517	5536	5555	5574
5518	5537	5556	

0-6-2T   5600 Class

Introduced 1924.
Weight : 68 tons 12 cwt.
Pressure : 200 lb. Cyls. 18″ × 26″.
Driving Wheels : 4′ 7½″. T.E. : 25800.

5600	5606	5612	5618
5601	5607	5613	5619
5602	5608	5614	5620
5603	5609	5615	5621
5604	5610	5616	5622
5605	5611	5617	5623

5600 Class—continued.

5624	5643	5662	5681
5625	5644	5663	5682
5626	5645	5664	5683
5627	5646	5665	5684
5628	5647	5666	5685
5629	5648	5667	5686
5630	5649	5668	5687
5631	5650	5669	5688
5632	5651	5670	5689
5633	5652	5671	5690
5634	5653	5672	5691
5635	5654	5673	5692
5636	5655	5674	5693
5637	5656	5675	5694
5638	5657	5676	5695
5639	5658	5677	5696
5640	5659	5678	5697
5641	5660	5679	5698
5642	5661	5680	5699

0-6-0T   5700 Class

Introduced 1929.
Weight : 49 tons 0 cwt.
Pressure : 200 lb. Cyls. 17½″×24″.
Driving Wheels : 4′ 7½″. T.E. : 22515.

(Continued from 4667)

5700	5721	5742	5763
5701	5722	5743	5764
5702	5723	5744	5765
5703	5724	5745	5766
5704	5725	5746	5767
5705	5726	5747	5768
5706	5727	5748	5769
5707	5728	5749	5770
5708	5729	5750	5771
5709	5730	5751	5772
5710	5731	5752	5773
5711	5732	5753	5774
5712	5733	5754	5775
5713	5734	5755	5776
5714	5735	5756	5777
5715	5736	5757	5778
5716	5737	5758	5779
5717	5738	5759	5780
5718	5739	5760	5781
5719	5740	5761	5782
5720	5741	5762	5783

5700 Class—*continued.*

5784	5788	5792	5796
5785	5789	5793	5797
5786	5790	5794	5798
5787	5791	5795	5799

(Class continued 6700)

0-4-2T　　　　4800 Class

NOT FITTED FOR AUTO TRAIN
WORKING.

(Continued from 4874)

5800	5805	5810	5815
5801	5806	5811	5816
5802	5807	5812	5817
5803	5808	5813	5818
5804	5809	5814	5819

"Hall" Class
4-6-0　　　　4900 Class

(Continued from 4999)

5900 Hinderton Hall
5901 Hazel Hall
5902 Howick Hall
5903 Keele Hall
5904 Kelham Hall
5905 Knowsley Hall
5906 Lawton Hall
5907 Marble Hall
5908 Moreton Hall
5909 Newton Hall

5910 Park Hall
5911 Preston Hall
5912 Queen's Hall
5913 Rushton Hall
5914 Ripon Hall
5915 Trentham Hall
5916 Trinity Hall
5917 Westminster Hall
5918 Walton Hall
5919 Worsley Hall
5920 Wycliffe Hall
5921 Bingley Hall
5922 Caxton Hall
5923 Colston Hall
5924 Dinton Hall
5925 Eastcote Hall
5926 Grotrian Hall
5927 Guild Hall
5928 Haddon Hall
5929 Hanham Hall
5930 Hannington Hall
5931 Hatherley Hall
5932 Haydon Hall
5933 Kinsgway Hall
5934 Kneller Hall
5935 Norton Hall
5936 Oakley Hall
5937 Stanford Hall
5938 Stanley Hall
5939 Tangley Hall
5940 Whitbourne Hall
5941 Campion Hall

No. 2166, ex B.P.G.V.

4900 Class—*continued*.
5942 Doldowlod Hall
5943 Elmdon Hall
5944 Ickenham Hall
5945 Leckhampton Hall
5946 Marwell Hall
5947 Saint Benet's Hall
5948 Siddington Hall
5949 Trematon Hall
5950 Wardley Hall
5951 Clyffe Hall
5952 Cogan Hall
5953 Dunley Hall
5954 Faendre Hall
5955 Garth Hall
5956 Horsley Hall
5957 Hutton Hall
5958 Knolton Hall
5959 Mawley Hall
5960 Saint Edmund Hall
5961 Toynbee Hall
5962 Wantage Hall
5963 Wimpole Hall
5964 Wolseley Hall
5965 Woollas Hall
5966 Ashford Hall
5967 Bickmarsh Hall
5968 Cory Hall
5969 Honington Hall
5970 Hengrave Hall
5971 Merevale Hall
5972 Olton Hall
5973 Rolleston Hall
5974 Wallsworth Hall
5975 Winslow Hall
5976 Ashwicke Hall
5977 Beckford Hall
5978 Bodinnick Hall
5979 Cruckton Hall
5980 Dingley Hall
5981 Frensham Hall
5982 Harrington Hall
5983 Henley Hall
5984 Linden Hall
5985 Mostyn Hall

5986 Arbury Hall
5987 Brocket Hall
5988 Bostock Hall
5989 Cransley Hall
5990 Dorford Hall
5991 Gresham Hall
5992 Horton Hall
5993 Kirby Hall
5994 Roydon Hall
5995 Wick Hall
5996 Mytton Hall
5997 Sparkford Hall
5998 Trevor Hall
5999 Wollaton Hall
(Class continued 6900)

"King" Class
4-6-0 (4-Cyl.) 6000 Class

Introduced 1927.
Weights : Loco. 89 tons 0 cwt.
Tender 46 tons 14 cwt.
Pressure : 250 lb. Cyls. $16\frac{1}{4}'' \times 28''$
Driving Wheels : 6' 6". T.E.: 40300.

6000 King George V
6001 King Edward VII
6002 King William IV
6003 King George IV
6004 King George III
6005 King George II
6006 King George I
6007 King William III
6008 King James II
6009 King Charles II
6010 King Charles I
6011 King James I
6012 King Edward VI
6013 King Henry VIII
6014 King Henry VII
6015 King Richard III
6016 King Edward V
6017 King Edward IV
6018 King Henry VI
6019 King Henry V
6020 King Henry IV
6021 King Richard II
6022 King Edward III

6000 Class—continued.
6023 King Edward II
6024 King Edward I
6025 King Henry III
6026 King John
6027 King Richard I
6028 King George VI
6029 King Edward VIII

2-6-2T   6100 Class
Introduced 1931.
Weight : 78 tons 9 cwt.
Pressure : 225 lb. Cyls. 18″ × 30″.
Driving Wheels : 5′ 8″. T.E.: 27340.

6100	6118	6136	6154
6101	6119	6137	6155
6102	6120	6138	6156
6103	6121	6139	6157
6104	6122	6140	6158
6105	6123	6141	6159
6106	6124	6142	6160
6107	6125	6143	6161
6108	6126	6144	6162
6109	6127	6145	6163
6110	6128	6146	6164
6111	6129	6147	6165
6112	6130	6148	6166
6113	6131	6149	6167
6114	6132	6150	6168
6115	6133	6151	6169
6116	6134	6152	
6117	6135	6153	

2-6-0   4300 Class
(Continued from 5399)

6300	6310	6320	6330
6301	6311	6321	6331
6302	6312	6322	6332
6303	6313	6323	6333
6304	6314	6324	6334
6305	6315	6325	6335
6306	6316	6326	6336
6307	6317	6327	6337
6308	6318	6328	6338
6309	6319	6329	6339

6340	6355	6370	6385
6341	6356	6371	6386
6342	6357	6372	6387
6343	6358	6373	6388
6344	6359	6374	6389
6345	6360	6375	6390
6346	6361	6376	6391
6347	6362	6377	6392
6348	6363	6378	6393
6349	6364	6379	6394
6350	6365	6380	6395
6351	6366	6381	6396
6352	6367	6382	6397
6353	6368	6383	6398
6354	6369	6384	6399

(Class continued 7300)

0-6-0T   6400 Class
Introduced 1932.
Weight : 45 tons 12 cwt.
Pressure : 165 lb. Cyls. 16½″ × 24″.
Driving Wheels : 4′ 7½″. T.E.: 16510.
FITTED FOR AUTO TRAIN
WORKING

6400	6410	6420	6430
6401	6411	6421	6431
6402	6412	6422	6432
6403	6413	6423	6433
6404	6414	6424	6434
6405	6415	6425	6435
6406	6416	6426	6436
6407	6417	6427	6437
6408	6418	6428	6438
6409	6419	6429	6439

0-6-2T   5600 Class
(Continued from 5699)

6600	6611	6622	6633
6601	6612	6623	6634
6602	6613	6624	6635
6603	6614	6625	6636
6604	6615	6626	6637
6605	6616	6627	6638
6606	6617	6628	6639
6607	6618	6629	6640
6608	6619	6630	6641
6609	6620	6631	6642
6610	6621	6632	6643

5600 Class—*continued.*

6644	6658	6672	6686
6645	6659	6673	6687
6646	6660	6674	6688
6647	6661	6675	6689
6648	6662	6676	6690
6649	6663	6677	6691
6650	6664	6678	6692
6651	6665	6679	6693
6652	6666	6680	6694
6653	6667	6681	6695
6654	6668	6682	6696
6655	6669	6683	6697
6656	6670	6684	6698
6657	6671	6685	6699

0-6-0T   5700 Class

(Continued from 5799)

6700	6713	6726	6739
6701	6714	6727	6740
6702	6715	6728	6741
6703	6716	6729	6742
6704	6717	6730	6743
6705	6718	6731	6744
6706	6719	6732	6745
6707	6720	6733	6746
6708	6721	6734	6747
6709	6722	6735	6748
6710	6723	6736	6749
6711	6724	6737	
6712	6725	6738	

(Class continued 7700)

" Grange " Class
4-6-0   6800 Class

Introduced 1936.
Weights : Loco. 74 tons 0 cwt.
        Tender 40 tons 0 cwt.
Pressure : 225 lbs. Cyls. 18½" × 30".
Driving Wheels : 5′ 8″. T.E. : 28875.

6800 Arlington Grange
6801 Aylburton Grange
6802 Bampton Grange
6803 Bucklebury Grange
6804 Brockington Grange
6805 Broughton Grange
6806 Blackwell Grange

6807 Birchwood Grange
6808 Beenham Grange
6809 Burghclere Grange
6810 Blakemere Grange
6811 Cranbourne Grange
6812 Chesford Grange
6813 Eastbury Grange
6814 Enbourne Grange
6815 Frilford Grange
6816 Frankton Grange
6817 Gwenddwr Grange
6818 Hardwick Grange
6819 Highnam Grange
6820 Kingstone Grange
6821 Leaton Grange
6822 Manton Grange
6823 Oakley Grange
6824 Ashley Grange
6825 Llanvair Grange
6826 Nannerth Grange
6827 Llanfrechfa Grange
6828 Trellech Grange
6829 Burmington Grange
6830 Buckenhill Grange
6831 Bearley Grange
6832 Brockton Grange
6833 Calcot Grange
6834 Dummer Grange
6835 Eastham Grange
6836 Estevarney Grange
6837 Forthampton Grange
6838 Goodmoor Grange
6839 Hewell Grange
6840 Hazeley Grange
6841 Marlas Grange
6842 Nunhold Grange
6843 Poulton Grange
6844 Penhydd Grange
6845 Paviland Grange
6846 Ruckley Grange
6847 Tidmarsh Grange
6848 Toddington Grange
6849 Walton Grange
6850 Cleeve Grange
6851 Hurst Grange

No. 6800 " Arlington Grange "

No. 7800 " Torquay Manor "

7200 Class

34

6800 Class—*continued.*

6852 Headbourne Grange
6853 Morehampton Grange
6854 Roundhill Grange
6855 Saighton Grange
6856 Stowe Grange
6857 Tudor Grange
6858 Woolston Grange
6859 Yiewsley Grange
6860 Aberporth Grange
6861 Crynant Grange
6862 Derwent Grange
6863 Dolhywel Grange
6864 Dymock Grange
6865 Hopton Grange
6866 Morfa Grange
6867 Peterston Grange
6868 Penrhos Grange
6869 Resolven Grange
6870 Bodicote Grange
6871 Bourton Grange
6872 Crawley Grange
6873 Caradoc Grange
6874 Haughton Grange
6875 Hindford Grange
6876 Kingsland Grange
6877 Llanfair Grange
6878 Longford Grange
6879 Overton Grange

" Hall " Class
4-6-0   4900 Class
(Continued from 5999)

6900 Abney Hall
6901 Arley Hall
6902 Butlers Hall
6903 Belmont Hall
6904 Charfield Hall
6905 Claughton Hall
6906 Chicheley Hall
6907 Davenham Hall
6908 Downham Hall
6909 Frewin Hall
6910 Gossington Hall
6911 Holker Hall

6912 Helmster Hall
6913 Levens Hall
6914 Langton Hall
6915 Mursley Hall

		6952	
		6953	
6916	6928	6940	6954
6917	6929	6941	6955
6918	6930	6942	6956
6919	6931	6943	6957
6920	6932	6944	6958
6921	6933	6945	6959
6922	6934	6946	6960
6923	6935	6947	6961
6924	6936	6948	6962
6925	6937	6949	6963
6926	6938	6950	6964
6927	6939	6951	6966

2-8-2T   7200 Class
Introduced 1934.
Weight : 92 tons 12 cwt.
Pressure : 200 lb. Cyls. 19″ × 30″.
Driving Wheels : 4′7½″. T.E. 33170.

7200	7214	7228	7242
7201	7215	7229	7243
7202	7216	7230	7244
7203	7217	7231	7245
7204	7218	7232	7246
7205	7219	7233	7247
7206	7220	7234	7248
7207	7221	7235	7249
7208	7222	7236	7250
7209	7223	7237	7251
7210	7224	7238	7252
7211	7225	7239	7253
7212	7226	7240	
7213	7227	7241	

2-6-0   4300 Class
(Continued from 6399)

7300	7306	7312	7318
7301	7307	7313	7319
7302	7308	7314	7320
7303	7309	7315	7321
7304	7310	7316	
7305	7311	7317	

(Class continued 8300)

0-6-0T   7400 Class

Introduced : 1936
Weight : 45 tons 9 cwt.
Pressure : 180 lb.
Cyls. : 16½″ × 24″.
Driving Wheels : 4′ 7½″.   T.E. : 18010

7400	7408	7416	7424
7401	7409	7417	7425
7402	7410	7418	7426
7403	7411	7419	7427
7404	7412	7420	7428
7405	7413	7421	7429
7406	7414	7422	
7407	7415	7423	

0-6-0T   5700 Class

(Continued from 6749)

7700	7725	7750	7775
7701	7726	7751	7776
7702	7727	7752	7777
7703	7728	7753	7778
7704	7729	7754	7779
7705	7730	7755	7780
7706	7731	7756	7781
7707	7732	7757	7782
7708	7733	7758	7783
7709	7734	7759	7784
7710	7735	7760	7785
7711	7736	7761	7786
7712	7737	7762	7787
7713	7738	7763	7788
7714	7739	7764	7789
7715	7740	7765	7790
7716	7741	7766	7791
7717	7742	7767	7792
7718	7743	7768	7793
7719	7744	7769	7794
7720	7745	7770	7795
7721	7746	7771	7796
7722	7747	7772	7797
7723	7748	7773	7798
7724	7749	7774	7799

(Class continued 8700)

" Manor " Class
4-6-0   7800 Class

Introduced 1938.
Weights : Loco. 68 tons 18 cwt.
            Tender 40 tons 0 cwt.
Pressure : 225 lb. Cyls. 18″× 30″.
Driving Wheels : 5′ 8″.   T.E.: 27340

7800 Torquay Manor
7801 Anthony Manor
7802 Bradley Manor
7803 Barcote Manor
7804 Baydon Manor
7805 Broome Manor
7806 Cockington Manor
7807 Compton Manor
7808 Cookham Manor
7809 Childrey Manor
7810 Draycott Manor
7811 Dunley Manor
7812 Erlestoke Manor
7813 Freshford Manor
7814 Fringford Manor
7815 Fritwell Manor
7816 Frilsham Manor
7817 Garsington Manor
7818 Granville Manor
7819 Hinton Manor

2-6-2T   8100 Class

Introduced 1938.
Weight : 76 tons 11 cwt.
Pressure : 225 lb.
Cyls. : 18″ × 30″.
Driving Wheels : 5′6″   T.E. : 28165

8100	8103	8106	8109
8101	8104	8107	
8102	8105	8108	

2-6-0   4300 Class

(Continued from 7321)

8300	8314	8326	8334
8302	8315	8327	8335
8305	8318	8328	8337
8307	8320	8331	8338
8309	8322	8332	8340
8313	8325	8333	8341

4300 Class—continued.

8343	8360	8373	8386
8344	8361	8374	8388
8350	8362	8376	8390
8351	8364	8378	8391
8353	8365	8379	8393
8357	8368	8381	
8358	8369	8382	
8359	8372	8384	

(Class continued 9300)

0-6-0T   5700 Class

(Continued from 7799)

8700	8715	8730	8745
8701	8716	8731	8746
8702	8717	8732	8747
8703	8718	8733	8748
8704	8719	8734	8749
8705	8720	8735	8750
8706	8721	8736	8751
8707	8722	8737	8752
8708	8723	8738	8753
8709	8724	8739	8754
8710	8725	8740	8755
8711	8726	8741	8756
8712	8727	8742	8757
8713	8728	8743	8758
8714	8729	8744	8759

8760	8770	8780	8790
8761	8771	8781	8791
8762	8772	8782	8792
8763	8773	8783	8793
8764	8774	8784	8794
8765	8775	8785	8795
8766	8776	8786	8796
8767	8777	8787	8797
8768	8778	8788	8798
8769	8779	8789	8799

(Class continued 9700)

2-6-0   4300 Class

(Continued from 8393)

9300	9305	9310	9315
9301	9306	9311	9316
9302	9307	9312	9317
9303	9308	9313	9318
9304	9309	9314	9319

0-6-0T   5700 Class

(Continued from 8799)

*9700	*9705	*9710	9715
*9701	*9706	9711	9716
*9702	*9707	9712	9717
*9703	*9708	9713	9718
*9704	*9709	9714	9719

* Fitted with condensers.

No. 9716, " 5700 " Class

37

Stream-lined Railcar No. 19

5700 Class—*continued.*

9720	9740	9760	9780
9721	9741	9761	9781
9722	9742	9762	9782
9723	9743	9763	9783
9724	9744	9764	9784
9725	9745	9765	9785
9726	9746	9766	9786
9727	9747	9767	9787
9728	9748	9768	9788
9729	9749	9769	9789
9730	9750	9770	9790
9731	9751	9771	9791
9732	9752	9772	9792
9733	9753	9773	9793
9734	9754	9774	9794
9735	9755	9775	9795
9736	9756	9776	9796
9737	9757	9777	9797
9738	9758	9778	9798
9739	9759	9779	9799

STREAM-LINED
DIESEL RAIL-CARS

1	11	21	31
2	12	22	32
3	13	23	33
4	14	24	34*
5	15	25	35
6	16	26	36
7	17*	27	37
8	18	28	38
9	19	29	
10	20	30	

* Parcels Cars

SERVICE LOCOS.
Oil and Petrol

0-4-0 : 23, 24, 26 and 27

LOCOMOTIVE RUNNING SHEDS AND CODES

Depot	Code	Depot	Code
Aberdare	ABDR	Llanelly	LLY
Aberbeeg ...	ABEEG	Llantrisant ...	LTS
Aberystwyth ...	ABH	Lydney	LYD
Banbury	BAN	Machynlleth ...	MCH
Birkenhead ...	BHD	Neath	NEA
Birmingham		Newport Dock ...	PILL
(Tyseley)	TYS	Newport ...	NPT
Brecon	BCN	Ebbw Jct. ...	EBBWJ
Bristol		Newton Abbot ...	NA
Bath Road ...	BL	Neyland	NEY
St. Philips		Old Oak Common.	PDN
Marsh ...	SPM	Oswestry	OSW
Burry Port ...	BP	Oxford	OXF
Cardiff	CDF	Oxley	OXY
Cardiff Valleys	CV Prefix	Pantyffynnon ...	PFN
Abercynon ...	(AYN)	Penzance	PZ
Barry	(BRY)	Plymouth (Laira)..	LA
Caeharris ...	(CH)	Pontypool Road ...	PPRᴰ
Cardiff East Dcks.	(CED)	Reading...	RDG
Cathays	(CYS)	Severn Tunnel Jct.	STJ
Dowlais Central	(DLIS)	Shrewsbury ...	SALOP
Ferndale	(FDL)	Slough	SLO
Merthyr	(MTHR)	Southall	SHL
Radyr Jct. ...	(RYR)	St. Blazey ...	STB
Rhymney	(RHY)	Stourbridge ...	STB
Treherbert ...	(TRT)	Swansea East Dock	SED
Carmarthen ...	CARM	Swindon	SDN
Chester	CHR	Taunton	TN
Croes Newydd ...	CNYD	Tondu	TDU
Danygraig ...	DG	Truro	TR
Didcot	DID	Wellington ...	WLN
Duffryn Yard ...	PT	Westbury ...	WES
Exeter	EXE	Weymouth ...	WEY
Fishguard		Wolverhampton ⎰	WPN
(Goodwick)	FGD	(Stafford Road) ⎱	SRD
Gloucester ...	GLO	Worcester	WOS
Hereford ...	HFD	Whitland	WTD
Kidderminster ...	KDR	Yeovil	YEO
Leamington ...	LMTN		
Llandore	LDR		

39

Principal Dimensions of G.W.R. Engines

Class	Wheels	Date	Weight (full) Loco. T. Cwt	Weight (full) Tender T. Cwt	Pressure Lb. per sq. in	Cylinders (2 unless otherwise shown)	Driving Wheels	Tractive Effort Lb	Power Class	Route Restriction Colour
517	0-4-2T	1868	35 4	— —	165	16"×24"	5' 2"	13,900	—	—
1101	0-4-0T	1926	38 4	— —	170	16"×24"	3' 9½"	19,512	B	Red
"Sir Dan."	0-6-0PT	1870	43 18	—	165	17"×24"	4' 7½"	17,525	A	—
1361	0-6-0ST	1910	35 4	—	150	16"×20"	3' 8"	14,835		Yellow
1366	0-6-0PT	1934	35 15	—	165	16"×20"	3' 8"	16,320		—
1501	0-6-0PT	1872	42 17	—	165	17"×24"	4' 7½"	17,525	A	—
1701	0-6-0PT	1891	46 13	—	180	17"×24"	4' 7½"	19,120	A	Blue
1813	0-6-0PT	1882	44 8	—	165	17"×24"	4' 7½"	17,525		Yellow
1901	0-6-0PT	1881	36 3	—	165	16"×24"	4' 1½"	17,410	A	—
2021 }2181*	0-6-0PT	1897	39 15	—	165	16½"×24"	4' 1½"	18,515	A	—
2251	0-6-0	1930	43 8	36 15	200	17½"×24"	5' 2"	20,155	B	Yellow
2301	0-6-0	1883	36 16	36 5	180	17½"×24"	5' 2"	18,140	A	—
2600	2-6-0	1900	56 15	47 14	200	18"×26"	4' 7½"	25,800	D	Blue
2700	0-6-0PT	1896	45 13	—	180	17½"×24"	4' 7½"	20,260	A	Blue
2800	2-8-0	1903	75 10	40 0	225	18½"×30"	4' 7½"	35,380	E	Blue
2900	4-6-0	1902	72 0	40 0	225	18½"×30"	6' 8½"	24,395	C	Red
3100	2-6-2T	1938	81 0	—	225	18½"×30"	5' 3"	31,170	D	Red
3150	2-6-2T	1907	81 12	—	200	18½"×30"	5' 8"	25,670	D	Red
3200	4-4-0	1936	49 6	40 0	180	18"×26"	5' 8"	18,955	B	Yellow
3252	4-4-0	1895	47 0	34 5	189	18"×26"	5' 8"	18,955	B	Yellow

THE
A B C
OF
L M S
LOCOMOTIVES

No. 6231. "Duchess of Atholl" near Liverpool with the pre-war up
"Merseyside Express".

Compiled by

IAN ALLAN & A. B. MACLEOD

April, 1944

SOME L.M.S. STANDARD LOCOS

Class 4P 4-4-0 Compound No. 1100.

Class 7F 0-8-0 No. 9666.

Class 5F 2.6-0 No. 13174. now renumbered 2874.

INTRODUCTION

The locomotive numbers shewn in this book have been arranged in numerical order, with dimensions at the head of each class. There is no definite way of distinguishing class from class on the L.M.S. except for a system of power classification. Each batch of locos. (with a few exceptions) is given a number followed by the letter " P," for passenger, or " F," for freight. The number denotes the haulage capacity of the loco with 0, the lowest, and 8, the highest, so that the smallest freight engine is classified " 0F " and the most powerful passenger " 7P," and so on.

The building dates shewn throughout the book (unless otherwise stated) apply to the date that the first locomotive of the class was put into service.

Against each class the pre-group owner is shewn (unless " LMS " appears, which denotes a standard class) in abbreviated form as under :—

Abbreviation	Company	Chief Mechanical or Locomotive Engineer
C.R.	Caledonian Railway ...	Dugald Drummond, J. Lambie, J. F. McIntosh and W. Pickersgill.
G.S.W.R. ...	Glasgow & South Western Railway	Peter Drummond and R. H. Whitelegg
F.R.	Furness Railway	W F. Pettigrew.
H.R.	Highland Railway ...	D. Jones, P. Drummond, F. G. Smith and C. Cumming.
L.N.W.R. ...	London & North Western Railway	F. W. Webb, G. Whale, C. J. Bowen-Cooke and H. P. M. Beames.
L.T. & S. ...	London, Tilbury & Southend Rly. (M.R.)	T. Whitelegg and R. H. Whitelegg.
L.Y.R.	Lancashire & Yorkshire Railway	W. Barton Wright, J. A. F. Aspinall and G. Hughes.
M.R.	Midland Railway ...	M. Kirtley, S. W. Johnson, R. M. Deeley and H. Fowler.
N.L.R.	North London Railway (L.N.W.R.)	J. C. Park.
S. & D.J.R. ...	Somerset & Dorset Joint Railway	S. W. Johnson and H. Fowler.
L.M.S.	London Midland & Scottish Railway	G. Hughes, Sir Henry Fowler and Sir William Stanier.

These are the constituents of the present L.M.S. Railway Group, with the Chief Mechanical or Locomotive Engineers, who designed the engines listed in this book.

The Locomotives shewn in this book are as running on the L.M.S.R. at 31st January, 1944 ; the total running stock standing at 7,818 engines.

3

Classified List of Locomotives in Numerical Order

2-6-2T   3P

Designed : Fowler, 1930. L.M.S.
Driving Wheels : 5′ 3″.
Outside Cyls. : 17½″ × 26″.
Tractive Effort : 21,486 lb.
Walschaerts Valve Gear and Super-
  heater (with parallel boilers).

1	19	37†	54
2	20	38†	55
3	21†	39†	56
4	22†	40†	57
5	23†	41	58
6	24†	42	59
7	25†	43	60
8	26†	44	61
9	27†	45	62
10	28†	46	63
11	29†	47	64
12	30†	48	65
13	31†	49	66
14	32†	50	67
15	33†	51	68
16	34†	52	69
17	35†	53	70
18	36†		Total 70

† Fitted with condensing apparatus.

2-6-2T   3P

Designed : Stanier, 1935. L.M.S.
Dimensions as locos. 1-70.
Walschaerts Valve Gear and Super-
  heater (with taper boilers).

71	84	97	110
72	85	98	111
73	86	99	112
74	87	100	113
75	88	101	114
76	89	102	115
77	90	103	116
78	91	104	117
79	92	105	118
80	93	106	119
81	94	107	120
82	95	108	121
83	96	109	122

123	145	167	189
124	146	168	190
125	147	169*	191
126	148*	170	192
127	149	171	193
128	150	172	194
129	151	173	195
130	152	174	196
131	153	175	197
132	154	176	198
133	155	177	199
134	156	178	200
135	157	179	201
136	158	180	202
137	159	181	203*
138	160	182	204
139	161	183	205
140	162	184	206
141	163*	185	207
142	164	186	208
143	165	187	209
144	166	188	Total 139

* Rebuilt with larger boilers.

4-4-0   2P

Designed : Fowler, 1914-21.
S. & D.J.R.
Driving Wheels : 7′ 0½″.
Cyls. : 20½″ × 26″ (Superheated).
Tractive Effort : 17,585 lb.

322	323	324	325
326			Total 5

4-4-0   2P

Built 1882
Designed : Johnson   Rebuilt from
  1910 onwards M.R.
Driving Wheels : 7′ 0½″.
Cyls. : 20½″ × 26″ (Superheated).
Tractive Effort : 17,585 lb.

332	359	378*	395
337	362	383*	396
351	364	385*	397
353	370	391*	
356	377	394	

Total 18

* Driving Wheels : 6′ 6½″.
  Cyls. : 18½″ × 26″ (non-superheated)
  Tractive Effort : 15,962 lb.

2-6-2T Standard 3P Class (with larger boiler)

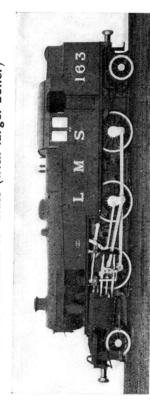

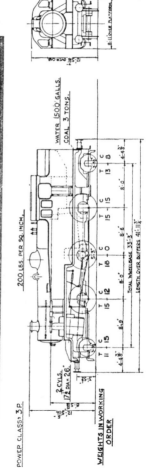

POWER CLASS: 3P

200 LBS. PER SQ. INCH.

2 CYLS.
17½ DIA. 26.

WATER 1500 GALLS.
COAL 3 TONS.

WEIGHTS IN WORKING ORDER

T C	T C	T C	T C	T C	T C
11 15	15 12	16 0	15 15	13 8	

4-4⅞" 8'0" 8'0" 8'6" 8'0" 4-4¾"

5'3½"

TOTAL WHEELBASE 33'3"

LENGTH OVER BUFFERS 41-11⅜"

12-2½ OVER

BULLNOSE PLATFORM

4-4-0   2P

Designed : Johnson, 1884-1901. M.R.
  Rebuilt Fowler, 1912-23.
Driving Wheels : 7′ 0½″.
Cyls. : 20½″ × 26.″ (Superheated).
Tractive Effort : 17,585 lb.

400	443	492	528
401	444	493	529
402	446	494	530
403	447	495	531
404	448	496	532
405	450	497	533
406	452	498	534
407	453	499	535
408	454	500	536
409	455	501	537
410	456	502	538
411	458	503	539
412	459	504	540
413	461	505	541
414	462	506	542
415	463	507	543
416	464	508	544
417	466	509	545
418	468	510	546
419	470	511	547
420	471	512	548
421	472	513	549
422	477	514	550
423	478	515	551
424	479	516	552
425	480	517	553
426	482	518	554
427	483	519	555
430	484	520	556
432	485	521	557
433	486	522	558
434	487	523	559
436	488	524	560
437	489	525	561
438	490	526	562
439	491	527	

Total 143

4-4-0   2P

Designed : Fowler, 1928-9, L.M.S.
Driving Wheels : 6′ 9″.
Cyls. : 19″ × 26″ (Superheated.)
Tractive Effort : 17,729 lb.

563	598	632	667
564	599	633*	668
565	600	634*	669
566	601	635*	670
567	602	636	671
568	603	637	672
569	604	638	673
570	605	640	674
571	606	641	675
572	607	642	676
573	608	643	677
574	609	644	678
575	610	645	679
576	611	646	680
577	612	647	681
578	613	648	682
579	614	649	683
580	615	650	684
581	616	651	685
582	617	652	686
583	618	653	687
584	619	654	688
585	620	655	689
586	621	656	690
587	622	657	691
588	623	658	692
589	624	659	693
590	625	660	694
592	626	661	695
593	627	662	696
594	628	663	697
595	629	664	698
596	630	665	699
597	631	666	700

Total 136

* Ex-S.D.J.R., Nos. 44, 45 and 46 (in
  same order).

4-4-0   3P

Designed : Johnson (Rebuilt), 1901
M.R.
Driving Wheels : 6′ 9″.
Cyls. : 20½″ × 26″.
(Superheated Fowler.)
Tractive Effort : 20,065 lb.

707	727	740	758
711	728	741	759
715	729	743	760
716	731	745	762
719	734	747	763
720	735	748	765
721	736	755	767
725	738	756	775
726	739	757	

Total 35

4-4-0 (3-Cyl. Compd.) 4P

Designed : Fowler, 1924, L.M.S.
Driving Wheels : 6′ 9″.
Cyls. : (2) 21″ × 26″, (1) 19″ × 26″
(Superheated).
Tractive Effort : 22,649 lb.

900	910	920	930
901	911	921	931
902	912	922	932
903	913	923	933
904	914	924	934
905	915	925	935
906	916	926	936
907	917	927	937
908	918	928	938
909	919	929	939

(*Continued*, 1045-1199)

4-4-0 (3-Cyl. Compd.) 4P

Designed : Deeley, 1905, M.R.
Driving Wheels : 7′ 0″.
Cyls. : (2) 21″ × 26″, (1) 19″ × 26″
(Superheated Fowler).
Tractive Effort : 21,840 lb.

1000	1011	1022	1033
1001	1012	1023	1034
1002	1013	1024	1035
1003	1014	1025	1036
1004	1015	1026	1037
1005	1016	1027	1038
1006	1017	1028	1039
1007	1018	1029	1040
1008	1019	1030	1041
1009	1020	1031	1042
1010	1021	1032	1043
			1044

Total 45

N.B.—1000 - 1004, built Johnson
1902-03. Rebuilt 1914-19.
1005, built Deeley 1905.
Rebuilt 1923.

The large photographs and diagrams throughout this book are by courtesy of the London Midland and Scottish Railway Company. The remainder are reproduced by kind permission of Messrs. A. W. Craughton, D. England and F. Moore, to whom the authors' thanks are extended.

4-4-0 Standard 2P Class

7

4-4-0 (3-Cyl. Compd.) 4P

Dimensions, etc., as locos. 900-939.

1045	1084	1123	1162
1046	1085	1124	1163
1047	1086	1125	1164
1048	1087	1126	1165
1049	1088	1127	1166
1050	1089	1128	1167
1051	1090	1129	1168
1052	1091	1130	1169
1053	1092	1131	1170
1054	1093	1132	1171
1055	1094	1133	1172
1056	1095	1134	1173
1057	1096	1135	1174
1058	1097	1136	1175
1059	1098	1137	1176
1060	1099	1138	1177
1061	1100	1139	1178
1062	1101	1140	1179
1063	1102	1141	1180
1064	1103	1142	1181
1065	1104	1143	1182
1066	1105	1144	1183
1067	1106	1145	1184
1068	1107	1146	1185
1069	1108	1147	1186
1070	1109	1148	1187
1071	1110	1149	1188
1072	1111	1150	1189
1073	1112	1151	1190
1074	1113	1152	1191
1075	1114	1153	1192
1076	1115	1154	1193
1077	1116	1155	1194
1078	1117	1156	1195
1079	1118	1157	1196
1080	1119	1158	1197
1081	1120	1159	1198
1082	1121	1160	1199
1083	1122	1161	

Total 195

0-4-4T   IP

Designed : Johnson, 1875, M.R.
Driving Wheels : 5′ 7″.
Cyls. : 18″×24″.
Tractive Effort : 13,611 lb.

1230*	1246	1251	1255
1239	1247	1252	1260
1240	1249	1253	1261

Total 12

* 2130—Ex-S.D.J.R. (No.52) Built 1877·
Driving Wheels : 5′ 4″.
Cyls.: 18″×24″.   T.E.: 16,524 lb.

0-4-4T   IP

Designed : Johnson, 1881, M.R.
Driving Wheels : 5′ 4″.
Cyls. : 18″×24″.
T.E. : 1267-1350 : 14,442 lb.
       1353-1430 : 15,491 lb.
Some locos. rebuilt with Belpaire boilers

1267	1334	1370	1403
1272	1337	1371	1404
1273	1338	1373	1406
1275	1340	1374	1407
1277	1341	1375	1408
1278	1342	1377	1409
1286	1344	1378	1411
1287	1346	1379	1413
1290	1348	1380	1416
1294	1350	1382	1420
1295	1353	1385	1421
1297	1357	1389	1422
1298	1358	1390	1423
1302	1360	1393	1424
1303	1361	1395	1425
1307	1365	1396	1426
1315	1366	1397	1428
1322	1367	1401	1429
1324	1368	1402	1430
1330			

Total 77

0-4-0ST   0 F

Designed : Johnson, M.R.
Driving Wheels : 3′ 10″.

	Date	Cyls.	T.E.
1516 ...	1897	13″×20″	8,743 lb.
1518 ...	1897	15″×20″	11,640 lb.
1523 ...	1903	15″×20″	12,472 lb.

Total 3

0-4-0T   0F

Designed : Deeley, 1907, M.R.
Driving Wheels : 3' 9¾".
Outside Cyls. : 15" × 22".
Tractive Effort : 14,635 lb.
Walschaerts Valve Gear.

1528	1531	1534	1536
1529	1532	1535	1537
1530	1533		

Total 10

0-6-0T   1F

Designed : Johnson, 1878, M.R.
Driving Wheels : 4' 7".
Cyls. : 17" × 24".
Tractive Effort : { 16,079 lb. / 15,007 lb.

1660	1727	1785	1850
1661	1734	1788	1852
1664	1738	1793	1853
1666	1739	1794	1854
1668	1742	1795	1855
1671	1745	1797	1856
1672	1747	1802	1857
1674	1748	1803	1859
1676	1749	1804	1860
1681	1751	1805	1864
1682	1752	1810	1865
1686	1753	1811	1869
1690	1754	1813	1870
1695	1755	1814	1871
1699	1756	1815	1873
1700	1759	1816	1874
1702	1762	1818	1875
1706	1763	1820	1876
1708	1767	1824	1878
1710	1768	1826	1879
1711	1769	1829	1884
1712	1770	1833	1885
1713	1771	1835	1889
1714	1773	1838	1890
1718	1777	1839	1891
1720	1778	1842	1893
1724	1779	1844	1895
1725	1780	1846	
1726	1781	1847	

Total 114

4-4-2T   2P

Designed : Whitelegg, 1900, M.R.
(L.T. & S. Section).
Driving Wheels : 6' 6".
Outside Cyls. : 19" × 26".
Tractive Effort : 17,388 lb.

2092	2097	2102	2106
2093	2098	2103	2107
2094	2099	2104	2108
2095	2100	2105	2109
2096	2101		

Total 18

4-4-2T   3P

Designed: Whitelegg/Fowler, 1923*,
L.M.S. (for L.T. & S. Section).
Driving Wheels : 6' 6".
Outside Cyls. : 19" × 26".
Tractive Effort : 17,388 lb.

2110	2123	2136	2149
2111	2124	2137	2150
2112	2125	2138	2151
2113	2126	2139	2152
2114	2127	2140	2153
2115	2128	2141	2154
2116	2129	2142	2155
2117	2130	2143	2156
2118	2131	2144	2157
2119	2132	2145	2158
2120	2133	2146	2159
2121	2134	2147	2160
2122	2135	2148	

Total 51

N.B.—Locos 2135—2146 L.T.S.R.
built from 1897, rebuilt from 1905.
Locos 2147—2150, L.T.S.R.
built 1909.
Locos 2110—2117 M.R., built
1923.

0-6-2T   3F

Designed : Whitelegg, 1903, M.R.
(L.T. & S. Section).
Driving Wheels : 5' 3".
Cyls. : 18" × 26".
Tractive Effort : 19,322 lb.

2180	2184	2188	2191
2181	2185	2189	2192
2182	2186	2190	2193
2183	2187		

Total 14

2-6-4T Standard 4P Class

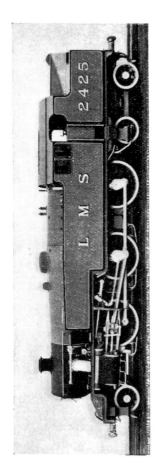

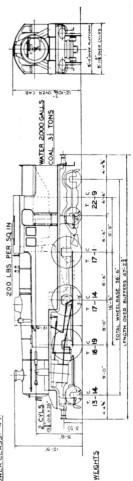

POWER CLASS: 4 P

2 CYLS
19½ DIA x 26"

200 LBS PER SQ IN

WATER 2000 GALLS
COAL 3½ TONS

WEIGHTS

T C	T C	T C	T C	T C	T C
13-14	16-19	17-14	17-1	22-9	

TOTAL WHEELBASE 36'-6"

LENGTH OVER BUFFERS 47'-2⅜"

0-10-0

Designed : Fowler, 1919, M.R.
Driving Wheels : 4′ 7½″.
Cyls. (4) : 16¾″×28″. T.E. : 43,313 lb.
Walschaerts Valve Gear.

| | 2290 | **Total 1** |

(Used for banking heavy trains up Lickey Incline)

2-6-4T   4P

Designed : Fowler, 1927, L.M.S.
Driving Wheels : 5′ 9″.
Outside Cyls. : 19″×26″.
Tractive Effort : 23,125 lb.
Walschaerts Valve Gear, Superheater and parallel boilers.

2300	2332	2364	2396
2301	2333	2365	2397
2302	2334	2366	2398
2303	2335	2367	2399
2304	2336	2368	2400
2305	2337	2369	2401
2306	2338	2370	2402
2307	2339	2371	2403
2308	2340	2372	2404
2309	2341	2373	2405
2310	2342	2374	2406
2311	2343	2375	2407
2312	2344	2376	2408
2313	2345	2377	2409
2314	2346	2378	2410
2315	2347	2379	2411
2316	2348	2380	2412
2317	2349	2381	2413
2318	2350	2382	2414
2319	2351	2383	2415
2320	2352	2384	2416
2321	2353	2385	2417
2322	2354	2386	2418
2323	2355	2387	2419
2324	2356	2388	2420
2325	2357	2389	2421
2326	2358	2390	2422
2327	2359	2391	2423
2328	2360	2392	2424
2329	2361	1393	
2330	2362	2394	
2331	2363	2395	

Total 125

N.B.—2395-2424 fitted with side-window cabs.

2-6-4T   4P

Designed : Stanier, 1935, L.M.S.
Driving Wheels : 5′ 9″.
Outside Cyls. 19⅝″×26″.
Tractive Effort : 24,670 lb.
Walschaerts Valve Gear, Superheater and taper boilers.

2425	2443	2461	2478
2426	2444	2462	2479
2427	2445	2463	2480
2428	2446	2464	2481
2429	2447	2465	2482
2430	2448	2466	2483
2431	2449	2467	2484
2432	2450	2468	2485
2433	2451	2469	2486
2434	2452	2470	2487
2435	2453	2471	2488
2436	2454	2472	2489
2437	2455	2473	2490
2438	2456	2474	2491
2439	2457	2475	2492
2440	2458	2476	2493
2441	2459	2477	2494
2442	2460		

(Continued, 2537-2672)

2-6-4T (3-Cyl.)   4P

Designed : Stanier, 1934, L.M.S.
Driving Wheels : 5′ 9″.
Cyls. (3) : 16″×26″.
Tractive Effort : 24,600 lb.
Walschaerts Valve Gear, Superheater and taper boiler.

2500	2510	2519	2528
2501	2511	2520	2529
2502	2512	2521	2530
2503	2513	2522	2531
2504	2514	2523	2532
2505	2515	2524	2533
2506	2516	2525	2534
2507	2517	2526	2535
2508	2518	2527	2536
2509			

Total 37

2-6-4T 4P

Dimensions, etc., as locos. 2425-94.

2537	2571	2605	2639
2538	2572	2606	2640
2539	2573	2607	2641
2540	2574	2608	2642
2541	2575	2609	2643
2542	2576	2610	2644
2543	2577	2611	2645
2544	2578	2612	2646
2545	2579	2613	2647
2546	2580	2614	2648
2547	2581	2615	2649
2548	2582	2616	2650
2549	2583	2617	2651
2550	2584	2618	2652
2551	2585	2619	2653
2552	2586	2620	2654
2553	2587	2621	2655
2554	2588	2622	2656
2555	2589	2623	2657
2556	2590	2624	2658
2557	2591	2625	2659
2558	2592	2626	2660
2559	2593	2627	2661
2560	2594	2628	2662
2561	2595	2629	2663
2562	2596	2630	2664
2563	2597	2631	2665
2564	2598	2632	2666
2565	2599	2633	2667
2566	2600	2634	2668
2567	2601	2635	2669
2568	2602	2636	2670
2569	2603	2637	2671
2570	2604	2638	2672

Total 206

2-6-0 5F

Designed: Hughes/Fowler, 1926, L.M.S.
Driving Wheels : 5' 6".
Outside Cyls. : 21" × 26".
Tractive Effort : 26,580 lb.
Walschaerts Valve Gear, Superheater and parallel boilers.

2700	2702	2704	2706
2701	2703	2705	2707
2708	2755	2802	2849
2709	2756	2803	2850
2710	2757	2804	2851
2711	2758	2805	2852
2712	2759	2806	2853
2713	2760	2807	2854
2714	2761	2808	2855
2715	2762	2809	2856
2716	2763	2810	2857
2717	2764	2811	2858
2718	2765	2812	2859
2719	2766	2813	2860
2720	2767	2814	2861
2721	2768	2815	2862
2722	2769	2816	2863
2723	2770	2817	2864
2724	2771	2818	2865
2725	2772	2819	2866
2726	2773	2820	2867
2727	2774	2821	2868
2728	2775	2822	2869
2729	2776	2823	2870
2730	2777	2824	2871
2731	2778	2825	2872
2732	2779	2826	2873
2733	2780	2827	2874
2734	2781	2828	2875
2735	2782	2829	2876
2736	2783	2830	2877
2737	2784	2831	2878
2738	2785	2832	2879
2739	2786	2833	2880
2740	2787	2834	2881
2741	2788	2835	2882
2742	2789	2836	2883
2743	2790	2837	2884
2744	2791	2838	2885
2745	2792	2839	2886
2746	2793	2840	2887
2747	2794	2841	2888
2748	2795	2842	2889
2749	2796	2843	2890
2750	2797	2844	2891
2751	2798	2845	2892
2752	2799	2846	2893
2753	2800	2847	2894
2754	2801	2848	2895

2896	2909	2921	2933
2897	2910	2922	2934
2898	2911	2923	2935
2899	2912	2924	2936
2900	2913	2925	2937
2901	2914	2926	2938
2902	2915	2927	2939
2903	2916	2928	2940
2904	2917	2929	2941
2905	2918	2930	2942
2906	2919	2931	2943
2907	2920	2932	2944
2908			

Total 245

2-6-0   5F

Designed : Stanier, 1933, L.M.S.
Driving Wheels : 5′ 6″.
Outside Cyls : 18″ × 28″
Tractive Effort : 26,288 lb.
Walschaerts Valve Gear, Superheater and taper boiler.

2945	2955	2965	2975
2946	2956	2966	2976
2947	2957	2967	2977
2948	2958	2968	2978
2949	2959	2969	2979
2950	2960	2970	2980
2951	2961	2971	2981
2952	2962	2972	2982
2953	2963	2973	2983
2954	2964	2974	2984

Total 40

0-6-0   2F

Designed : Johnson, 1876, M.R.
Driving Wheels : 4′ 11″.
Cyls. : 18″ × 26″.
Tractive Effort : 19,417 lb.

2987	2992	2996	3000
2988	2993	2997	3001
2989	2994	2998	3002
2990	2995	2999	3003

3005	3008	3011	3014
3006	3009	3012	3016
3007	3010	3013	3018

Total 28

Several rebuilt with small non-super-heater Belpaire boilers.
(Class continued on p. 52, locos. 22900-22984)

0-6-0   2F

Designed : Johnson, 1878, M.R.
Driving Wheels : 5′ 3″.
Cyls. : 18″ × 26″.
Tractive Effort : 18,815 lb.

3021	3051	3078	3108
3023	3052	3079	3109
3027	3054	3081	3110
3031	3055	3083	3113
3035	3056	3084	3114
3037	3057	3085	3115
3038	3058	3090	3116
3039	3061	3094	3118
3042	3062	3095	3119
3044	3064	3096	3121
3045	3066	3098	3123
3047	3071	3099	3124
3048	3073	3101	3126
3049	3074	3103	3127
3050			

Total 57

Several rebuilt with small non-super-heater Belpaire boilers.

0-6-0   2F

Designed : Johnson, 1878, M.R.
Driving Weels : 4′ 11″.
Cyls. : 18″ × 26″.
Tractive Effort : 19,417 lb.

3130	3144	3156	3168
3131	3149	3157	3171
3134	3150	3161	3173
3138	3151	3164	3175
3139	3153	3166	3176
3140	3154	3167	3177
3141			

Total 25

Several rebuilt with small non-super-heater Belpaire boilers.

13

0-6-0   3F

Designed : Johnson, 1885, M.R.
Driving Wheels : 4' 11".
Cyls. : 18" × 26".
Tractive Effort : 21,238 lb.
Rebuilt with non-superheater Belpaire boilers.

3137	3180	3185	3188
3174	3181	3186	3189
3178	3183	3187	

Total 11

0-6-0   3F

Designed : Johnson, 1896, S. & D.J.R.
Driving Wheels : 5' 3".
Cyls. : 18" × 26". T.E. : 19,890 lb.

3194	3204	3218	3248
3198	3211	3228	3260
3201	3216		Total 10

Rebuilds with non-superheater Belpaire boilers.

0-6-0   2F

Designed : Johnson, 1878, M.R.
Driving Wheels : 5' 3".
Cyls. : 18" × 26". T.E. : 18,815 lb.

3190	3384	3485	3551
3195	3385	3489	3554
3196	3391	3492	3559
3220	3412	3493	3561
3227	3416	3503	3564
3229	3420	3508	3566
3230	3423	3511	3571
3262	3424	3512	3577
3264	3425	3516	3590
3270	3430	3517	3592
3280	3432	3518	3601
3311	3434	3519	3602
3343	3437	3525	3603
3347	3438	3526	3616
3352	3445	3527	3617
3353	3451	3533	3632
3358	3466	3535	3635
3360	3470	3536	3642
3366	3473	3537	3646
3372	3477	3539	3648
3377	3478	3543	3649
3382	3479	3545	3655

3666	3695	3707	3739
3677	3696	3725	3744
3688	3699	3726	3746
3689	3703	3732	3758
3691	3704	3738	3764

Total 108

Several rebuilt with small non-superheater Belpaire boilers.

0-6-0   3F

Designed : Johnson/Deeley, 1885, M.R.
Driving Wheels : 5' 3".
Cyls. : 18" × 26".
Tractive Effort : 19,890 lb.
All rebuilt with non-superheated Belpaire boilers.

3191	3242	3277	3314
3192	3243	3278	3315
3193	3244	3281	3316
3200	3245	3282	3317
3203	3246	3283	3318
3205	3247	3284	3319
3207	3249	3286	3321
3208	3250	3287	3323
3210	3251	3290	3324
3212	3252	3292	3325
3213	3253	3293	3326
3214	3254	3294	3327
3219	3256	3295	3329
3222	3257	3296	3330
3223	3258	3297	3331
3224	3259	3298	3332
3225	3261	3299	3333
3226	3263	3300	3334
3231	3265	3301	3335
3232	3266	3305	3336
3233	3267	3306	3337
3234	3268	3307	3338
3235	3269	3308	3339
3237	3271	3309	3340
3239	3273	3310	3341
3240	3274	3312	3342
3241	3275	3313	3344

> For the purposes of classification the locos on this page are not in numerical order.

3351	3446	3565	3645
3355	3448	3568	3650
3356	3449	3570	3651
3357	3453	3572	3652
3359	3454	3573	3653
3361	3456	3574	3656
3364	3457	3575	3657
3367	3458	3578	3658
3368	3459	3579	3660
3369	3462	3580	3661
3370	3463	3581	3662
3371	3464	3582	3664
3373	3467	3583	3665
3374	3468	3584	3667
3378	3469	3585	3668
3379	3474	3586	3669
3381	3476	3587	3673
3386	3482	3593	3674
3387	3484	3594	3675
3388	3490	3595	3676
3389	3491	3596	3678
3392	3494	3598	3679
3394	3496	3599	3680
3395	3497	3600	3681
3396	3499	3604	3682
3398	3502	3605	3683
3399	3506	3607	3684
3400	3507	3608	3686
3401	3509	3612	3687
3402	3510	3615	3690
3405	3514	3618	3693
3406	3515	3619	3698
3408	3520	3620	3705
3410	3521	3621	3709
3411	3522	3622	3710
3419	3523	3623	3711
3427	3524	3624	3712
3428	3529	3627	3714
3429	3531	3629	3715
3431	3538	3630	3717
3433	3540	3631	3721
3435	3544	3633	3723
3436	3546	3634	3724
3439	3548	3636	3727
3440	3550	3637	3728
3441	3553	3638	3729
3443	3558	3639	3731
3444	3562	3644	3734

3735	3751	3760	3769
3737	3753	3762	3770
3742	3754	3763	3771
3745	3755	3765	3772
3747	3756	3766	3773
3748	3757	3767	3774
3749	3759	3768	

Total 327

0-6-0   3F

Designed : Deeley, 1906 M.R.
Driving Wheels : 5′ 3″.
Cyls. : 18″ × 26″.
Tractive Effort : 21,010 lb.
Non-superheater Belpaire boilers.

3775	3790	3805	3820
3776	3791	3806	3821
3777	3792	3807	3822
3778	3793	3808	3823
3779	3794	3809	3824
3780	3795	3810	3825
3781	3796	3811	3826
3782	3797	3812	3827
3783	3798	3813	3828
3784	3799	3814	3829
3785	3800	3815	3830
3786	3801	3816	3831
3787	3802	3817	3832
3788	3803	3818	3833
3789	3804	3819	3834

Total 60

0-6-0   4F

Designed : Fowler, 1911, M.R.
Driving Wheels : 5′ 3″.
Cyls. : 20″ × 26″ (superheated).
Tractive Effort : 24,555 lb.

3835	3846	3857	3868
3836	3847	3858	3869
3837	3848	3859	3870
3838	3849	3860	3871
3839	3850	3861	3872
3840	3851	3862	3873
3841	3852	3863	3874
3842	3853	3864	3875
3843	3854	3865	3876
3844	3855	3866	3877
3845	3856	3867	3878

0-6-0 Standard 4 F Class

L M S

4562

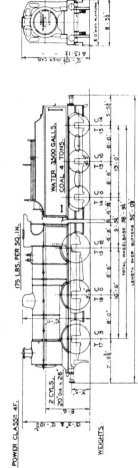

POWER CLASS^{S.} 4F.

175 LBS. PER SQ. IN.

2 CYLS.
20 DIA × 26"

WATR 3500 GALLS.
COAL 4 TONS.

WEIGHTS.

TOTAL WHEELBASE 38'-9¼"

LENGTH OVER BUFFERS 52'-0¼"

8'-0" OPEN PLATFORM.

8'-5½"

3879	3916	3953	3990	4039	4087	4135	4183
3880	3917	3954	3991	4040	4088	4136	4184
3881	3918	3955	3992	4041	4089	4137	4185
3882	3919	3956	3993	4042	4090	4138	4186
3883	3920	3957	3994	4043	4091	4139	4187
3884	3921	3958	3995	4044	4092	4140	4188
3885	3922	3959	3996	4045	4093	4141	4189
3886	3923	3960	3997	4046	4094	4142	4190
3887	3924	3961	3998	4047	4095	4143	4191
3888	3925	3962	3999	4048	4096	4144	4192
3889	3926	3963	4000	4049	4097	4145	4193
3890	3927	3964	4001	4050	4098	4146	4194
3891	3928	3965	4002	4051	4099	4147	4195
3892	3929	3966	4003	4052	4100	4148	4196
3893	3930	3967	4004	4053	4101	4149	4197
3894	3931	3968	4005	4054	4102	4150	4198
3895	3932	3969	4006	4055	4103	4151	4199
3896	3933	3970	4007	4056	4104	4152	4200
3897	3934	3971	4008	4057	4105	4153	4201
3898	3935	3972	4009	4058	4106	4154	4202
3899	3936	3973	4010	4059	4107	4155	4203
3900	3937	3974	4011	4060	4108	4156	4204
3901	3938	3975	4012	4061	4109	4157	4205
3902	3939	3976	4013	4062	4110	4158	4206
3903	3940	3977	4014	4063	4111	4159	4207
3904	3941	3978	4015	4064	4112	4160	4208
3905	3942	3979	4016	4065	4113	4161	4209
3906	3943	3980	4017	4066	4114	4162	4210
3907	3944	3981	4018	4067	4115	4163	4211
3908	3945	3982	4019	4068	4116	4164	4212
3909	3946	3983	4020	4069	4117	4165	4213
3910	3947	3984	4021	4070	4118	4166	4214
3911	3948	3985	4022	4071	4119	4167	4215
3912	3949	3986	4023	4072	4120	4168	4216
3913	3950	3987	4024	4073	4121	4169	4217
3914	3951	3988	4025	4074	4122	4170	4218
3915	3952	3989	4026	4075	4123	4171	4219

Total 192

0-6-0   4F

Designed : Fowler, 1924, L.M.S.
Driving Wheels : 5′ 3″.
Cyls. : 20″ × 26″ (superheated).
Tractive Effort : 24,555 lb.
[Including Nos. 4557 to 4561, ex
S. & D.J.R., new 1922]

4027	4030	4033	4036
4028	4031	4034	4037
4029	4032	4035	4038

4076	4124	4172	4220
4077	4125	4173	4221
4078	4126	4174	4222
4079	4127	4175	4223
4080	4128	4176	4224
4081	4129	4177	4225
4082	4130	4178	4226
4083	4131	4179	4227
4084	4132	4180	4228
4085	4133	4181	4229
4086	4134	4182	4230

4231	4279	4327	4375	4423	4469	4515	4561
4232	4280	4328	4376	4424	4470	4516	4562
4233	4281	4329	4377	4425	4471	4517	4563
4234	4282	4330	4378	4426	4470	4518	4564
4235	4283	4331	4379	4427	4473	4519	4565
4236	4284	4332	4380	4428	4474	4520	4566
4237	4285	4333	4381	4429	4475	4521	4567
4238	4286	4334	4382	4430	4476	4522	4568
4239	4287	4335	4383	4431	4477	4523	4569
4240	4288	4336	4384	4432	4478	4524	4570
4241	4289	4437	4385	4433	4479	4525	4571
4242	4290	4338	4386	4434	4480	4526	4572
4243	4291	4339	4387	4435	4481	4527	4573
4244	4292	4340	4388	4436	4482	4528	4574
4245	4293	4341	4389	4437	4483	4529	4575
4246	4294	4342	4390	4438	4484	4530	4576
4247	4295	4343	4391	4439	4485	4531	4577
4248	4296	4344	4392	4440	4486	4532	4578
4249	4297	4345	4393	4441	4487	4533	4579
4250	4298	4346	4394	4442	4488	4534	4580
4251	4299	4347	4395	4443	4489	4535	4581
4252	4300	4348	4396	4444	4490	4536	4582
4253	4301	4349	4397	4445	4491	4537	4583
4254	4302	4350	4398	4446	4492	4538	4584
4255	4303	4351	4399	4447	4493	4539	4585
4256	4304	4352	4400	4448	4494	4540	4586
4257	4305	4353	4401	4449	4495	4541	4587
4258	4306	4354	4402	4450	4496	4542	4588
4259	4307	4355	4403	4451	4497	4543	4589
4260	4308	4356	4404	4452	4498	4544	4590
4261	4309	4357	4405	4453	4499	4545	4591
4262	4310	4358	4406	4454	4500	4546	4592
4263	4311	4359	4407	4455	4501	4547	4593
4264	4312	4360	4408	4456	4502	4548	4594
4265	4313	4361	4409	4457	4503	4549	4595
4266	4314	4362	4410	4458	4504	4550	4596
4267	4315	4363	4411	4459	4505	4551	4597
4268	4316	4364	4412	4460	4506	4552	4598
4269	4317	4365	4413	4461	4507	4553	4599
4270	4318	4366	4414	4462	4508	4554	4600
4271	4319	4367	4415	4463	4509	4555	4601
4272	4320	4368	4416	4464	4510	4556	4602
4273	4321	4369	4417	4465	4511	4557*	4603
4274	4322	4370	4418	4466	4512	4558*	4604
4275	4323	4371	4419	4467	4513	4559*	4605
4276	4324	4372	4420	4468	4514	4560*	4606
4277	4325	4373	4421				
4278	4326	4374	4422				

Total 580

* Ex S. & D.J.R., Nos. 57-61 (in same order) built 1922.

18

4-6-0   5P5F

Designed : Stanier, 1934, L.M.S.
Driving Wheels : 6′ 0″.
Outside Cyls. : 18½″ × 28″.
Superheated Taper Boiler,
    Walschaerts Valve Gear.
Tractive Effort : 25,455 lb.

5000	5042	5084	5126
5001	5043	5085	5127
5002	5044	5086	5128
5003	5045	5087	5129
5004	5046	5088	5130
5005	5047	5089	5131
5006	5048	5090	5132
5007	5049	5091	5133
5008	5050	5092	5134
5009	5051	5093	5135
5010	5052	5094	5136
5011	5053	5095	5137
5012	5054	5096	5138
5013	5055	5097	5139
5014	5056	5098	5140
5015	5057	5099	5141
5016	5058	5100	5142
5017	5059	5101	5143
5018	5060	5102	5144
5019	5061	5103	5145
5020	5062	5104	5146
5021	5063	5105	5147
5022	5064	5106	5148
5023	5065	5107	5149
5024	5066	5108	5150
5025	5067	5109	5151
5026	5068	5110	5152
5027	5069	5111	5153
5028	5070	5112	5154*
5029	5071	5113	5155
5030	5072	5114	5156*
5031	5073	5115	5157*
5032	5074	5116	5158*
5033	5075	5117	5159
5034	5076	5118	5160
5035	5077	5119	5161
5036	5078	5120	5162
5037	5079	5121	5163
5038	5080	5122	5164
5039	5081	5123	5165
5040	5082	5124	5166
5041	5083	5125	5167

5168	5211	5254	5297
5169	5212	5255	5298
5170	5213	5256	5299
5171	5214	5257	5300
5172	5215	5258	5301
5173	5216	5259	5302
5174	5217	5260	5303
5175	5218	5261	5304
5176	5219	5262	5305
5177	5220	5263	5306
5178	5221	5264	5307
5179	5222	5265	5308
5180	5223	5266	5309
5181	5224	5267	5310
5182	5225	5268	5311
5183	5226	5269	5312
5184	5227	5270	5313
5185	5228	5271	5314
5186	5229	5272	5315
5187	5230	5273	5316
5188	5231	5274	5317
5189	5232	5275	5318
5190	5233	5276	5319
5191	5234	5277	5320
5192	5235	5278	5321
5193	5236	5279	5322
5194	5237	5280	5323
5195	5238	5281	5324
5196	5239	5282	5325
5197	5240	5283	5326
5198	5241	5284	5327
5199	5242	5285	5328
5200	5243	5286	5329
5201	5244	5287	5330
5202	5245	5288	5331
5203	5246	5289	5332
5204	5247	5290	5333
5205	5248	5291	5334
5206	5249	5292	5335
5207	5250	5293	5336
5208	5251	5294	5337
5209	5252	5295	5338
5210	5253	5296	5339

* 5154 Lanarkshire Yeomanry.
  5156 Ayrshire Yeomanry.
  5157 Glasgow Highlander.
  5158 Glasgow Yeomanry.

4-6-0 Standard 5P5F Class

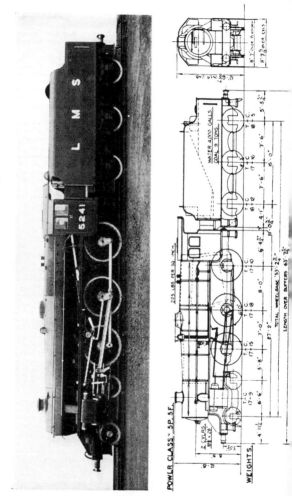

POW'R CLASS ~ 5P 5F

225 LBS PER SQ INCH

WATER 4000 GALLS
COAL 9 TONS

2 CYLRS
18¾ x 28"

TOTAL WHEELBASE 53'-2¾"

LENGTH OVER BUFFERS 63'-7¾"

WEIGHTS

5340	5379	5418	5457
5341	5380	5419	5458
5342	5381	5420	5459
5343	5382	5421	5460
5344	5383	5422	5461
5345	5384	5423	5462
5346	5385	5424	5463
5347	5386	5425	5464
5348	5387	5426	5465
5349	5388	5427	5466
5350	5389	5428	5467
5351	5390	5429	5468
5352	5391	5430	5469
5353	5392	5431	5470
5354	5393	5432	5471
5355	5394	5433	5472
5356	5395	5434	5473
5357	5396	5435	5474
5358	5397	5436	5475
5359	5398	5437	5476
5360	5399	5438	5477
5361	5400	5439	5478
5362	5401	5440	5479
5363	5402	5441	5480
5364	5403	5442	5481
5365	5404	5443	5482
5366	5405	5444	5483
5367	5406	5445	5484
5368	5407	5446	5485
5369	5408	5447	5486
5370	5409	5448	5487
5371	5410	5449	5488
5372	5411	5450	5489
5373	5412	5451	5490
5374	5413	5452	5491
5375	5414	5453	5492
5376	5415	5454	5493
5377	5416	5455	5494
5378	5417	5456	

Total 495

(Still being delivered)

4-6-0   5XP
"Patriot" Class

Designed : Fowler, 1930-34, L.M.S.
Driving Wheels : 6' 9".
Cyls. (3) : 18" × 26".
Superheated. Parallel Boiler.
Walschaerts Valve Gear.
Tractive Effort : 26,520 lb.

5500 Patriot
5501 St. Dunstan's
5502 Royal Naval Division
5503 The Leicestershire
      Regiment
5504 Royal Signals
5505
5506
5507 Royal Tank Corps
5508
5509
5510
5511 Isle of Man
5512 Bunsen
5513
5514
5515 Caernarvon
5516 The Bedfordshire and
      Hertfordshire Regiment
5517
5518
5519 Lady Godiva
5520 Llandudno
5521 Rhyl
5522 Prestatyn
5523 Bangor
5524 Blackpool
5525 Colwyn Bay
5526 Morecambe and Heysham
5527 Southport
5528
5529
5530 Sir Frank Ree
5531 Sir Frederick Harrison
5532 Illustrious
5533 Lord Rathmore
5534 E. Tootal Broadhurst
5535 Sir Herbert Walker,
      K.C.B.
5536 Private W. Wood, V.C.

4-6-0 "Patriot" Class (5 XP)

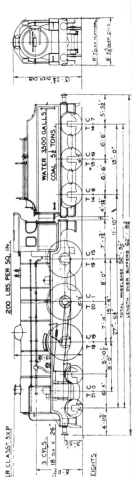
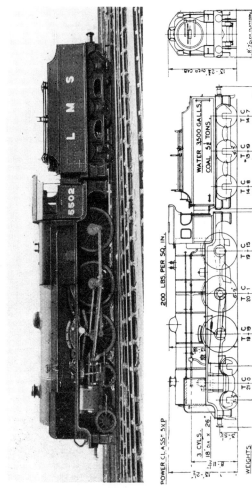

POWER CLASS" 5XP

3 CYLS.
18 DIA × 26"

WEIGHTS

200 LBS. PER SQ. IN.

WATER 3500 GALLS.
COAL 5½ TONS.

TOTAL WHEELBASE 52' 3½"
LENGTH OVER BUFFERS 62' 8½"

Patriot " Class—*continued*.
37 Private E. Sykes, V.C.
538 Giggleswick
539 E. C. Trench
540 Sir Robert Turnbull
541 Duke of Sutherland
42
543 Home Guard
44
45
46 Fleetwood
47
48 Lytham St. Annes
49
50
51

Total 52

" Jubilee " Class
-6-0   **5XP**
Designed : Stanier, 1934, L.M.S.
Driving Wheels : 6′ 9″.
Cyls. (3) : 17″ × 26″.
Tractive Effort : 26,610 lb.
Superheated Taper Boiler.
Walschaerts Valve Gear.
552 Silver Jubilee
553 Canada
554 Ontario
555 Quebec
556 Nova Scotia
557 New Brunswick
558 Manitoba
559 British Columbia
560 Prince Edward Island
561 Saskatchewan
562 Alberta
563 Australia
564 New South Wales
565 Victoria
566 Queensland
567 South Australia
568 Western Australia
569 Tasmania

5570 New Zealand
5571 South Africa
5572 Eire
5573 Newfoundland
5574 India
5575 Madras
5576 Bombay
5577 Bengal
5578 United Provinces
5579 Punjab
5580 Burma
5581 Bihar and Orissa
5582 Central Provinces
5583 Assam
5584 North West Frontier
5585 Hyderabad
5586 Mysore
5587 Baroda
5588 Kashmir
5589 Gwalior
5590 Travancore
5591 Udaipur
5592 Indore
5593 Kolhapur
5594 Bhopal
5595 Southern Rhodesia
5596 Bahamas
5597 Barbados
5598 Basutoland
5599 Bechuanaland
5600 Bermuda
5601 British Guiana
5602 British Honduras
5603 Solomon Islands
5604 Ceylon
5605 Cyprus
5606 Falkland Islands
5607 Fiji
5608 Gibraltar
5609 Gilbert and Ellice Islands

4-6-0 " Jubilee " Class (5XP)

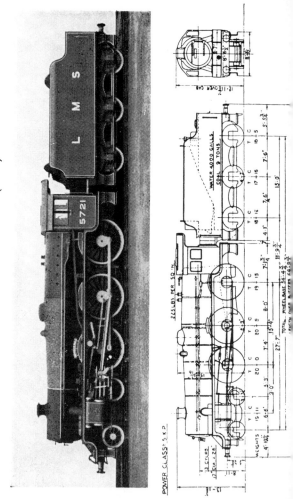

" Jubilee " Class—*continued.*

5610 Gold Coast
5611 Hong Kong
5612 Jamaica
5613 Kenya
5614 Leeward Islands
5615 Malay States
5616 Malta G. C.
5617 Mauritius
5618 New Hebrides
5619 Nigeria
5620 North Borneo
5621 Northern Rhodesia
5622 Nyasaland
5623 Palestine
5624 St. Helena
5625 Sarawak
5626 Seychelles
5627 Sierra Leone
5628 Somaliland
5629 Straits Settlements
5630 Swaziland
5631 Tanganyika
5632 Tonga
5633 Trans-Jordan
5634 Trinidad
5635 Tobago
5636 Uganda
5637 Windward Islands
5638 Zanzibar
5639 Raleigh
5640 Frobisher
5641 Sandwich
5642 Boscawen
5643 Rodney
5644 Howe
5645 Collingwood
5646 Napier
5647 Sturdee
5648 Wemyss
5649 Hawkins
5650 Blake
5651 Shovell
5652 Hawke
5653 Barham
5654 Hood
5655 Keith
5656 Cochrane

5657 Tyrwhitt
5658 Keyes
5659 Drake
5660 Rooke
5661 Vernon
5662 Kempenfelt
5663 Jervis
5664 Nelson
5665 Lord Rutherford of Nelson
5666 Cornwallis
5667 Jellicoe
5668 Madden
5669 Fisher
5670 Howard of Effingham
5671 Prince Rupert
5672 Anson
5673 Keppel
5674 Duncan
5675 Hardy
5676 Codrington
5677 Beatty
5678 De Robeck
5679 Armada
5680 Camperdown
5681 Aboukir
5682 Trafalgar
5683 Hogue
5684 Jutland
5685 Barfleur
5686 St. Vincent
5687 Neptune
5688 Polyphemus
5689 Ajax
5690 Leander
5691 Orion
5692 Cyclops
5693 Agamemnon
5694 Bellerophon
5695 Minotaur
5696 Arethusa
5697 Achilles
5698 Mars
5699 Galatea
5700 Britannia
5701 Conqueror
5702 Colossus
5703 Thunderer

Ex-L.Y.R. 0-6-0ST, No. 11363 (now withdrawn)

McIntosh 0-6-0T No. 16268, ex-C.R.

McIntosh 0-4-4 T No. 15175, ex-C.R.

704 Leviathan
705 Seahorse
706 Express
707 Valiant
708 Resolution
709 Implacable
710 Irresistible
711 Courageous
712 Victory
713 Renown
714 Revenge
715 Invincible
716 Swiftsure
717 Dauntless
718 Dreadnought
719 Glorious
720 Indomitable
721 Impregnable
722 Defence
723 Fearless
724 Warspite
725 Repulse
726 Vindictive
727 Inflexible
728 Defiance
729 Furious
730 Ocean
731 Perseverance
732 Sanspareil
733 Novelty
734 Meteor
735*Comet
736*Phœnix
737 Atlas
738 Samson
739 Ulster
740 Munster
741 Leinster
742 Connaught

Total 191

* Rebuilt with larger, superheated taper Boilers in 1942, and reclassified 6P. T.E. 29,590 lb.

" Claughton " Class
4-6-0   5XP

Designed : B. Cooke, 1921.
Driving Wheels : 6' 9".
Cyls. (4) : $15\frac{3}{4}" \times 26"$.
Tractive Effort : 27,072 lb.
Superheated. Walschaerts Valve Gear.
Rebuilt 1928 with larger Belpaire
  Boiler.

6004

Total 1

" Royal Scot " Class
4-6-0   6P

Designed : Fowler, 1927, L.M.S.
Driving Wheels : 6' 9".
Cyls. (3) : $18" \times 26"$.
Tractive Effort : 33,150 lb.
Superheated. Walschaerts Valve Gear.
Parallel Boilers.

6100 Royal Scot
6101 Royal Scots Grey
6102 Black Watch
6103†Royal Scots Fusilier
6104 Scottish Borderer
6105 Cameron Highlander
6106 Gordon Highlander
6107 Argyll and Sutherland
       Highlander
6108†Seaforth Highlander
6109†The Royal Engineer
6110 Grenadier Guardsman
6111 Royal Fusilier
6112†Sherwood Forester
6113 Cameronian
6114 Coldstream Guardsman
6115 Scots Guardsman
6116 Irish Guardsman
6117†Welsh Guardsman
6118 Royal Welch Fusilier
6119 Lancashire Fusilier
6120 Royal Inniskilling Fusilier
6121 H.L.I.
6122 Royal Ulster Rifleman
6123 Royal Irish Fusilier
6124†London Scottish
6125†3rd Carabinier

4-6-0 "Royal Scot" Class (6 P)

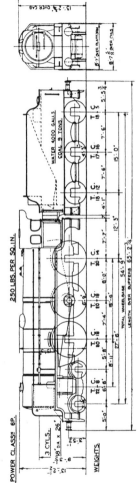

POWER CLASS: 6P

3 CYLS.

250 LBS. PER SQ. IN.

WATER 4000 GALLS.
COAL 9 TONS.

WEIGHTS:

TOTAL WHEELBASE 54'·9"
LENGTH OVER BUFFERS 65'·2¾"

4-6-0 Rebuilt "Royal Scot" Class (6P)

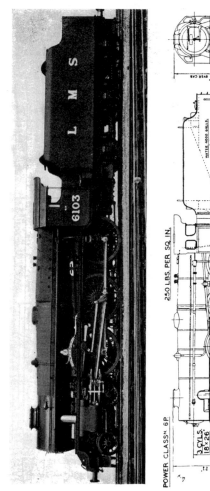

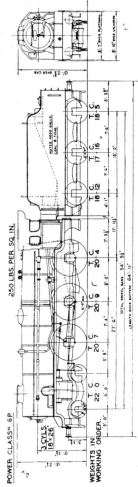

POWER CLASS^{N.} 6P   250 LBS. PER SQ. IN.

3 CYLS.
18"×26"

WEIGHTS IN
WORKING ORDER.

4-6-2 "Princess Royal" Class (7 P)

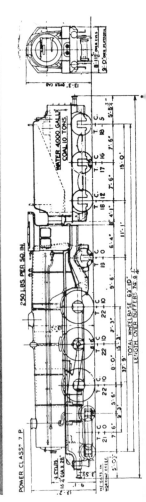

POWER CLASS" 7 P

250 LBS PER SQ. IN.

WATER 4000 GALLS
COAL 10 TONS

13'-3" OVER CAB

8'-1½" PIN LINES
9'-0" OVER PLATFORM

4 CYLRS.
16¼ DIA. X 28"

DRIVING WHEELS
6'-6"

TOTAL WHEELBASE 63'-10"
LENGTH OVER BUFFERS 74'-4⅝"

" Royal Scot " Class—contd.
6126 Royal Army Service Corps
6127 The Old Contemptibles
6128 The Lovat Scouts
6129 The Scottish Horse
6130 The West Yorkshire Regiment
6131 The Royal Warwickshire Regiment
6132†The King's Regiment (Liverpool)
6133 The Green Howards
6134 The Cheshire Regiment
6135 The East Lancashire Regiment
6136 The Border Regiment
6137 The Prince of Wales' Volunteers (South Lancs.)
6138 The London Irish Rifleman
6139 The Welch Regiment
6140 The King's Royal Rifle Corps
6141 The North Staffordshire Regiment
6142 The York and Lancaster Regiment
6143 The South Staffordshire Regiment
6144
6145†The Duke of Wellington's Regiment (West Riding)
6146†The Rifle Brigade
6147 The Northamptonshire Regiment
6148 The Manchester Regiment
6149 The Middlesex Regiment
6150 The Life Guardsman
6151 The Royal Horse Guardsman
6152 The King's Dragoon Guardsman
6153 The Royal Dragoon
6154 The Hussar
6155 The Lancer

6156 The South Wales Borderer
6157 The Royal Artilleryman
6158 The Loyal Regiment
6159 The Royal Air Force
6160 Queen Victoria's Rifleman
6161 The King's Own
6162 Queen's Westminster Rifleman
6163 Civil Service Rifleman
6164 The Artists' Rifleman.
6165 The Ranger (12th London Regiment)
6166 London Rifle Brigade
6167 The Hertfordshire Regiment
6168 The Girl Guide
6169 The Boy Scout
6170 British Legion
(rebuilt " Fury," 1935, Stanier, with taper boiler)
Total 71

† Rebuilt with superheated taper boiler and new cylinders 18″ x 26″ (3). First engine 6103 in 1943.

"Princess Royal" Class 4-6-2   7P
Designed : Stanier, 1933-5, L.M.S.
Driving Wheels : 6′ 6″.
Cyls. (4) : 16¼″ x 28″.
Tractive Effort : 40,300 lb.
Superheated. Walschaerts Valve Gear.
6200 The Princess Royal
6201 Princess Elizabeth
6202 *
6203 Princess Margaret Rose
6204 Princess Louise
6205 Princess Victoria
6206 Princess Marie Louise
6207 Princess Arthur of Connaught
6208 Princess Helena Victoria
6209 Princess Beatrice
6210 Lady Patricia
6211 Queen Maud
6212 Duchess of Kent
Total 13
N.B.—6200 and 6201 built 1933, the rest 1935.
* Turbine driven locomotive.

31

4-6-2 "Princess Coronation" Class (7 P)

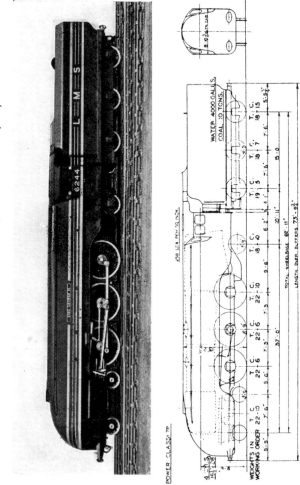

POWER CLASS 7P

WATER 4000 GALLS

COAL 10 TONS.

WEIGHTS IN
WORKING ORDER

4-6-2 "Princess Coronation" Class (Non-Streamlined) (7 P)

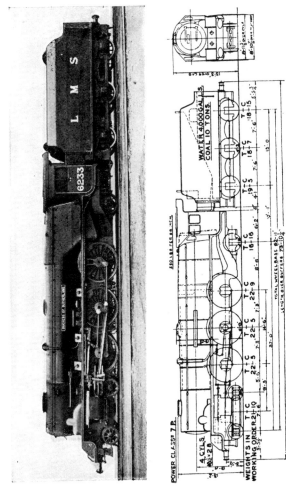

"Princess Coronation"
4-6-2   7P

Designed : Stanier, 1937, L.M.S.
Driving Wheels : 6' 9".
Cyls. (4) : 16¼"×28".
Tractive Effort : 40,000 lb.
Superheated. Walschaerts Valve Gear
Streamlined.
6220 Coronation
6221 Queen Elizabeth
6222 Queen Mary
6223 Princess Alice
6224 Princess Alexandra
6225 Duchess of Gloucester
6226 Duchess of Norfolk
6227 Duchess of Devonshire
6228 Duchess of Rutland
6229 Duchess of Hamilton
6230*Duchess of Buccleuch
6231*Duchess of Atholl
6232*Duchess of Montrose
6233*Duchess of Sutherland
6234*Duchess of Abercorn
6235 City of Birmingham
6236 City of Bradford
6237 City of Bristol
6238 City of Carlisle
6239 City of Chester
6240 City of Coventry
6241 City of Edinburgh
6242 City of Glasgow
6243 City of Lancaster
6244 King George VI
6245 City of London
6246 City of Manchester
6247 City of Liverpool
6248 City of Leeds

Total 29

* Not streamlined.
(Still being delivered.)

0-4-4T   2P

Designed : Stanier, 1932, L.M.S.
Driving Wheels : 5' 7".
Cyls. : 18"×26".
Tractive Effort : 17,099 lb.

6400	6403	6406	6408
6401	6404	6407	6409
6402	6405		

Total 10

2-4-0T

Designed : Webb, 1877, L.N.W.R.
Driving Wheels : 4' 8½".
Cyls. : 17"×20".
Tractive Effort : 13,043 lb.

6428

Total

2-4-2T

Designed : Webb, 1890, L.N.W.R
Driving Wheels : 5' 8½".
Cyls. : 17"×24".
Tractive Effort : 12,910 lb.

6601	6652	6683	672
6603	6653	6685	672
6604	6654	6686	672
6605	6656	6687	672
6607	6657	6688	672
6616	6658	6689	673
6619	6659	6690	673
6620	6660	6691	673
6627	6661	6692	674
6628	6663	6699	674
6632	6666	6700	674
6635	6667	6701	674
6636	6669	6703	674
6637	6673	6704	674
6639	6674	6710	674
6641	6676	6711	674
6643	6679	6712	675
6645	6680	6713	675
6646	6681	6718	675
6650	6682	6722	

Total

2-4-2T   2

Designed : Aspinall 1890, Wirral R
Driving Wheels : 5' 8".
Cyls. : 17½"×26".
Tractive Effort : 17,914 lb.
(Purchased from L.Y.R.)

6762

Total

0-6-2T　　　　　2P

Designed : Webb, 1898, L.N.W.R.
Driving Wheels : 5' 2½".
Cyls. : 18" × 24".
Tractive Effort : 15,502 lb.

6866	6890	6912	6927
6869	6893	6917	6930
6870	6894	6919	6931
6871	6899	6920	6933
6876	6900	6922	6935
6878	6904	6924	6936
6881	6906	6925	
6883	6909	6926	

Total 30

0-4-0ST　　　　0 F

Designed : Stanier, 1932, L.M.S.
Driving Wheels : 3' 10".
Outside Cyls. : 15½" × 20".
Tractive Effort : 14,200 lb.
(Saddle tanks, built by Kitsons)

7000	7002	7003	7004
7001			

Total 5

0-6-0　　　　Diesel

Tractive Effort : 10,250 lb.

7051

Total 1

0-6-0　　Diesel Electric

Tractive Effort : 7058, 24,000 lb.
7059-79, 30,000 lb.
7080-7119, 35,000 lb.

7058	7080	7090	7110
7059	7081	7091	7111
7061	7082	7092	7112
7062	7083	7093	7113
7063	7084	7094	7114
7064	7085	7095	7115
7067	7086	7096	7116
7074	7087	7097	7117
7076	7088	7098	7118
7079	7089	7099	7119

Total 40

0-6-0T　　　　2F

Designed : Fowler, 1928, L.M.S.
Driving Wheels : 3' 11".
Outside Cyls. : 17" × 22".
Tractive Effort : 18,400 lb.
With Walschaerts Valve Gear.
For use in dockyards.

7160	7163	7166	7168
7161	7164	7167	7169
7162	7165		

Total 10

0-4-0T　Sentinel

Built : 1929/30.
Tractive Effort : 11,800 lb.

7180	7182	7184*	7191†
7181	7183	7190†	

Total 7

* Tractive Effort : 13,570 lb.
† ex S.D.J.R. Nos. 101 and 102 Tractive Effort 15,500 lb.

0-6-0T　　　　3F

Designed : Johnson, 1899, M.R.
Driving Wheels : 4' 7".
Cyls. : 18" × 26".
Tractive Effort : 20,834 lb.

7200	7215	7230	7245
7201	7216	7231	7246
7202	7217	7232	7247
7203	7218	7233	7248
7204	7219	7234	7249
7205	7220	7235	7250
7206	7221	7236	7251
7207	7222	7237	7252
7208	7223	7238	7253
7209	7224	7239	7254
7210	7225	7240	7255
7211	7226	7241	7256
7212	7227	7242	7257
7213	7228	7243	7258
7214	7229	7244	7259

Total 60

0-6-0T   3F

Designed : Fowler, 1924, L.M.S.
Driving Wheels : 4' 7".
Cyls. : 18" × 26".
Tractive Effort : 20,834 lb.

7260	7303	7346	7389
7261	7304	7347	7390
7262	7305	7348	7391
7263	7306	7349	7392
7264	7307	7350	7393
7265	7308	7351	7394
7266	7309	7352	7395
7267	7310*	7353	7396
7268	7311*	7354	7397
7269	7312*	7355	7398
7270	7313*	7356	7399
7271	7314*	7357	7400
7272	7315*	7358	7401
7273	7316*	7359	7402
7274	7317	7360	7403
7275	7318	7361	7404
7276	7319	7362	7405
7277	7320	7363	7406
7278	7321	7364	7407
7279	7322	7365	7408
7280	7323	7366	7409
7281	7324	7367	7410
7282	7325	7368	7411
7283	7326	7369	7412
7284	7327	7370	7413
7285	7328	7371	7414
7286	7329	7372	7415
7287	7330	7373	7416
7288	7331	7374	7417
7289	7332	7375	7418
7290	7333	7376	7419
7291	7334	7377	7420
7292	7335	7378	7421
7293	7336	7379	7422
7294	7337	7380	7423
7295	7338	7381	7424
7296	7339	7382	7425
7297	7340	7383	7426
7298	7341	7384	7427
7299	7342	7385	7428
7300	7343	7386	7429
7301	7344	7387	7430
7302	7345	7388	7431

7432	7480	7528	75..
7433	7481	7529	752
7434	7482	7530	75.
7435	7483	7531	752
7436	7484	7532	758
7437	7485	7533	758
7438	7486	7534	758
7439	7487	7535	758
7440	7488	7536	758
7441	7489	7537	758
7442	7490	7538	758
7443	7491	7539	758
7444	7492	7540	758
7445	7493	7541	759
7446	7494	7542	759
7447	7495	7543	759
7448	7496	7544	759
7449	7497	7545	759
7450	7498	7546	759
7451	7499	7547	759
7452	7500	7548	759
7453	7501	7549	759
7454	7502	7550	759
7455	7503	7551	760.
7456	7504	7552	760
7457	7505	7553	760.
7458	7506	7554	760.
7459	7507	7555	760.
7460	7508	7556	760.
7461	7509	7557	760.
7462	7510	7558	760.
7463	7511	7559	760.
7464	7512	7560	761(
7465	7513	7561	761.
7466	7514	7562	761.
7467	7515	7563	761.
7468	7516	7564	761.
7469	7517	7565	761.
7470	7518	7566	761.
7471	7519	7567	762.
7472	7520	7568	762.
7473	7521	7569	762.
7474	7522	7570	762.
7475	7523	7571	762.
7476	7524	7572	762.
7477	7525	7573	762.
7478	7526	7574	762.
7479	7527	7575	762.

6-0T 3F—continued.

'629	7642	7655	7670
'630	7643	7656	7671
'631	7644	7657	7672
'632	7645	7658	7673
'633	7646	7661	7674
'634	7647	7662	7675
'635	7648	7664	7676
'636	7649	7665	7677
'637	7650	7666	7678
'638	7651	7667	7679
'639	7652	7668	7680
'640	7653	7669	7681
'641	7654		

Total 414

Ex S. & D.J.R., Nos. 19-25 built 1929.

6-2T 2F

Designed : Webb, 1882, L.N.W.R.
Driving Wheels : 4' 5½".
Cyls. : 17" × 24".
Tractive Effort : 16,530 lb.
For coal traffic.

'682	7733	7769	7807
'690	7737	7772	7808
'692	7740	7773	7812
'699	7741	7778	7816
'700	7742	7780	7821
'703	7746	7782	7822
'705	7751	7787	7823
'709	7752	7789	7824
'710	7755	7791	7827
711	7756	7794	7829
715	7757	7795	7830
717	7759	7796	7833
720	7761	7797	7834
721	7763	7799	7836
722	7765	7802	7840
730	7768	7803	7841

Total 64

(Class continued on p. 53,
locos. 27552-27681)

0-4-2ST 1F

Designed : Webb, 1901, L.N.W.R.
Driving Wheels : 4' 5½".
Cyls. : 17" × 24".
Tractive Effort : 16,530 lb.
(Square saddle ; Bissel truck.)

7862	7865

Total 2

0-8-2T 6F

Designed : Bowen Cooke, 1911,
L.N.W.R.
Driving Wheels : 4' 5½".
Cyls. : 20½" × 24".
Tractive Effort : 27,242 lb.

7870	7878	7886	7892
7875	7881	7887	7896
7876	7884	7888	7897
7877	7885	7891	7898

Total 16

0-8-4T 7F

Designed : Beames, 1923, L.M.S.
Driving Wheels : 4' 5½". L.N.W.R.
Cyls. : 20½" × 24".
Tractive Effort : 29,814 lb.

7930	7938	7946	7953
7931	7939	7947	7954
7932	7940	7948	7955
7933	7941	7949	7956
7934	7942	7950	7957
7935	7943	7951	7958
7936	7944	7952	7959
7937	7945		

Total 30

2-6-6-2T

Designed : Fowler, 3 in 1927, 30 in
1930, L.M.S.
Driving Wheels : 5' 3".
Cyls. (4) : 18½" × 26".
(Beyer-Garratt : Walschaerts Valve
Gear and Superheater.)
Tractive Effort : 45,620 lb.

7967	7972	7977	7982
7968	7973	7978	7983
7969	7974	7979	7984
7970	7975	7980	7985
7971	7976	7981	7986

2-8-0 Standard 8F Class

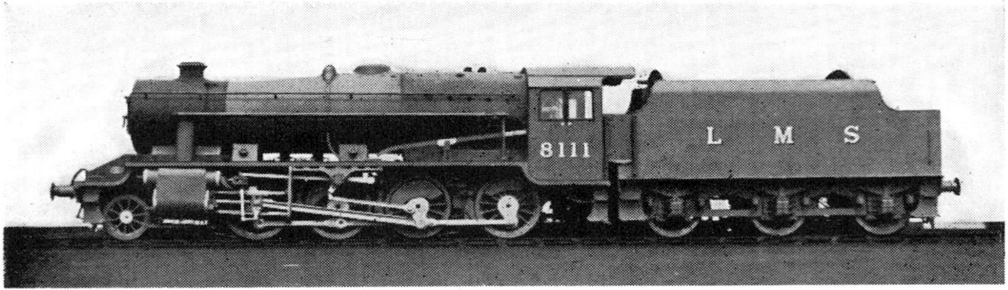
8111
L M S

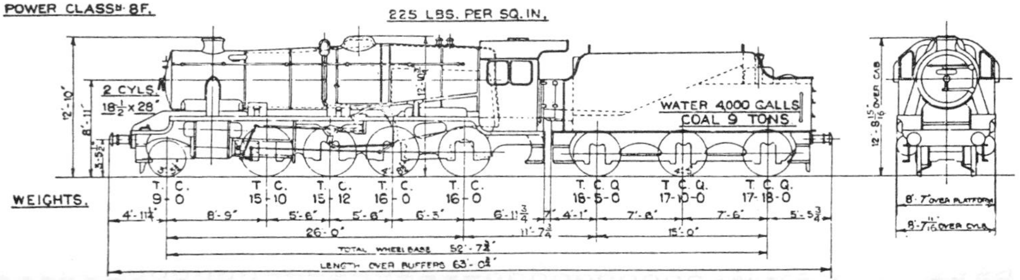
POWER CLASSN. 8F.
225 LBS. PER SQ. IN.
2 CYLS.
18½ x 28"
WATER 4000 GALLS
COAL 9 TONS
WEIGHTS.
T. C. 9-0
T. C. 15-10
T. C. 15-12
T. C. 16-0
T. C. 16-0
T. C. Q. 16-5-0
T. C. Q. 17-10-0
T. C. Q. 17-18-0
4'-11¼"
8'-9"
5'-6"
5'-6"
6'-5"
6'-11¾"
7"
4'-1"
7'-8"
7'-6"
5'-5¾"
26'-0"
11'-7¾"
15'-0"
TOTAL WHEELBASE 52'-7¾"
LENGTH OVER BUFFERS 63'-0¾"
12'-10"
8'-11"
3'-5½"
12'-8 15/16" OVER CAB
8'-7" OVER PLATFORM
8'-7 11/16" OVER CYLS.

6-2T—continued.

7	7991	7994	7997
8	7992	7995	7998
9	7993	7996	7999
0			

Total 33

0   **8F**

gned : Stanier, 1935, L.M.S.
ng Wheels : 4' 8½".
ide Cyls. : 18½"×28".
tive Effort : 32,438 lb.
erheated : Walschaerts Valve
ar.)

0	8033	8067	8104	8137	8185	8271‖	8402†
)1	8034	8069	8105	8138	8186	8272‖	8403†
)2	8035	8070	8106	8139	8187	8273‖	8404†
)3	8036	8072	8107	8140	8188	8274‖	8405†
)4	8037	8073	8108	8141	8189	8275‖	8406†
)5	8038	8074	8109	8142	8190	8276‖	8407†
)6	8039	8075	8110	8143	8191	8277‖	8408†
)7	8040	8076	8111	8144	8192	8278‖	8409†
)8	8041	8078	8112	8145	8193	8279‖	8410†
)9	8042	8079	8113	8146	8194	8280‖	8411†
0	8043	8080	8114	8147	8195	8281‖	8412†
1	8044	8081	8115	8148	8196	8282‖	8413†
2	8045	8082	8116	8149	8197	8283‖	8414†
3	8046	8083	8117	8150	8198	8284‖	8415†
4	8047	8084	8118	8151	8199	8285‖	8416†
5	8048	8085	8119	8152	8200	8293‖	8417†
6	8049	8086	8120	8153	8201	8301	8418†
7	8050	8088	8121	8154	8202	8302	8419†
8	8051	8089	8122	8155	8203	8303	8420†
9	8052	8090	8123	8156	8204	8304	8421†
20	8053	8091	8124	8157	8205	8305	8422†
21	8054	8092	8125	8158	8206	8306	8423†
22	8055	8093	8126	8159	8207	8307	8424†
23	8056	8094	8127	8160	8208	8308	8425†
24	8057	8095	8128	8161	8209	8309	8426†
25	8058	8096	8129	8162	8210	8310	8427†
26	8059	8097	8130	8163	8211	8311	8428†
27	8060	8098	8131	8164	8212	8312	8429†
28	8061	8099	8132	8165	8213	8313	8510‡
29	8062	8100	8133	8166	8214	8314	8600*
30	8063	8101	8134	8167	8215	8315	8601*
31	8064	8102	8135	8168	8216	8316	8602*
32	8065	8103	8136	8169	8217	8317	8603*
				8170	8218	8318	8604*
				8171	8219	8319	8605*
				8172	8220	8331	8606*
				8173	8221	8332	8607*
				8174	8222	8333	8608*
				8175	8223	8334	8609*
				8176	8224	8335	8610*
				8177	8225	8336	8611*
				8178	8264‖	8337	8612*
				8179	8265‖	8338	8613*
				8180	8266‖	8339	8614*
				8181	8267‖	8340	8615*
				8182	8268‖	8400†	8616*
				8183	8269‖	8401†	8617*
				8184	8270‖		

8618*	8631*	8644*	8657*	9159	9202	9261	9337
8619*	8632*	8645*	8658*	9160	9204	9263	9338
8620*	8633*	8646*	8659*	9162	9206	9267	9340
8621*	8634*	8647*	8660*	9164	9208	9269	9346
8622*	8635*	8648*	8671*	9165	9210	9272	9349
8623*	8636*	8649*	8672*	9166	9213	9273	9350
8624*	8637*	8650*	8679*	9167	9215	9274	9353
8625*	8638*	8651*	8680*	9171	9218	9277	9354
8626*	8639*	8652*	8681*	9173	9219	9279	9359
8627*	8640*	8653*	8683*	9175	9221	9282	9362
8628*	8641*	8654*	8684*	9178	9222	9283	9364
8629*	8642*	8655*		9179	9225	9285	9367
8630*	8643*	8656*		9182	9227	9286	9369
				9183	9229	9287	9370
				9184	9230	9295	9371
				9187	9231	9297	9372
				9188	9232	9302	9373
				9189	9233	9303	9374
				9190	9236	9305	9380
				9191	9241	9307	9383
				9193	9248	9309	9384
				9194	9250	9314	9385
				9195	9251	9320	9391
				9196	9253	9324	
				9197	9254	9326	
				9199	9255	9328	
				9200	9257	9332	
				9201	9259	9334	

Total 372

Still being delivered.

* S.R. built. † G.W.R. built.

‡ L.N.E.R. built. ‖ Ex War Dept.

Total 191

0-8-0 6F

Designed : Webb, 1892. Rebuilt and built, 1908, Whale, L.N.W.R.
Driving Wheels : 4' 5½".
Cyls. : 20½" × 24".
Tractive Effort : 25,639 lb.

G.1 Class

8892	8929	9052	9102
8894	8931	9053	9103
8895	8934	9054	9107
8897	8935	9056	9108
8901	8939	9058	9118
8902	8962	9059	9125
8904	8966	9060	9128
8906	9006	9063	9129
8907	9011	9067	9131
8908	9012	9071	9133
8910	9013	9075	9135
8911	9015	9076	9136
8912	9017	9081	9138
8913	9030	9083	9140
8915	9032	9085	9142
8917	9038	9089	9144
8918	9040	9091	9145
8922	9041	9092	9151
8924	9043	9095	9152
8926	9049	9098	9154
8927	9050	9100	9156

4-6-0 4F

Designed : Whale. 1908, L.N.W.R.
Driving Wheels : 5' 2½".
Cyls. : 19" × 26".
Tractive Effort : 22,338 lb.
(Some rebuilt with Belpaire Boilers.

8801	8824	8858
8815	8834	28786

Total 6

40

-8-0   7F

Designed : Webb/Whale/B. Cooke
  L.N.W.R.
Driving Wheels : 4′ 5½″.
Cyls. : 20½″ × 24″.
Tractive Effort : 28,043 lb.
Superheater. Many with Belpaire
  Boilers (Rebuilds, etc.).

G2a Class

8893	9019	9078	9139
8896	9020	9079	9141
8898	9021	9080	9143
8899	9022	9082	9146
8903	9023	9084	9147
8905	9024	9086	9148
8909	9025	9087	9149
8914	9026	9088	9150
8920	9027	9090	9153
8921	9028	9093	9155
8925	9029	9094	9157
8930	9031	9096	9158
8932	9033	9097	9161
8933	9034	9099	9163
8936	9035	9101	9168
8940	9036	9104	9169
8941	9037	9105	9170
8942	9039	9106	9172
8943	9042	9109	9174
8944	9044	9110	9176
8945	9045	9111	9177
8948	9046	9112	9180
8950	9047	9113	9181
8951	9048	9114	9185
8952	9051	9115	9186
8953	9055	9116	9192
8954	9057	9117	9198
8964	9061	9119	9203
9002	9062	9120	9205
9003	9064	9121	9207
9004	9065	9122	9209
9005	9066	9123	9211
9007	9068	9124	9212
9008	9069	9126	9214
9009	9070	9127	9216
9010	9072	9130	9217
9014	9073	9132	9220
9016	9074	9134	9223
9018	9077	9137	9224

9226	9275	9316	9356
9228	9276	9317	9357
9234	9278	9318	9358
9235	9280	9319	9360
9237	9281	9321	9361
9238	9284	9322	9363
9239	9288	9323	9365
9240	9289	9325	9366
9242	9290	9327	9368
9243	9291	9329	9375
9244	9292	9330	9376
9245	9293	9331	9377
9246	9294	9333	9378
9247	9296	9335	9379
9249	9298	9336	9381
9252	9299	9339	9382
9256	9300	9341	9386
9258	9301	9342	9387
9260	9304	9343	9388
9262	9306	9344	9389
9264	9308	9345	9390
9265	9310	9347	9392
9266	9311	9348	9393
9268	9312	9351	9394
9270	9313	9352	
9271	9315	9355	

Total 258

0-8-0   7F

Designed : Bowen-Cooke, 1921,
  L.N.W.R.
Driving Wheels : 4′ 5½″.
Cyls. : 20½″ × 24″.
Tractive Effort : 28,043 lb.
Superheater. Many with Belpaire
  Boilers.

G2 Class

9395	9405	9415	9425
9396	9406	9416	9426
9397	9407	9417	9427
9398	9408	9418	9428
9399	9409	9419	9429
9400	9410	9420	9430
9401	9411	9421	9431
9402	9412	9422	9432
9403	9413	9423	9433
9404	9414	9424	9434

7F Class G2—continued.

9435	9440	9445	9450
9436	9441	9446	9451
9437	9442	9447	9452
9438	9443	9448	9453
9439	9444	9449	9454

Total 60

0-8-0   7F

Designed : Fowler, 1929, L.M.S.
Driving Wheels : 4' 8½".
Cyls. : 19½" × 26".
Tractive Effort : 29,747 lb.
Superheated.

9500	9533	9566	9599
9501	9534	9567	9600
9502	9535	9568	9601
9503	9536	9569	9602
9504	9537	9570	9603
9505	9538	9571	9604
9506	9539	9572	9605
9507	9540	9573	9606
9508	9541	9574	9607
9509	9542	9575	9608
9510	9543	9576	9609
9511	9544	9577	9610
9512	9545	9578	9611
9513	9546	9579	9612
9514	9547	9580	9613
9515	9548	9581	9614
9516	9549	9582	9615
9517	9550	9583	9616
9518	9551	9584	9617
9519	9552	9585	9618
9520	9553	9586	9619
9521	9554	9587	9620
9522	9555	9588	9621
9523	9556	9589	9622
9524	9557	9590	9623
9525	9558	9591	9624
9526	9559	9592	9625
9527	9560	9593	9626
9528	9561	9594	9627
9529	9562	9595	9628
9530	9563	9596	9629
9531	9564	9597	9630
9532	9565	9598	9631

9632	9643	9654	9665
9633	9644	9655	9666
9634	9645	9656	9667
9635	9646	9657	9668
9636	9647	9658	9669
9637	9648	9659	9670
9638	9649	9660	9671
9639	9650	9661	9672
9640	9651	9662	9673
9641	9652	9663	9674
9642	9653	9664	

Total 175

4-6-0   5P

Designed : Hughes, 1908, Rebuilt
1921, L.Y.R.
Driving Wheels : 6' 3".
Cyls. (4), 16½" × 26", and 15¾" × 26".
Tractive Effort : 28,879 lb. and
26,314 lb.
(With Walschaerts Valve Gear and
Superheater.)

	Bldg. Date	Cyls.
10412	1908	
10423	1921	} 16½ × 26
10429	1921	
10432	1922	{
10437	1923	
10442	1923	} 15¾ × 26
10446	1923	
10448	1923	}
10455	1924	} 16½ × 26
10460	1924	

Total 10

0-4-0T   Rail Motors

Designed : Hughes, 1906, L.Y.R.
Driving Wheels : 5' 7⅞".
Outside Cyls. : 12" × 16".
Tractive Effort :
(With Walschaerts Valve Gear.)

10600	10617

Total 2

2-4-2T   2P

Designed : Aspinall, 1889, L.Y.R.
Driving Wheels : 5′ 8″.
Cyls. : 18″ × 26″.
Tractive Effort : 18,954 lb.

10621	10687	10759	10840*
10622	10689	10762	10841*
10623	10692	10764	10842*
10625	10693	10765	10843*
10630	10695	10766†	10844*
10631	10696	10776	10847*
10633	10697	10777	10849*
10634†	10703	10778	10850*
10636	10704†	10780	10852*
10639	10705	10781	10855*†
10640	10707*	10787†	10856*
10642	10711	10788	10857*
10643†	10712	10793	10859*
10644	10714†	10795†	10861*
10646	10715†	10796	10864*
10647	10717	10798	10865*†
10648	10719	10799†	10869*
10650	10720	10800†	10871
10651	10721	10801	10872
10652†	10722	10802	10873
10653†	10724	10803†	10874
10654†	10725	10804†	10875
10655	10728	10806	10876
10656†	10729	10807†	10878
10660	10731	10809	10879
10661	10732	10810	10880
10664	10735	10812	10881
10665†	10736	10813	10883
10667	10737	10815†	10884
10669†	10738	10818	10886
10670	10742	10819	10887
10671	10743	10821†	10888
10674	10746	10822*	10889
10675†	10748	10823*	10892
10676	10749	10825*†	10896
10677	10750	10827*†	10897
10678†	10752†	10829*	10898
10681	10755	10831*	10899
10686	10757		

Total 154

* These locos. have larger bunkers,
but are otherwise similar to the rest.
† Cyls. 17½″ × 26″.

2-4-2T   3P

Designed : Aspinall and Hughes, 1898,
L.Y.R.
Driving Wheels : 5′ 8″.
Cyls. : 20½″ × 26″.
Tractive Effort : 24,584 lb.
(Rebuilt with Belpaire boilers 1912.
Some superheated 1914-21).

10835	10903*	10934	10944
10882	10909	10935	10945*
10885	10910	10938*	10950
10890	10911	10939	10951
10891	10921	10941	10952*
10893	10923*	10942	10953
10901	10925*	10943*	

Total 27

* Cyls. : 19½″ × 26″.
T.E. : 22,244 lb.

0-4-0ST   0F

Designed : Aspinall, 1891.
                     L.Y.R. "Pugs."
Driving Wheels : 3′ 0¾″.
Outside Cyls. : 13″ × 18″.
Tractive Effort : 11,335 lb.

11202	11217	11230	11240
11204	11218	11231	11241
11206	11221	11232	11244
11207	11222	11234	11246
11212	11227	11235	11253
11216	11229	11237	

Total 23

0-6-0 ST   2F

Designed : Barton Wright, 1877,
L.Y.R. (Cl. 23) Rebuilt Aspinall.
Driving Wheels : 4′ 6″.
Cyls. : 17½″ × 26″.
Tractive Effort : 17,547 lb.

11307	11323	11345	11375
11313	11325	11348	11376
11316	11327	11353	11379
11318	11336	11358	11381
11319	11338	11361	11390
11320	11342	11366	11396
11321	11343	11371	11397

0-6-0ST 2F—continued.

11400	11439	11472	11498
11404	11441	11474	11499
11405	11443	11475	11500
11408	11444	11477	11503
11410	11445	11479	11504
11412	11446	11481	11506
11413	11447	11482	11508
11415	11448	11484	11510
11418	11453	11486	11511
11419	11457	11487	11512
11423	11458	11488	11513
11424	11460	11489	11514
11425	11462	11490	11516
11427	11464	11491	11519
11429	11467	11492	11521
11432	11468	11495	11524
11434	11469	11496	11526
11436	11470	11497	11530
11438	11471		

Total 102

0-6-0 T 1F

Designed: Aspinall, 1897. L.Y.R.(Cl. 24)
Driving Wheels : 4′ 6″.
Outside Cyls.: 17″×24″.
Tractive Effort : 15,285 lb.

11535 11537 11544 11546
11536

Total 5

0-6-2 T 3F

Designed : Pettigrew, 1904.   F.R.
Driving Wheels : 5′ 1″.
Cyls.: 18″×26″.
Tractive Effort : 17,781 lb.

11628 **Total 1**

0-6-0 2 F

Designed : Barton Wright, 1887.
L.Y.R. (Cl. 25)
Driving Wheels : 4′ 6″.
Cyls.: 17½″×26″.
Tractive Effort : 17,545 lb.

12016	12030	12041	12051
12019	12031	12043	12053
12021	12032	12044	12056
12022	12034	12045	12059
12023	12036	12046	12063
12024	12037	12047	12064
12025	12038	12049	
12026	12039		

Total 29

0-6-0 3 F

Designed : Aspinall, 1889.   L.Y.R
Driving Wheels : 5′ 1″.
Cyls.: 18″×26″.
Tractive Effort : 21,129 lb.

12086	12117	12150	12181
12087	12118	12152	12182
12088	12119	12154	12183
12089	12120	12155	12184
12090	12121	12156	12186
12091	12123	12157	12187
12092	12124	12159	12189
12093	12125	12160	12191
12094	12126	12161	12192
12095	12127	12162	12194
12098	12128	12163	12196
12099	12129	12164	12197
12100	12130	12165	12201
12101	12131	12166	12203
12102	12132	12167	12205
12103	12133	12169	12206
12104	12135	12170	12207
12105	12136	12171	12208
12106	12137	12172	12212
12107	12138	12174	12214
12108	12139	12175	12215
12110	12140	12176	12216
12111	12141	12177	12217
12112	12143		12218
12114	12146	12179	12219
12116	12149	12180	12220

0-6-0 3F—continued.

12224	12288	12363	12430
12225	12289	12364	12431
12227	12290	12365	12432
12229	12293	12366	12433
12230	12294	12367	12435
12231	12295	12368	12436
12232	12296	12369	12437
12233	12299	12374	12438
12235	12300	12375	12439
12236	12304	12376	12440
12237	12305	12378	12441
12238	12306	12379	12442
12239	12309	12381	12443
12240	12311	12382	12444
12241	12312	12383	12445
12243	12317	12386	12446
12244	12319	12387	12447
12245	12321	12388	12448
12246	12322	12389	12449
12247	12324	12390	12450
12248	12326	12393	12452
12250	12328	12394	12453
12252	12330	12395	12454
12253	12331	12397	12455
12254	12332	12399	12456
12255	12333	12400	12457
12256	12334	12401	12458
12257	12336	12403	12459
12258	12337	12404	12460
12260	12338	12405	12461
12262	12340	12407	12463
12263	12341	12408	12464
12265	12343	12410	12465
12266	12345	12411	12466
12268	12348	12412	12467
12269	12349	12413	12515
12270	12350	12414	12517
12271	12351	12415	12518
12272	12352	12416	12521
12273	12353	12417	12522
12275	12354	12418	12523
12278	12355	12420	12524
12279	12356	12422	12525
12280	12357	12424	12526
12282	12358	12427	12527
12284	12360	12428	12529
12285	12362	12429	

Total 290

0-6-0   **3 F**

Designed: Pettigrew, 1913.   F.R.
Driving Wheels: 4' 7½".
Cyls.: 18"×26".
Tractive Effort: 21,933 lb.

12494	12501	12509	12510
12499	12508		

Total 6

0-6-0   **3 F**

Designed: Hughes, 1909.   L.Y.R
Driving Wheels: 5' 1".
Cyls.: 20½"×26".
Superheated.
Tractive Effort: $\begin{cases} 27,405 \text{ lb. (43).} \\ 24,797 \text{ lb. (3).} \end{cases}$

12528	12559	12581	12605
12538	12561	12582	12606
12541	12562	12583	12607
12542	12568	12584	12608
12545	12569	12586	12609
12546	12572	12587	12614
12549	12574	12588	12615
12550	12575	12590	12616
12551	12576	12592	12617
12554	12578	12598	12618
12557	12579	12602	12619
12558	12580		

Total 46

0-8-0   **6 F**

Designed: Aspinall, 1901.
       L.Y.R. (Cl. 30)
Driving Wheels: 4' 6".
Cyls.: 20"×26".
Tractive Effort: 29,466 lb.

12710	12771	12822	12831
12723	12782	12824	12834
12725	12790	12825	12837
12727	12806	12827	12838
12729	12821	12828	12839

Total 20

0-8-0   7 F

Designed: Hughes, 1912. L.Y.R.(Cl.31)
Driving Wheels: 4' 6".
Cyls.: 21½" × 26".   Superheated.
Tractive Effort: 34,052 lb.

12841	12877	12916	12956
12856	12886	12920	12958
12857	12887	12928	12962
12861	12902	12935	12964
12870	12906	12945	12971
12873	12910	12948	12981
12875	12913	12952	

Total 27

2-8-0   7 F

Designed: Fowler, 1914.   S.& D.J.R.
Driving Wheels: 4' 8½".
Outside Cyls.: 21" × 28". Superheated
Tractive Effort: 35,932 lb.
             Walschaerts valve gear.

13800	13803	13806	13809
13801	13804	13807	13810
13802	13805	13808	

Total 11

N.B.—13806–10: built 1925.

4-4-0   2 P

Designed: McIntosh, 1898, etc. C.R.
Driving Wheels: 6' 6".
Cyls.: 19" × 26".
Tractive Effort: 18,411 lb.

14331	(Dunalastair II Cl.)
14332	(,, ,, ,,)
14333	(,, ,, ,,)
14337	(,, ,, III Cl. 1900)
14338	(,, ,, ,,)
14340	(,, ,, ,,)
14348	(,, ,, ,,)
14350	(,, ,, IV Cl. 1904)
14355	(,, ,, ,, 1905)
14363	(,, ,, ,, 1910)

Total 10

4-4-0 "Loch" Class   2P

Designed: Jones, 1896. H.R.
Driving Wheels: 6' 3½".
Outside Cyls.: 19" × 24".
Tractive Effort: 17,557 lb.
(Rebuilt with C. Rly. non-superheater
             boilers.)

14379	Loch Insh
14385	Loch Tay
14392	Loch Naver

Total 3

4-4-0 "Ben" Class   2P

Designed: P. Drummond, 1898. H.R.
Driving Wheels: 6'. 0".
Cyls.: 18½" × 26".
Tractive Effort: 18,402 lb.

14397	Ben-y-Gloe
14398	Ben Alder
14399	Ben Wyvis
14400	Ben More
14401	Ben Vrackie
14403	Ben Attow
14404	Ben Clebrig
14405	Ben Rinnes
14406	Ben Slioch
14408	Ben Hope
14409	Ben Alisky
14410	Ben Dearg
14412	Ben Avon
14415	Ben Bhach Ard
14416	Ben A'Bhuird

Total 15

4-4-0   3 P

Designed: McIntosh, 1900.   C.R.
Driving Wheels: 6' 6".
Cyls.: 19½" × 26".
Superheated. (Dunalastair III Cl.
                             rebuild)
Tractive Effort: 19,393 lb.

14434	Rebuilt 1916

Total 1

4-4-0   3 P

Designed : McIntosh, 1907.   C.R.
Driving Wheels : 6′ 6″.
Cyls.: 20½″×26″.
Superheated, (Dunalastair IV Class,
    Non-Superheater rebuilds.)
Tractive Effort : 20,913 lb.

| 14438 | Rebuilt 1917 |
| 14439 | ,, 1915 |

Total 2

4-4-0   3 P

Designed : McIntosh, 1910.   C.R.
Driving Wheels : 6′ 6″.
Cyls.: 20½″×26″.
Tractive Effort : 20,913 lb.
Superheated (Dunalastair IV Class)

14440	14446	14451	14456
14441	14447	14452	14457
14442	14448	14453	14458
14443	14449	14454	14459
14444	14450	14455	14460
14445			

Total 21

4-4-0   3 P

Designed : Pickersgill, 1916.   C.R.
Driving Wheels : 6′ 6″.
Cyls.: 20″×26″.
Tractive Effort : 20,400 lb.
         21,432 lb. (cyls. :
             20½″×26″)

Superheated.

14461	14465	14469	14473
14462	14466	14470	14474
14463	14467	14471	14475
14464	14468	14472	14476

With Cyls.: 20½″×26″ Built 1920.

14477	14485	14493	14501
14478	14486	14494	14502
14479	14487	14495	14503
14480	14488	14496	14504
14481	14489	14497	14505
14482	14490	14498	14506
14483	14491	14499	14507
14484	14492	14500	14508

Total 48

4-6-0   3 P

Designed : Pickersgill, 1922.
         C.R. (" Oban " Class)
Driving Wheels : 5′ 6″.
Outside Cyls.: 19½″×26″.
Tractive Effort: 23,555 lb.
(With Walschaerts Valve Gear.)

14621

Total 1

4-6-0   4 P

Designed : Pickersgill, 1925.   L.M.S.
Driving Wheels : 6′ 1″.
Outside Cyls. : 20½″×26″.
Tractive Effort : 22,900 lb.
    (Superheated.)

14630	14637	14644	14651*
14631	14638	14645	14652*
14632	14639	14646	14653*
14633	14640	14647	14654*
14634	14641	14648	
14635	14642	14649	
14636	14643	14650*	

Total 25

* Built 1916. C.R. with cyls. 20″×26″
" 60 " Class. Tractive Effort : 21,797 lb

4-6-0 " Castle " Class 3P

Designed : P. Drummond, 1900. H.R.
         (" Castle " Class.)
Driving Wheels : 5′ 9″.
Outside Cyls. : 19½″×26″.
Tractive Effort : 21,922 lb.

14678	Gordon Castle
14681	Skibo Castle
14685	Dunvegan Castle
14686	Urquhart Castle
14689	Cluny Castle
14690	Dalcross Castle
14692†	Darnaway Castle

Total 7

† Designed by Cumming, 1917, with
6′ 0″ driving wheels. Tractive Effort :
20,425 lb.

4-6-0   4P

Designed : Smith (H. Rly.), 1915. C.R.
Driving Wheels : 6′ 0″.
Outside Cyls. : 21″ × 28″.
Tractive Effort : 23,324 lb.
(Superheated, Walschaert's valve gear.)

         14758   14760

Total 2

4-6-0 " Clan " Class   4 P

Designed : Cumming, 1919.   H.R.
Driving Wheels : 6′ 0″.
Outside Cyls. : 21″ × 26″.
Tractive Effort : 23,688 lb.
(With Walschaert's valve gear and superheater.)

14762	Clan Campbell
14763	Clan Fraser
14764	Clan Munro
14765	Clan Stewart
14766	Clan Chattan
14767	Clan Mackinnon
14768	Clan Mackenzie

Total 7

0-4-2ST   0P

Designed : D. Drummond, 1885. C.R.
            (For Killin Branch.)
Driving Wheels : 3′ 8″.
Outside Cyls. : 14″ × 20″.
Tractive Effort : 10,600 lb.

        15001   **Total 1**

0-4-4T   0P

Designed : P. Drummond, 1905. H.R.
Driving Wheels : 4′ 6″.
Cyls. : 14″ × 20″.
Tractive Effort : 9,255 lb.

   15051   15053   15054

Total 3

0-4-4T   1 P

Designed : D. Drummond, 1886. C.R.
Driving Wheels : 5′ 0″.
Cyls. : 16″ × 22″.
Reboilered 1924, L.M.S.
Tractive Effort : 11,968 lb.

    15103   **Total 1**

0-4-4T   2 P

Designed : McIntosh, 1895.   C.R.
Driving Wheels : 5′ 9″.
Cyls. : 18″ × 26″.
(Originally fitted with condensing apparatus.)
Tractive Effort : 18,679 lb.

15115	15123	15131	15139
15116	15124	15132	15140
15117	15125	15133	15141
15118	15126	15134	15142
15119	15127	15135	15143
15120	15128	15136	15144
15121	15129	15137	15145
15122	15130	15138	15146

Total 32

0-4-4T   2 P

Designed : McIntosh, 1900.   C.R.
Driving Wheels : 5′ 9″.
Cyls. : 18″ × 26″.
Tractive Effort : 18,679 lb.

15159	15180	15201	15222
15160	15181	15202	15223
15161	15182	15203	15224
15162	15183	15204	15225
15163	15184	15205	15226
15164	15185	15206	15227
15165	15186	15207	15228
15166	15187	15208	15229
15167	15188	15209	15230
15168	15189	15210	15231
15169	15190	15211	15232
15170	15191	15212	15233
15171	15192	15213	15234
15172	15193	15214	15235
15173	15194	15215	15236
15174	15195	15216	15237*
15175	15196	15217	15238*
15176	15197	15218	15239*
15177	15198	15219	15240*
15178	15199	15220	
15179	15200	15221	

Total 82

* Cyls.: 18½″ × 26″. Tractive Effort: 19,201 lb. Fitted with cast-iron front buffer beams for banking purposes. Built : Pickersgill 1922.

0-4-4T 2 P

Designed : McIntosh C.R. type, 1925,
enlarged.   L.M.S.
Driving Wheels : 5' 9".
Cyls. : 18¼"×26".
Tractive Effort : 19,201 lb.

15260	15263	15266	15269
15261	15264	15267	
15262	15265	15268	

Total 10

4-6-2T 4 P

Designed : Pickersgill, 1917.   CR.
Driving Wheels : 5' 9".
Outside Cyls. : 19½"×26".
    Superheated.
Tractive Effort : 21,922 lb.

15350	15353	15356	15359
15351	15354	15357	15360
15352	15355	15358	15361

Total 12

0-4-0ST 0F

Designed : D. Drummond, 1885. C.R.
Driving Wheels : 3' 8".
Outside Cyls. : 14"×20".
Tractive Effort : 12,116 lb.

16009	16026	16030	16035
16010	16027	16031	16038
16011	16028	16032	16039
16020	16029		

Total 14

0-6-0T 2 F

Designed : McIntosh, 1912.   C.R.
    (" Dock " Class)
Driving Wheels : 4' 0".
Outside Cyls. : 17"×22".
Tractive Effort : 18,014 lb.

16151	16157	16163	16169
16152	16158	16164	16170
16153	16159	16165	16171
16154	16160	16166	16172
16155	16161	16167	16173
16156	16162	16168	

Total 23

0-6-0 T 3 F

Designed : McIntosh, 1896.   C.R.
Driving Wheels : 4' 6".
Cyls. : 18"×26".
Tractive Effort : 21,216 lb.

16230	16267	16304	16341
16231	16268	16305	16342
16232	16269	16306	16343
16233	16270	16307	16344
16234	16271	16308	16345
16235	16272	16309	16346
16236	16273	16310	16347
16237	16274	16311	16348
16238	16275	16312	16349
16239	16276	16313	16350
16240	16277	16314	16351
16241	16278	16315	16352
16242	16279	16316	16353
16243	16280	16317	16354
16244	16281	16318	16355
16245	16282	16319	16356
16246	16283	16320	16357
16247	16284	16321	16358
16248	16285	16322	16359
16249	16286	16323	16360
16250	16287	16324	16361
16251	16288	16325	16362
16252	16289	16326	16363
16253	16290	16327	16364
16254	16291	16328	16365
16255	16292	16329	16366
16256	16293	16330	16367
16257	16294	16331	16368
16258	16295	16332	16369
16259	16296	16333	16370
16260	16297	16334	16371
16261	16298	16335	16372
16262	16299	16336	16373
16263	16300	16337	16374
16264	16301	16338	16375
16265	16302	16339	16376
16266	16303	16340	

Total 147

0-6-2 T   3 F

Designed : P. Drummond, 1915.
                      (G. & S.W.R.)
Driving Wheels : 5' 0".
Cyls. : 18½" × 26".
Tractive Effort : 22,082 lb.

16901*	16907*	16920	16922
16905*	16911	16921	16926

Total 8

* Designed, Whitelegg, 1919).

0-6-0   2 F

Designed : D. Drummond, 1883. C.R.
Driving Wheels : 5' 0".
Cyls. : 18" × 26".
Tractive Effort : 21,481 lb.
(102 engines fitted with Westinghouse brakes for working passenger trains.)

17230	17259	17288	17317
17231	17260	17289	17318
17232	17261	17290	17319
17233	17262	17291	17320
17234	17263	17292	17321
17235	17264	17293	17322
17236	17265	17294	17323
17237	17266	17295	17324
17238	17267	17296	17325
17239	17268	17297	17326
17240	17269	17298	17327
17241	17270	17299	17328
17242	17271	17300	17329
17243	17272	17301	17330
17244	17273	17302	17331
17245	17274	17303	17332
17246	17275	17304	17333
17247	17276	17305	17334
17248	17277	17306	17335
17249	17278	17307	17336
17250	17279	17308	17337
17251	17280	17309	17338
17252	17281	17310	17339
17253	17282	17311	17340
17254	17283	17312	17341
17255	17284	17313	17342
17256	17285	17314	17343
17257	17286	17315	17344
17258	17287	17316	17345
17346	17378	17410	17442
17347	17379	17411	17443
17348	17380	17412	17444
17349	17381	17413	17445
17350	17382	17414	17446
17351	17383	17415	17447
17352	17384	17416	17448
17353	17385	17417	17449
17354	17386	17418	17450
17355	17387	17419	17451
17356	17388	17420	17452
17357	17389	17421	17453
17358	17390	17422	17454
17359	17391	17423	17455
17360	17392	17424	17456
17361	17393	17425	17457
17362	17394	17426	17458
17363	17395	17427	17459
17364	17396	17428	17460
17365	17397	17429	17461
17366	17398	17430	17462
17367	17399	17431	17463
17368	17400	17432	17464
17369	17401	17433	17465
17370	17402	17434	17466
17371	17403	17435	17467
17372	17404	17436	17468
17373	17405	17437	17469
17374	17406	17438	17470
17375	17407	17439	17471
17376	17408	17440	17472
17377	17409	17441	17473

Total 244

N.B. 17325-17473 built by Lambie and McIntosh.

0-6-0   3 F

Designed : McIntosh, 1899.   C.R.
                      ("812" Class.)
Driving Wheels : 5' 0".
Cyls. : 18½" × 26".
Tractive Effort : 22,691 lb.
(20 engines fitted with Westinghouse brakes for working passenger trains)

17550	17556	17562	17568
17551	17557	17563	17569
17552	17558	17564	17570
17553	17559	17565	17571
17554	17560	17566	17572
17555	17561	17567	17573

0-6-0 3F Class—continued.

17574	17592	17610	17628
17575	17593	17611	17629
17576	17594	17612	17630
17577	17595	17613	17631
17578	17596	17614	17632
17579	17597	17615	17633
17580	17598	17616	17634
17581	17599	17617	17635
17582	17600	17618	17636
17583	17601	17619	17637
17584	17602	17620	17638
17585	17603	17621	17639
17586	17604	17622	17640
17587	17605	17623	17641
17588	17606	17624	17642
17589	17607	17625	17643
17590	17608	17626	17644
17591	17609	17627	17645

Total 96

0-6-0 3 F

Designed : McIntosh, 1912. C.R.
("30" Class)
Driving Wheels : 5' 0".
Cyls. : $19\frac{1}{2}" \times 26"$.
Superheated : Westinghouse brakes.
Tractive Effort : 22,409 lb.

17647　17648　17649

Total 3

0-6-0 3 F

Designed : Pickersgill, 1918. C.R.
Driving Wheels : 5' 0".
Cyls. : $18\frac{1}{2}" \times 26"$.
Superheated.
Tractive Effort : 22,691 lb.

17650	17658	17666	17672
17651	17659	17667	17673
17652	17661	17668	17674
17653	17662	17669	17679
17654	17663	17670	17681
17655	17665	17671	17682

Total 24

0-6-0 3 F

Designed : Pickersgill, 1919. C.R.
Driving Wheels : 5' 0".
Cyls. : $18\frac{1}{2}" \times 26"$.
(All now superheated, except 17687.)
Tractive Effort : 22,691 lb.

17684	17687	17689	17 69
17686	17688	17690	

Total 7

0-6-0 3 F

Designed : P. Drummond, 1900. H.R.
Driving Wheels : 5' 0".
Cyls. : $18\frac{1}{2}" \times 26"$.
Tractive Effort : 21,468 lb.

17693	17696	17699	17703
17694	17697	17700	17704
17695	17698	17702	

Total 11

2-6-0 4 F

Designed : P. Drummond, 1915.
G. & S.W.R.
Driving Wheels : 5' 0".
Cyls. : $19\frac{1}{2}" \times 26"$.
Superheated.
Tractive Effort : 25,210 lb.

17821　17822　17826　17829

Total 4

4-6-0 3 F

Designed : McIntosh, 1913. C.R.
("179" Class.)
Driving Wheels : 5' 9".
Cyls. : $19\frac{1}{2}" \times 26"$.
Tractive Effort : 20,704 lb.
Superheated.
17905　17908　**Total 2**

4-6-0 4 F

Designed : Cumming, 1918. H.R.
("Clan" Goods Class)
Driving Wheels : 5' 3".
Outside Cyls. : $20\frac{1}{2}" \times 26"$.
Tractive Effort : 25,799 lb.
Walschaerts valve gear. Superheated.

17950	17952	17954	17956
17951	17953	17955	17957

Total 8

2-4-0   1P

Designed : Kirtley, 1866.   M.R.
(Double Frames)
Reboilered by Johnson.
Driving Wheels : 6′ 3″.
Cyls. : 18″ × 24″.
Tractive Effort : 12,338 lb.

20002   20012

Total 2

2-4-0   1 P

Designed : Johnson, 1876.   M.R
Driving Wheels : As shown.
Cyls. : 18″ × 24″.
Tractive Effort : As shown.

20155   6′ 3″
     Tractive Effort : 12,338 lb.
20185   6′ 6⅛″
     Tractive Effort : 12,770 lb.
20216   6′ 9″
     Tractive Effort : 12,376 lb.

Total 3

0-6-0   2 F

Designed : Kirtley, 1868.   M.R.
Driving Wheels : 5′ 3″.
Cyls. : 18″ × 24″.
(Double Frames. Reboilered).
Tractive Effort : 16,786 lb.

22567	22630*	22834*	22853
22579	22818*	22846	22863
22589	22822	22849	

Total 11

* Round top boilers ; the remainder Belpaire boilers.

0-6-0   2 F

Designed : Johnson, 1876.   M.R·
Driving Wheels : 4′ 11″.
Cyls. : 18″ × 26″.
Tractive Effort : 19,417 lb.

22900	22915	22928	22940
22901	22916	22929	22941
22902	22918	22930	22943
22904	22920	22931	22944
22907	22921	22932	22945
22911	22924	22933	22946
22912	22926	22934	22947
22913	22927	22935	22950
22951	22963	22971	2297
22953	22965	22974	2297
22954	22967	22975	2298
22955	22968	22976	2298
22958	22969	22977	2298
22959	22970		

Total 5·

Many rebuilt with non-super-heater Belpaire boilers.

" Precursor " Class

4-4-0   3

Designed : Whale, 1904.   L.N.W.
Driving Wheels : 6′ 9″.
Cyls. : 20½″ × 26″.
Tractive Effort : 20,639 lb.
Rebuilt with superheated Belpaire boilers.

25277 Oberon
25292 Medusa
25297 Sirocco
25304 Greyhound

Total ·

" George the Fifth "

4-4-0   Class   3

Designed : B. Cooke, 1910. L.N.W.
Driving Wheels : 6′ 9″.
Cyls. : 20½″ × 26″.
Tractive Effort : 20,639 lb.
Rebuilt superheated Belpaire boilers

25321 Lord Loch
25350
25373 Ptarmigan
25376 Snipe

Total ·

" Prince of Wales "

4-6-0   Class   4

Designed : B. Cooke, 1911. L.N.W.
Driving Wheels : 6′ 3″.
Cyls. : 20½″ × 26″.
Tractive Effort : 22,690 lb.
Superheated.
Some rebuilt with Belpaire boilers.

25648 Queen of the Belgians
25673 Lusitania
25674 Scott
25683 Falaba

Prince of Wales " Class—
continued.

694	25752	25798	25818
722	25775	25802	25827
725	25787	25804	25841
749	25791	25805	25845*
751	25797		

Total 22

* Built in 1924 with Walschaerts gear.

4-2 ST Crane Engine

(Square saddle)

Designed : Sharp-Stewart, 1858, as 0-4-0T. L.N.W.R. (N.L.R.)
Driving Wheels : 3′ 10″.
Cyls. : 13″ × 17″.
Tractive Effort : 6,376 lb.

27217

Total 1

6-0 ST 2 F

Designed : Webb, 1891. L.N.W.R.
Rebuilt, Whale, 1906, from 0-6-0 tender engines
Driving Wheels : 4′ 5½″.
Cyls. : 17″ × 24″
Tractive Effort : 16,530 lb.

27480 27484

Total 2

6-0T 2 F

Designed : Park 1879. L.N.W.R. (N.L.R.)
Driving Wheels : 4′ 4″.
Outside Cyls. : 17″ × 24″.
Tractive Effort : 18,140 lb.

505	27513	27520	27528
509	27514	27522	27530
510	27515	27525	27532
512	27517	27527	

Total 15

0-6-2T 2 F

Designed : Webb, 1882. L.N.W.R.
Driving Wheels : 4′ 5½″.
Cyls. : 17″ × 24″.
Tractive Effort : 16,530 lb.
For Coal Traffic.

27552	27590	27619	27648
27553	27591	27621	27650
27555	27596	27623	27654
27558	27597	27624	27662
27561	27602	27625	27663
27562	27603	27626	27664
27571	27604	27627	27666
27572	27605	27631	27669
27577	27606	27635	27672
27580	27609	27636	27674
27585	27616	27640	27678
27586	27618	27645	27681

Total 48

0-6-0 2 F

Designed : Webb, 1873. L.N.W.R.
Driving Wheels : 4′ 5½″.
Cyls. : 17″ × 24″.
Tractive Effort : 16,530 lb.
(For Coal Traffic.)

28088	28138	28209	28261
28091	28139	28216	28262
28093	28141	28221	28263
28095	28145	28226	28271
28097	28152	28227	28278
28100	28153	28230	28288
28104	28158	28233	28289
28105	28166	28234	28295
28106	28172	28239	28296
28107	28186	28240	28303
28115	28187	28245	28308
28116	28191	28246	28309
28117	28199	28247	28312
28128	28202	28251	28313
28129	28204	28253	
28133	28205	28256	

Total 62

0-6-0   2 F

Designed : Webb, 1887.   L.N.W.R.
Driving Wheels : 5' 2½".
Cyls. : 18" × 24".
("Cauliflowers.")
Tractive Effort : 15,502 lb.

28315	28423	28512	28555
28318	28428	28513	28556
28333	28429	28515	28559
28335	28430	28518	28561
28337	28441	28521	28575
28338	28442	28524	28580
28339	28443	28525	28583
28343	28450	28526	28585
28345	28451	28527	28586
28347	28457	28529	28587
28350	28458	28531	28588
28367	28460	28532	28589
28369	28464	28533	28592
28370	28482	28535	28594
28372	28484	28538	28597
28385	28485	28542	28598
28392	28487	28543	28601
28401	28492	28544	28603
28403	28494	28546	28608
28404	28499	28547	28610
28408	28503	28548	28611
28410	28505	28549	28614
28415	28507	28550	28616
28417	28508	28551	28618
28420	28509	28552	28619
28422	28511	28553	28622

Total 104

Leyland Diesel Railcar

Built : 1933.
Four Wheels : Non-coupled.
Diesel Engine : 95 h.p.
Wheel Diameter : 3' 0".
6 Cyls. : 4⅝" diam. × 6" stroke.

29950   29951   29952

Total 3

0-4-0   Rail Motors

Designed : Whale, 1905.   L.N.W.
Driving Wheels : 3' 9".
Cyls. : 9½" × 15".

Coach No. 29988.

Total 1

Diesel Articulated 3-ca
Set

Built : 1938.
Four 4-wheel Bogies.
6 Cyls. : 4½" × 5½".
125 h.p.

Car numbers :

80000   80001   80002

Total

Standard 0-0-9 No. 7143 now renumbered 7303

54

Ex-Caledonian Railway 0-6-0 No. 17257.

Aspinall ex-L.Y.R. 0-6-0 No. 12193.

Johnson/Dedey 0-6-0 No. 3624 ex M.R.

Ex L.N.W.R. 0-6-0 No. 8484, now renumbered 28484.

3P Class 4-4-2T, No. 2112.

Webb/Whale 0-8-0 No. 9190, ex-L.N.W.R.

THE A B C OF
L.N.E.R.
LOCOMOTIVES

[Photo : H. C. Casserly

4-0 D 16 class loco. 8833 hauling a stopping train, near Littlebury

IAN ALLAN, STAINES

(Second Edition)

August, 1944

A locomotive of the D 49 (Hunt) class, 366 " The Oakley "

[Photo : S. Oborne]

PREFACE

At the time of the Railway Grouping of 1923 the locomotive stock of the constituent companies of the London and North Eastern Railway Group comprised : 1,359 Great Northern locomotives, 1,358 Great Central locomotives, 1,336 Great Eastern locomotives, 2,156 North Eastern locomotives, 1,074 North British locomotives, 122 Great North of Scotland locomotives. Since that time many of these old locomotives have been superseded and between then and the end of 1942, 1,850 new locomotives have been placed in traffic. Of these, 390 have been built in the Doncaster shops, 728 in the shops at Darlington, 65 at Gorton, 30 at Stratford and 30 at Cowlairs, whilst the remainder have been supplied by various locomotive building contractors. The present stock stands at about 6,500 locos.

The most important of the locomotives built subsequent to 1923 are the Gresley "Pacific" type engines, the "Mikado" engines and the 2-6-2 type locomotives classified as V 2. The Pacific engines were solely responsible for hauling the high speed light-weight trains of the immediate pre-war period, and it was one of this type which in 1938 attained a speed of 125 miles per hour, which was, and is still, retained as a world speed record for a steam locomotive and train.

In the same period also the first Garratt type engine for the British Railways was introduced on to the L.N.E.R. system. With its tractive power of over 72,000 lbs., it was, and still remains, the most powerful locomotive at work in this country.

With regard to electrification, the L.N.E.R. had in hand the scheme to electrify the main line between Sheffield and Manchester. A series of Bo-Bo locomotives was planned, and but for the intervention of the war would have been proceeded with. Only one locomotive, however, was turned out ; this was given certain tests on the M.S.J. & A. line, but must await more favourable times before it can be put to work on the lines for which it was designed.

The general classification of locomotives on the L.N.E.R. is as follows :—

A	4-6-2	J	0-6-0	S	0-8-4
B	4-6-0	K	2-6-0	T	4-8-0
C	4-4-2	L	2-6-4	U	2-8-8-2
D	4-4-0	M	0-6-4	V	2-6-2
E	2-4-0	N	0-6-2	W	4-6-4
F	2-4-2	O	2-8-0	Y	0-4-0
G	0-4-4	P	2-8-2	Z	0-4-2
H	4-4-4	Q	0-8-0		

3

As in the early days of the Grouping, there was more necessity to retain the engines of the constituent companies within their own section, the renumbering was carried out on a sectional basis. Locomotives of the old North Eastern Railway retained their own numbers; locomotives of the Great Northern had 3000 added to their original number. To the Great Central engine numbers 5000 was added, to the Great Eastern 7000, to the North British 9000 and to the Great North of Scotland 6800. Locomotives of the subsidiary companies took vacant numbers in the Great Northern and Great Eastern series.

Sincere thanks are extended to the L.N.E.R. Company for having checked the information contained herein and for having supplied many of the photographs. Other photographs are by kind courtesy of Mr. H. C. Casserly and Mr. Sidney Oborne.

No. 7160 (J 69 class) of Stratford fame

PRINCIPAL LOCOMOTIVE RUNNING DEPOTS

SOUTHERN AREA

EASTERN SECTION

Cambridge
Bury
Ely

Colchester
Parkeston

Ipswich

March

Kings Lynn
South Lynn

Norwich
Cromer
Lowestoft
Melton Constable
Yarmouth Beach
Yarmouth (S.T.)

Stratford
Bishops Stortford
Brentwood

Enfield Town
Hertford
Palace Gates
Epping
Wood Street
Southend

WESTERN SECTION

Ardsley
Bradford
Leeds (Copley Hill)

Colwick
Woodford
Annesley
Leicester
Staveley

Doncaster
Mexborough
Sheffield
Barnsley
Retford

Gorton
Trafford Park

Liverpool
Stockport (Heaton Mersey)
Northwich
Wrexham
Chester

Immingham
Louth
New Holland
Frodingham
Langwith
Lincoln
Tuxford

King's Cross
Hornsey
Hatfield
Hitchin

Neasden

Peterborough (New England)
Boston
Grantham

NORTH-EASTERN AREA

Darlington
Northallerton
Kirkby Stephen
West Auckland
Wearhead
Middleton-in-Teesdale

Gateshead
Borough Gardens
Tyne Dock
Sunderland
Durham
Waskerley
Hexham

Pelton Level
Bowes Bridge
Consett Junction
Alston

Heaton
Blaydon
Percy Main
Blyth South
North Blyth
Alnmouth
Tweedmouth
Duns
Reedsmouth
Rothbury

Hull (Dairycoates)
Hull (Springhead)
Hull (Botanic Gdns.)
Hull (Alexandra Dock)
Cudworth
Bridlington
Leeds (Neville Hill)
Starbeck
Ilkley
Manningham
Pateley Bridge
Middlesbrough
Newport
West Hartlepool

Stockton	**York**	Malton
Haverton Hill	Selby	Pickering
Saltburn	Scarborough	Normanton
Guisborough	Whitby	

SCOTTISH AREA

Aberdeen (Kitty- Keith brewster)	**Dunfermline U.**	**Kipps** (Coatbridge
Elgin	**Edinburgh**	**Perth**
Aberdeen (Ferryhill)	(St. Margarets) Haymarket	
Bathgate		**Polmont**
Carlisle	**Glasgow** (Eastfield)	
Hawick	Parkhead Galashiels	**Stirling**
Dundee	Fort William	**Thornton Junctn**

LOCOMOTIVE SUPERINTENDENTS
AND CHIEF MECHANICAL ENGINEERS

Great Northern Railway

A. Sturrock	1850 – 1866
P. Stirling	1866 – 1895
H. A. Ivatt	1896 – 1911
H. N. Gresley	1911 – 1922

North Eastern Railway

E. Fletcher	1854 – 1882
A. McDonnell	1882 – 1885
T.W.Worsdell	1885 – 1890
W. Worsdell	1890 – 1910
Sir Vincent Raven	1910 – 1922

Great Eastern Railway

R. Sinclair	1862 – 1866
S. W. Johnson	1866 – 1873
W. Adams	1873 – 1878
M. Bromley	1878 – 1881
T.W.Worsdell	1881 – 1885
J. Holden	1885 – 1907
S. D. Holden	1908 – 1912
A. J. Hill	1912 – 1922

Great Central Railway

H. Pollitt	1897 – 1900
J. G. Robinson	1900 – 1922

Hull and Barnsley

M. Stirling	1885 – 1922

North British Railway

T. Wheatley	1867 – 1874
D. Drummond	1875 – 1882
M. Holmes	1882 – 1903
W. P. Reid	1903 – 1914
W. Chalmers	1919 – 1922

Gt. North of Scotland Rly.

D. K. Clark	1853 – 1855
— Ruthven	1855 – 1857
W. Cowan	1857 – 1883
J. Manson	1883 – 1890
J. Johnson	1890 – 1894
W. Pickersgill	1894 – 1914
T. E. Heywood	1914 – 1922

London & North Eastern Rly.

Sir Nigel Gresley	1923 – 1941
E. Thompson	From 1941

NUMERICAL LIST OF ENGINES AND CLASSES

This list is officially correct up to June, 1944.

No.	Class	No.	Class	No.	Class	No.	Class	No.	Class
1	Electric*	52	K 3	102	J 21	154	Y 3	203	K 3
2	Electric*	53	K 3	103	J 71	155	Y 3	204	K 3
3	Electric†	54	J 71	105	J 77	156	K 3	205	D 49
4	Electric†	55	Y 3	106	Y 1	158	K 3	206	K 3
5	Electric†	57	J 77	108	Y 1	159	K 3	207	K 3
6	Electric†	58	K 3	109	K 3	161	J 71	208	K 3
7	Electric†	59	Y 1	111	K 3	162	Q 5	209	J 21
8	Electric†	60	Y 3	112	K 3	163	K 3	210	N 8
9	Electric†	61	Y 3	113	K 3	165	J 71	211	D 49
10	Electric†	62	Y 3	114	K 3	166	J 77	212	N 8
11	Electric†	63	Y 3	116	K 3	167	K 3	214	D 49
12	Electric†	64	Y 3	117	Y 3	168	J 71	217	D 49
13	Electric§	65	Y 3	118	K 3	170	K 3		
		67	J 26	119	Y 1	171	Y 1	219	N 8
15	J 77	68	J 21	120	K 3	172	Y 3	220	D 49
16	J 21	69	K 3	121	K 3	174	Y 1	221	J 71
17	K 3	70	J 71	123	J 21	175	Y 1	222	D 49
18	Y 3	71	J 77	124	Y 1	176	J 71	224	J 71
19	Y 1	73	K 3	125	K 3	177	J 71	226	D 49
21	Y 3	74	N 8	126	K 3	178	K 3	227	K 3
23	Y 3	75	K 3	127	K 3	179	J 71	228	K 3
25	J 25	76	N 8	130	Q 5	180	K 3	229	K 3
26	J 21	77	J 71	132	J 26	181	J 71	230	D 49
28	K 3	78	Y 3	134	K 3	183	Y 1	231	K 3
29	J 25	79	Y 1	135	K 3	184	K 3	232	D 49
30	J 21	80	Y 3	136	N 8	186	K 3	233	J 26
32	K 3	81	K 3	137	J 71	187	Y 1	234	D 49
33	K 3	83	Q 5	138	J 77	188	K 3	235	D 49
35	Y 3	86	Y 3	139	J 21	189	Y 3	236	D 49
36	K 3	87	Y 3	140	K 3	191	K 3	237	J 71
37	J 77	89	N 10	141	K 3	192	Y 3	238	D 49
38	K 3	90	Y 3	142	Y 1	193	Y 3	239	J 71
39	K 3	91	K 3	143	K 3	195	K 3	240	J 71
42	Y 3	92	K 3	145	J 77	196	Y 3	241	J 71
43	J 77			146	K 3	197	Y 3	243	J 26
44	Y 1	94	Y 3	147	J 21	198	Y 3	244	J 71
45	Y 1	96	Y 3	148	Y 3	199	J 77	245	D 49
46	K 3	97	J 21	149	G 5			246	D 49
47	J 77	98	Y 3	150	Y 1	200	K 3	247	D 49
49	Y 3			151	J 77	201	D 49	248	J 71
50	J 71	100	Y 1	153	K 3	202	K 3	249	D 49

* Bo-Bo Shunting   † Bo-Bo Shildon.   § 2 Co 2 Express.

C 7 Class

Q 4 Class

Q I Class

8

250	D 49	306	D 49	380	G 5	427	G 5	472	V 3
251	D 49	307	D 49	381	G 5	428	V 1	473	N 7
252	J 71	309	D 49	383	N 9	429	N 10	474	Q 5
253	D 49	310	D 49	384	G 5	430	Q 5	475	N 7
254	J 71	311	D 49	387	G 5			476	D 20
255	D 49	312	J 21	390	V 3	432	J 21		
256	D 49	313	J 21	391	V 3	433	G 5	477	V 1
257	J 25	314	J 21	392	V 3	434	J 26	478	V 1
258	D 49	318	D 49	393	V 3	435	G 5	479	V 1
260	J 71	319	J 77	394	G 5	436	G 5	480	V 1
261	J 71	320	D 49	395	V 3	437	G 5	481	V 1
264	D 49	322	D 49	396	V 3	438	J 26	482	J 71
265	D 49	324	J 77	397	V 3	439	G 5	483	V 3
266	D 49	326	J 71	398	V 3	440	V 1	484	V 1
267	N 8	327	D 49	399	V 3	441	G 5	485	V 1
269	D 49	329	D 49			442	J 26	486	V 1
270	D 49	335	D 49	400	J 71	443	Q 5	487	V 1
271	N 8	336	D 49	401	V 3	444	Q 5	488	V 1
272	J 71	338	J 71	402	V 1	445	N 8	489	V 1
273	D 49	342	J 26	403	J 71	446	V 1	490	V 1
274	D 49	344	J 77	404	V 1	447	V 1	491	V 1
275	J 71	345	N 8	405	G 5	448	V 1	492	J 71
276	J 77	346	N 8	406	J 26	449	J 71	494	J 71
277	D 49	347	J 71	407	V 1	450	J 71	495	J 71
279	D 49	348	N 8	408	G 5	451	V 3	496	V 1
280	J 71	352	D 49	409	N 7	452	J 71	497	V 1
281	D 49	353	D 49	410	Q 5	454	V 1	498	V 1
282	D 49	354	J 77	411	Q 5	455	V 1	499	J 71
283	D 49	357	D 49	412	J 26	456	N 7		
286	J 71	359	D 49	413	G 5	457	N 7	500	J 72
288	D 49	361	D 49	414	V 1	459	J 25	501	J 71
290	J 77	362	D 49	415	V 1	460	N 7	503	N 8
292	D 49	363	D 49	416	V 1	461	V 1	505	G 5
293	N 8	364	D 49	417	V 3	462	J 72	512	J 72
294	J 21	365	D	418	V 1	463	J 25	513	J 21
		366	D 49	419	V 1	464	N 7	515	N 8
297	D 49	368	D 49	420	V 1	465	V 1	516	J 72
298	D 49	370	D 49	421	N 7	466	V 1	517	J 26
299	J 71	374	D 49	422	V 1	467	V 1	524	J 72
		375	D 49	423	V 1	468	G 5	525	J 26
300	J 21	376	D 49	424	V 1	469	V 1	526	G 5
301	J 71	377	D 49	425	V 1	470	J 21	527	Q 5
305	J 77	379	J 26	426	N 7	471	N 7	529	G 5

533 J 71	589 J 50	633 Q 7	700 C 6	778 J 21
535 N 8	590 J 50	634 Q 7	701 C 6	780 N 8
536 J 25	591 J 50		702 C 6	
540 G 5	592 D 20		703 C 6	781 Q 5
541 J 71	593 J 50	635 J 50	704 C 6	782 B 15
542 J 72	594 J 50	636 J 50	706 C 7	783 Q 5
543 J 26	595 J 50		707 D 20	784 C 6
	596 J 50	642 Q 5	708 D 20	785 Q 5
544 J 73	597 J 77	643 Q 5	709 C 7	787 B 15
545 J 73	598 J 50	644 Q 5	711 D 20	789 Q 5
546 J 73	599 J 50	645 Q 5	712 D 20	790 J 27
547 J 73	600 J 50	646 Q 5	713 D 20	792 Q 5
548 J 73	601 J 50	647 Q 5	715 Q 5	793 Q 5
549 J 73	602 J 50	648 Q 5	716 C 7	794 Q 5
550 J 73	603 J 50	650 Q 5	718 C 7	795 B 15
551 J 73	604 J 77	651 Q 5	720 C 7	796 B 15
552 J 73	605 J 50	652 Q 5	722 C 7	798 B 15
553 J 73	606 J 50	653 Q 5	723 D 20	800 J 21
	607 J 77	654 Q 5	724 D 20	802 J 71
554 J 26	608 J 50	655 Q 5	725 D 20	806 J 21
555 J 26	609 J 50	656 Q 5		807 J 21
559 Y 8	610 J 50	657 Q 5	728 C 7	810 J 21
560 Y 8	611 J 50	658 Q 5	729 C 7	814 J 27
566 J 72	612 J 77	659 Q 5	732 C 7	815 B 15
569 J 21	613 J 21	660 Q 5	733 C 7	816 J 26
570 J 21	614 J 77	661 Q 5	734 C 7	817 B 15
571 J 72	615 J 50		735 C 7	818 J 26
572 J 71	616 J 50	665 J 21	736 C 7	819 B 15
573 N 8	617 J 50	669 Q 5	737 C 7	820 B 15
574 J 72	618 J 50	686 A 6		821 B 15
576 J 72	619 J 21	687 A 6	742 C 6	823 B 15
577 J 71	621 J 50	688 A 6	761 B 13	824 B 15
578 Q 5	622 J 50	689 A 6	764 Q 5	
580 G 5	623 J 77	690 A 6	765 J 26	826 N 7
581 J 72		691 A 6		827 N 7
582 J 21	624 Q 7	692 A 6	767 Q 5	828 N 7
	625 Q 7	693 A 6	769 Q 5	829 N 7
583 J 50	626 Q 7	694 A 6	770 Q 5	830 N 7
584 J 50	628 Q 7	695 A 6	771 Q 5	831 J 26
585 J 50	629 Q 7		772 Q 5	832 N 7
586 J 50	630 Q 7	696 C 6	773 Q 5	833 N 7
587 J 50	631 Q 7	697 C 6	774 Q 5	834 N 7
588 J 50	632 Q 7	698 C 6		835 J 26
		699 C 6		

836	J 27	895	N 2	941	N 7	1005	J 27	1052	J 27
837	N 7	896	N 2	942	B 16	1006	J 27	1053	J 27
838	N 7	897	N 2	943	B 16	1007	J 27	1054	Q 5
839	J 27	899	J 21	944	J 21	1008	J 27	1056	J 27
840	B 16			947	N 7	1009	Q 5	1057	J 26
841	B 16	901	Q 7	948	J 77	1010	J 27	1058	J 50
842	B 16	902	Q 7	950	N 7	1011	J 27	1060	J 27
843	B 16	903	Q 7	952	N 7	1012	J 27	1061	J 27
844	B 16	904	Q 7	953	J 77	1013	J 27	1062	Q 5
845	B 16	905	Q 7	954	J 77	1014	J 27	1063	J 50
846	B 16	906	B 16	956	J 77	1015	J 27	1064	J 27
847	B 16	907	N 7	958	J 77	1016	J 27	1065	J 27
848	B 16	908	B 16	961	N 8	1017	J 27	1066	J 27
849	B 16	909	B 16	964	N 7	1018	J 27	1067	J 27
850	N 7	911	N 7	965	J 21	1022	J 27	1068	J 50
851	N 7	912	N 7	966	N 7	1023	J 27	1069	J 50
852	N 7	913	N 7	967	N 7	1024	J 27	1070	J 50
853	N 7	914	B 16	968	N 7	1025	J 27	1072	N 8
856	N 8	915	B 16	970	N 7	1026	D 20	1074	J 50
859	N 8	916	N 7	971	N 7	1027	J 27	1078	D 20
861	N 8	917	J 27	972	J 71	1028	J 27	1079	J 50
862	N 8	918	N 7	973	J 21	1029	J 27	1081	J 50
863	N 8	919	N 7	976	J 21	1030	J 27	1082	J 50
864	N 8	920	B 16	977	J 71	1031	Q 5	1083	J 71
865	N 7	921	B 16	978	J 71	1032	Q 5	1084	J 71
866	N 7	922	B 16	980	J 71	1033	J 77	1085	J 71
867	N 7	923	B 16	981	J 21	1034	J 27	1086	J 50
868	N 7	924	B 16	982	Y 7	1035	J 27	1091	N 8
870	N 7	926	B 16	983	Y 7	1036	J 27	1095	J 71
873	N 7	927	B 16	985	Y 7	1037	J 50	1096	G 5
		928	B 16	986	Y 7	1039	J 27	1098	J 26
874	J 21	929	B 16	987	N 7	1040	J 27		
875	J 21	930	B 16	988	N 7	1041	J 50	1100	K 3
876	J 21	931	B 16	993	J 21	1042	D 20	1101	K 3
880	J 27	932	B 16	997	J 21	1043	J 26	1102	K 3
881	J 26	933	B 16			1044	J 27	1103	J 71
883	J 27	934	B 16			1045	J 50	1104	N 8
888	J 27	935	N 7			1046	J 27	1105	N 8
891	J 27	936	B 16	1000	J 77	1047	J 27	1106	K 3
		937	B 16	1001	J 27	1048	J 27	1108	K 3
892	N 2	938	J 27	1002	Q 5	1049	J 27	1109	N 10
893	N 2	939	Q 5	1003	J 27	1050	J 27	1110	Q 5
894	N 2	940	N 7	1004	J 27	1051	D 20	1111	Q 5

No.	Code	No.	Code	No.	Code	No.	Code	No.	Code
1112	N 10	1159	J 26	1209	D 20	1255	J 39	1296	J
1113	A 7	1162	K 3	1210	D 20	1256	J 27	1298	J
1114	A 7	1164	K 3	1211	J 27	1257	Q 6		
1115	J 77	1166	K 3	1212	J 27	1258	D 20	1300	K .
1116	J 77	1167	J 71	1213	J 27	1259	J 39	1302	K .
1117	K 3	1169	G 5	1214	J 27	1260	D 20	1304	K :
1118	K 3	1170	A 7			1261	Q 6	1305	J
1119	K 3	1172	J 26			1262	Q 6	1306	K
1121	K 3	1173	Q 5	1215	Q 5	1263	J 39	1307	K
1122	J 21	1174	A 7	1216	J 27	1264	Q 6	1308	K .
1123	J 71	1175	A 7	1217	D 20			1310	K :
1125	K 3	1176	A 7	1218	Q 5	1265	J 39	1311	Q .
1126	A 7	1177	Q 5	1219	J 27	1266	J 39	1312	K :
1127	N 8	1178	Q 5	1220	J 27	1267	J 39	1313	J :
1128	Q 5	1179	A 7	1221	J 27	1268	J 39	1315	J :
1129	A 7	1180	A 7	1222	J 27	1269	J 39	1316	G :
1130	J 26	1181	A 7	1223	D 20	1270	J 39	1317	N
1131	J 26	1182	A 7	1224	J 27			1318	K 3
1132	N 10	1183	A 7	1225	J 27	1271	Q 6	1319	G :
1133	K 3	1184	D 20	1226	J 27	1272	J 39	1320	Q 5
1134	J 71	1185	A 7	1227	J 27	1273	J 39	1321	N
1135	K 3	1186	Q 5	1228	J 27	1274	J 39	1322	K 3
1136	A 7	1189	J 27	1229	J 27	1275	J 39	1323	J 2
1137	K 3	1190	A 7	1230	J 27	1276	Q 6	1324	K 3
1138	N 10	1191	A 7	1231	J 27	1277	J 39	1325	K 3
1139	J 26	1192	A 7	1232	D 20	1278	Q 6	1326	A 8
1140	J 71	1193	A 7	1233	J 39	1279	Q 6	1327	A 8
1141	K 3	1194	J 26	1235	D 20	1280	Q 6	1328	A 8
1142	J 71	1195	A 7	1236	D 20	1281	J 39	1329	A 8
1143	J 71	1196	J 71	1237	D 21	1282	J 39	1330	A 8
1146	J 26	1197	J 71	1238	D 21	1283	Q 6	1331	K 3
		1198	J 71	1242	D 21	1284	Q 6	1332	K 3
1148	N 10	1199	J 71	1243	D 21	1285	Q 6	1333	K 3
1149	Q 5			1244	D 21	1286	J 39	1334	G :
1150	Q 5	1200	J 26	1245	D 21	1287	J 39	1335	Q 6
1151	J 71	1201	J 27	1247	Q 6	1288	Q 6	1337	J 2
1152	N 8	1202	J 26	1248	Q 6	1289	J 39	1339	K 3
1153	J 71	1203	J 27	1249	Q 6	1290	J 39	1340	J 7
1154	K 3	1204	J 27	1250	Q 6	1291	Q 6	1341	J 7
1155	J 71	1205	J 27	1251	Q 6	1292	Q 6	1342	J 7
1156	K 3	1206	D 20	1252	Q 6	1293	Q 6	1344	J 7
1157	J 71	1207	D 20	1253	Q 6	1294	Q 6	1345	K 3
1158	K 3	1208	J 26	1254	Q 6	1295	J 39	1346	J 7

1347	J 77	1392	K 3	1434	J 38	1478	J 39	1520	A 8
1348	J 77	1393	J 27	1435	J 77	1479	J 39	1521	A 8
1349	J 77	1394	K 3	1436	J 39	1480	J 39	1522	A 8
1350	T 1	1395	K 3	1437	J 38	1481	J 39	1523	A 8
1351	T 1	1396	K 3	1438	J 77	1482	J 39	1524	A 8
1352	T 1	1397	K 3	1440	J 38	1483	J 39	1525	A 8
1353	T 1	1398	K 3	1441	J 38	1484	J 39	1526	A 8
1354	T 1	1399	K 3	1442	J 38	1485	J 39	1527	A 8
1356	T 1			1443	J 38	1486	J 39	1528	A 8
1357	T 1	1400	J 38	1444	J 38	1487	J 39	1529	A 8
1359	T 1	1401	J 38	1445	J 38	1488	J 39	1530	A 8
1360	J 26	1402	J 27	1446	J 38	1489	J 39	1531	A 8
1361	Q 6	1403	J 38	1447	J 38	1490	J 39	1532	J 39
1362	Q 6	1404	J 38	1448	J 39	1491	J 39	1533	J 39
1363	Q 6	1405	J 38	1449	J 39	1492	J 39	1534	J 39
1364	K 3	1406	J 38	1450	J 39	1493	J 39	1535	J 39
1365	K 3	1407	J 38	1451	J 39	1494	J 39	1536	J 39
1366	J 26	1408	J 38	1452	J 39	1495	J 39	1537	J 39
1367	K 3	1409	J 38	1453	J 39	1496	J 39	1538	J 39
1368	K 3	1410	J 38	1454	J 39	1497	J 39	1539	J 39
1369	J 26	1411	J 38	1455	J 39	1498	J 39	1540	J 39
1370	J 26	1412	J 39	1456	J 39	1499	A 8	1541	J 39
1371	B 16	1413	J 38	1457	J 39			1542	J 39
1372	B 16	1414	J 38	1458	J 39	1500	A 8	1543	J 39
1373	B 16	1415	J 38	1459	J 39	1501	A 8	1544	J 39
1374	B 16	1416	J 38	1460	J 39	1502	A 8	1545	J 39
1375	B 16	1417	J 38	1461	J 77	1503	A 8	1546	J 39
1376	B 16	1418	J 39	1462	J 77	1504	J 39	1547	J 39
1377	B 16	1419	J 38	1463	J 39	1505	J 39	1548	J 39
1378	B 16	1420	J 38	1464	J 39	1506	J 39	1549	J 21
1379	B 16	1421	J 38	1465	J 39	1507	J 21	1550	J 21
1380	B 16	1422	J 38	1466	J 39	1508	J 39	1551	J 39
1381	B 16	1423	J 38	1467	J 39	1509	J 39	1552	J 21
1382	B 16	1424	J 38	1468	J 39	1510	J 21	1553	J 21
1383	B 16	1425	J 39	1469	J 39	1511	J 21	1554	J 21
1384	B 16	1426	J 38	1470	J 39	1512	J 21	1555	J 21
1385	B 16	1427	J 38	1471	J 39	1513	J 21	1556	J 21
1386	K 3	1428	J 38	1472	J 39	1514	J 21	1557	J 21
1387	K 3	1429	J 39	1473	J 39	1515	J 21	1558	J 39
1388	K 3			1474	J 39	1516	J 21	1559	J 21
1389	K 3	1431	J 77	1475	J 39	1517	A 8	1560	J 39
1390	J 26	1432	J 77	1476	J 39	1518	A 8	1561	J 21
1391	K 3	1433	J 77	1477	J 39	1519	A 8	1562	J 21

Electric 0-4-4-0 Mixed Traffic Loco.

563	J 39	1646	N 9	1699	N 10	1744	J 72	1789	J 71
564	J 21	1647	N 9			1745	G 5	1790	A 5
565	J 21	1648	N 9	1700	Q 5	1746	J 72	1791	G 5
566	J 21	1649	N 9	1701	G 5	1747	J 72	1792	C 6
567	J 21	1650	N 9	1702	G 5	1748	G 5	1793	G 5
569	J 21	1651	N 9	1703	G 5	1749	J 72	1795	G 5
573	J 21	1652	N 9	1704	Q 5	1750	A 5		
574	J 21	1653	N 9	1705	N 9	1751	G 5	1796	J 71
575	J 21	1654	N 9	1706	N 10	1752	G 5	1797	J 71
576	J 21	1655	N 9	1707	N 10	1753	C 6	1798	Y 7
577	J 39	1656	T 1	1708	Q 5	1754	G 5	1799	Y 7
580	J 39	1657	T 1	1709	Q 5	1755	G 5		
584	J 39	1658	T 1	1710	N 10	1756	Q 5	1800	Y 7
585	J 39	1659	T 1	1711	N 10	1757	Q 5		
586	J 39	1660	T 1	1712	A 5	1759	G 5	1803	J 39
587	J 39	1665	D 20	1713	G 5	1760	A 5	1804	J 39
588	J 21	1667	N 10	1715	J 72	1761	J 72	1805	J 21
589	J 21	1669	Q 5	1716	N 10	1762	G 5	1806	J 21
590	J 21	1670	J 26	1717	Q 5	1763	J 72	1808	J 39
591	J 21	1671	J 26	1718	J 72	1764	G 5		
593	J 21	1672	D 20	1719	A 5	1765	G 5	1810	J 21
594	J 21	1673	J 26	1720	J 72	1766	A 5	1811	J 21
595	J 21	1674	J 26	1721	J 72	1767	A 5	1812	J 21
596	J 21	1676	J 26	1722	J 72	1768	A 5	1813	J 39
		1678	J 26	1723	J 25	1769	G 5	1814	J 21
		1680	C 6	1725	J 25	1770	J 72		
1608	J 21	1682	Q 5	1726	J 25	1771	A 5	1819	J 21
1609	J 21	1683	N 10	1728	J 72	1772	G 5	1820	J 21
1610	J 21	1684	Q 5	1729	Q 5	1773	J 26	1821	J 24
1611	J 21	1685	Q 5	1730	G 5	1774	N 10	1822	J 24
1613	J 21	1686	J 27	1731	Q 5	1775	G 5	1823	J 24
1614	J 21	1687	G 5	1732	J 72			1824	J 39
1615	J 21	1688	J 71	1733	J 72	1777	J 26	1825	J 24
1617	N 9	1689	J 71	1734	J 72	1778	G 5	1826	J 24
1618	N 9	1690	J 71	1735	J 71	1779	N 10	1827	J 24
1621	D 17	1691	G 5	1736	J 72	1780	G 5	1828	J 39
1629	D 17	1692	G 5	1737	G 5	1781	J 26	1829	J 24
1640	N 9	1693	G 5	1738	A 5	1782	A 5	1830	J 24
1641	N 9	1694	Q 5	1739	G 5	1783	G 5	1831	J 71
1642	N 9	1695	G 5	1740	G 5	1784	A 5	1832	J 71
1643	N 9	1696	Q 5	1741	J 72	1785	N 10	1833	J 71
1644	N 9	1697	N 10	1742	J 72	1786	G 5	1834	J 71
1645	N 9	1698	J 26	1743	J 25	1788	G 5	1835	J 39

N 2 Class

T I Class

A 5 Class

Year	Code	Year	Code	Year	Code	Year	Code	Year	Code
1836	J 71	1888	G 5	1943	J 39	1993	J 25	2045	J 25
1837	G 5	1889	G 5	1945	J 24	1994	J 25	2046	J 25
1838	G 5	1890	G 5	1946	J 24	1995	J 25	2047	J 25
1839	G 5			1948	J 24	1996	J 39	2048	J 25
1840	G 5	1891	J 24	1950	J 24	1997	J 39	2051	J 25
		1892	J 24	1951	J 24			2053	J 25
1843	J 24	1894	J 39	1952	J 39	2000	J 25	2055	J 25
1844	J 24	1895	J 24	1954	J 24	2001	A 2	2056	J 25
1845	J 24	1896	J 39	1955	J 24	2002	P 2	2057	J 25
1847	J 24	1897	J 24	1956	J 24	2003	P 2	2058	J 25
1850	J 24	1898	J 39			2004	P 2	2059	J 25
1851	J 24	1899	J 24	1960	J 24	2005	A 2	2060	J 25
1852	J 24			1961	J 25	2006	A 2	2061	J 25
1853	J 24	1900	J 24	1962	J 25	2011	D 20	2065	J 25
1854	J 39	1901	D 17	1963	J 25	2012	D 20	2067	J 25
1856	J 39	1902	D 17	1964	J 25	2013	D 20	2068	J 25
1857	J 39	1903	J 39	1965	J 39	2014	D 20	2069	J 25
1858	J 24	1911	G 5	1967	J 25	2015	D 20	2070	J 25
1859	J 24	1912	G 5			2016	D 20	2071	J 25
1860	J 24	1913	G 5	1969	J 25	2017	D 20	2072	J 25
1861	J 71	1914	G 5	1970	J 25	2018	D 20	2073	J 25
1862	J 39	1915	G 5	1971	J 39	2019	D 20	2075	J 25
1863	J 39	1916	G 5	1972	J 25	2020	D 20	2076	J 25
1864	J 71	1917	G 5	1973	J 25	2021	D 20	2078	J 25
1865	G 5	1918	G 5	1974	J 39	2022	D 20	2079	J 25
1866	G 5	1919	G 5	1976	J 25	2023	D 20	2080	J 25
1867	G 5	1920	G 5			2024	D 20	2081	G 5
1868	G 5			1977	J 39	2025	D 20	2082	G 5
		1922	J 39	1979	J 25	2026	D 20	2083	G 5
1869	J 39	1926	J 39	1980	J 39	2027	D 20	2084	G 5
1870	J 39	1927	J 39	1981	J 25	2028	D 20	2085	G 5
1873	D 17	1928	J 39	1982	J 25	2029	D 20	2086	G 5
1875	J 39	1930	J 39	1983	J 25	2030	D 20	2087	G 5
1880	J 39	1931	J 24	1984	J 39	2032	J 25	2088	G 5
		1932	J 24	1985	J 25	2033	J 25	2089	G 5
1881	G 5	1933	J 39	1986	J 25	2034	J 25	2090	G 5
1882	G 5	1934	J 24	1987	J 25	2037	J 25	2091	G 5
1883	G 5	1935	J 24	1988	J 25	2038	J 25	2092	G 5
1884	G 5			1989	J 25	2040	J 25	2093	G 5
1885	G 5	1937	J 24			2041	J 25	2094	G 5
1886	G 5	1940	J 39	1990	J 25	2042	J 25	2095	G 5
1887	G 5	1941	J 24	1991	J 25	2043	J 25	2096	G 5
		1942	J 39	1992	J 25	2044	J 25	2097	G 5

2098	G 5	2149	A 8	2193	C 7	2235	Q 6	2278	Q 6
2099	G 5	2150	A 8	2194	C 7	2236	Q 6	2279	Q 6
		2151	A 8	2195	C 7	2237	Q 6	2280	Q 6
2100	G 5	2152	A 8	2196	C 7	2238	Q 6	2281	Q 6
2101	D 20	2153	A 8	2197	C 7	2239	Q 6	2282	Q 6
2102	D 20	2154	A 8	2198	C 7	2240	Q 6	2283	Q 6
2103	D 20	2155	A 8	2199	C 7	2241	Q 6	2284	Q 6
2104	D 20	2156	A 8			2242	Q 6	2285	Q 6
2105	D 20	2157	A 8	2200	C 7	2243	Q 6	2286	Q 6
2106	D 20	2158	A 8	2201	C 7	2244	Q 6	2287	Q 6
2107	D 20	2159	A 8	2203	C 7	2245	Q 6	2288	Q 6
2108	D 20	2160	A 8	2204	C 7	2246	Q 6	2289	Q 6
		2161	A 8	2205	C 7	2247	Q 6	2290	Q 6
2110	D 20	2162	A 8	2206	C 7	2248	Q 6	2291	Q 6
2116	Q 5	2163	C 7	2207	C 7	2249	Q 6	2292	Q 6
2117	Q 5	2164	C 7	2208	C 7	2250	Q 6	2293	Q 6
2118	Q 5	2165	C 7	2210	C 7	2251	Q 6	2294	Q 6
2119	Q 5	2166	C 7	2211	C 7	2252	Q 6	2295	Q 6
2120	Q 5	2167	C 7	2212	C 7	2253	Q 6	2296	Q 6
2121	Q 5	2168	C 7			2254	Q 6	2297	Q 6
2122	Q 5	2169	C 7			2255	Q 6	2298	Q 6
2123	Q 5			2213	Q 6	2256	Q 6	2299	Q 6
2124	Q 5	2172	C 7	2214	Q 6	2257	Q 6		
2125	Q 5	2173	J 72	2215	Q 6	2258	Q 6	2300	Q 6
2126	J 25	2174	J 72	2216	Q 6	2259	Q 6	2301	Q 6
2128	J 25	2175	J 72	2217	Q 6	2260	Q 6	2302	Q 6
2130	J 25	2176	J 72	2218	Q 6	2261	Q 6	2303	J 72
2131	J 25	2177	J 72	2219	Q 6	2262	Q 6	2304	J 72
2133	J 25	2178	J 72	2220	Q 6	2263	Q 6	2305	J 72
2134	J 25	2179	J 72	2221	Q 6	2264	Q 6	2306	J 72
2135	J 25	2180	J 72	2222	Q 6	2265	Q 6	2307	J 72
2136	J 25	2181	J 72	2223	Q 6	2266	Q 6	2308	J 72
2138	J 25	2182	J 72	2224	Q 6	2267	Q 6	2309	J 72
2139	J 25	2183	J 72	2225	Q 6	2268	Q 6	2310	J 72
2140	J 25	2184	J 72	2226	Q 6	2269	Q 6	2311	J 72
2141	J 25	2185	J 72	2227	Q 6	2270	Q 6	2312	J 72
2142	J 25	2186	J 72	2228	Q 6	2271	Q 6	2313	J 72
2143	A 8	2187	J 72	2229	Q 6	2272	Q 6	2314	J 72
2144	A 8	2188	J 72	2230	Q 6	2273	Q 6	2315	J 72
2145	A 8	2189	J 72	2231	Q 6	2274	Q 6	2316	J 72
2146	A 8	2190	J 72	2232	Q 6	2275	Q 6	2317	J 72
2147	A 8	2191	J 72	2233	Q 6	2276	Q 6	2318	J 72
2148	A 8	2192	J 72	2234	Q 6	2277	Q 6	2319	J 72

Class U I Garratt 2-8-2 loco. No. 2395

O 2 Class loco. No. 3834

2320	J 72	2363	B 16	2428	K 3	2499	K 3	2565	A 1
2321	J 72	2364	B 16	2429	K 3			2566	A 3
2322	J 72	2365	B 16	2430	O 2	2500	A 3	2567	A 1
2323	J 72	2366	B 16	2431	O 2	2501	A 3	2568	A 3
2324	J 72	2367	B 16	2432	O 2	2502	A 3	2569	A 1
2325	J 72	2368	B 16	2433	O 2	2503	A 3	2570	A 1
2326	J 72	2369	B 16	2434	O 2	2504	A 3	2571	A 3
2327	J 72	2370	B 16	2435	O 2	2505	A 3	2572	A 1
2328	J 72	2371	B 16	2436	O 2	2506	A 3	2573	A 3
2329	J 72	2372	B 16	2437	O 2	2507	A 3	2574	A 3
2330	J 72	2373	B 16	2438	K 3	2508	A 3	2575	A 3
2331	J 72	2374	B 16	2439	K 3	2509	A 4	2576	A 3
2332	J 72	2375	B 16	2440	K 3	2510	A 4	2577	A 3
2333	J 72	2376	B 16	2442	K 3	2511	A 4	2578	A 3
2334	J 72	2377	B 16	2443	K 3	2512	A 4	2579	A 3
2335	J 72	2378	B 16	2445	K 3	2532	J 75	2580	A 3
2336	J 72	2379	B 16	2446	K 3	2533	N 13	2581	A 3
2337	J 72	2380	B 16	2447	K 3	2534	N 13	2582	A 3
2338	J 27	2381	B 16	2448	K 3	2535	N 13	2583	N 2
2339	J 27	2382	B 16	2449	K 3	2536	N 13	2584	N 2
2340	J 27	2383	J 27	2450	K 3	2537	N 13	2585	N 2
2341	J 27	2384	J 27	2451	K 3	2543	A 1	2586	N 2
2342	J 27	2385	J 27	2453	K 3	2544	A 3	2587	N 2
2343	J 27	2386	J 27	2455	K 3	2545	A 3	2588	N 2
2344	J 27	2387	J 27	2458	K 3	2546	A 1	2589	N 2
2345	J 27	2388	J 27	2459	K 3	2547	A 1	2590	N 2
2346	J 27	2389	J 27	2461	K 3	2548	A 1	2591	N 2
2347	J 27	2390	J 27	2463	K 3	2549	A 3	2592	N 2
2348	J 27	2391	J 27	2465	K 3	2550	A 1	2593	N 2
2349	J 27	2392	J 27	2466	K 3	2551	A 3	2594	N 2
2350	J 27	2393	P 1	2467	K 3	2552	A 3	2595	A 3
2351	J 27	2394	P 1	2468	K 3	2553	A 3	2596	A 3
2352	J 27	2395	U 1	2470	K 3	2554	A 3	2597	A 3
2353	J 27			2471	K 3	2555	A 1	2598	A 3
2354	J 27	2405	N 13	2472	K 3	2556	A 1	2599	A 3
2355	J 27	2407	N 13	2473	K 3	2557	A 1		
2356	J 27	2410	N 13			2558	A 3	2600	N 7
2357	J 27	2415	N 13	2479	N 11	2559	A 3	2601	N 7
2358	J 27	2417	K 3	2480	N 11	2560	A 3	2602	N 7
2359	J 27	2419	N 13	2481	N 11	2561	A 3	2603	N 7
2360	J 27	2425	K 3	2482	N 11	2562	A 1	2604	N 7
2361	J 27	2426	K 3	2486	N 12	2563	A 3	2605	N 7
2362	J 27	2427	K 3	2498	K 3	2564	A 1	2606	N 7

2607	N 7	2650	N 7	2693	J 39	2735	J 39	2778	J 39
2608	N 7	2651	N 7	2694	J 39	2736	J 39	2779	J 39
2609	N 7	2652	N 7	2695	J 39	2737	J 39	2780	J 39
2610	N 7	2653	N 7	2696	J 39	2738	J 39	2781	J 39
2611	N 7	2654	N 7	2697	J 39	2739	J 39	2782	J 39
2612	N 7	2655	N 7	2698	J 39	2740	J 39	2783	J 39
2613	N 7	2656	N 7	2699	J 39	2741	J 39	2784	J 39
2614	N 7	2657	N 7			2742	J 39	2785	J 39
2615	N 7	2658	N 7	2700	J 39	2743	A 3	2786	J 39
2616	N 7	2659	N 7	2701	J 39	2744	A 3	2787	J 39
2617	N 7	2660	N 7	2702	J 39	2745	A 3	2788	J 39
2618	N 7	2661	N 7	2703	J 39	2746	A 3	2789	J 50
2619	N 7	2662	N 2	2704	J 39	2747	A 3	2790	J 50
2620	N 7	2663	N 2	2705	J 39	2748	A 3	2791	J 50
2621	N 7	2664	N 2	2706	J 39	2749	A 3	2792	J 50
2622	N 7	2665	N 2	2707	J 39	2750	A 3	2793	J 50
2623	N 7	2666	N 2	2708	J 39	2751	A 3	2794	J 50
2624	N 7	2667	N 2	2709	J 39	2752	A 3	2795	A 3
2625	N 7	2668	N 2	2710	J 39	2753	D 49	2796	A 3
2626	N 7	2669	N 2	2711	J 39	2754	D 49	2797	A 3
2627	N 7	2670	N 2	2712	J 39	2755	D 49	2798	S 1
2628	N 7	2671	N 2	2713	J 39	2756	D 49	2799	S 1
2629	N 7	2672	N 2	2714	J 39	2757	D 49		
2630	N 7	2673	N 2	2715	J 39	2758	D 49	2800	B 17
2631	N 7	2674	N 2	2716	J 39	2759	D 49	2801	B 17
2632	N 7	2675	N 2	2717	J 39	2760	D 49	2802	B 17
2633	N 7	2676	N 2	2718	J 39	2761	K 3	2803	B 17
2634	N 7	2677	N 2	2719	J 39	2762	K 3	2804	B 17
2635	N 7	2678	N 5	2720	J 39	2763	K 3	2805	B 17
2636	N 7	2679	N 2	2721	J 39	2764	K 3	2806	B 17
2637	N 7	2680	N 2	2722	J 39	2765	K 3	2807	B 17
2638	N 7	2681	N 2	2723	J 39	2766	K 3	2808	B 17
2639	N 7	2682	N 2	2724	J 39	2767	K 3	2809	B 17
2640	N 7	2683	N 2	2725	J 39	2768	K 3	2810	B 17
2641	N 7	2684	N 2	2726	J 39	2769	K 3	2811	B 17
2642	N 7	2685	N 2	2727	J 39	2770	J 39	2812	B 17
2643	N 7	2686	N 2	2728	J 39	2771	J 39	2813	B 17
2644	N 7	2687	N 2	2729	J 39	2772	J 39	2814	B 17
2645	N 7	2688	N 2	2730	J 39	2773	J 39	2815	B 17
2646	N 7	2689	N 2	2731	J 39	2774	J 39	2816	B 17
2647	N 7	2690	N 2	2732	J 39	2775	J 39	2817	B 17
2648	N 7	2691	J 39	2733	J 39	2776	J 39	2818	B 17
2649	N 7	2692	J 39	2734	J 39	2777	J 39	2819	B 17

2820	B 17	2863	B 17	2929	V 1	2972	J 39	3014	J 1
2821	B 17	2864	B 17	2930	V 1	2973	J 39	3015	J 1
2822	B 17	2865	B 17	2931	V 1	2974	J 39	3021	J 5
2823	B 17	2866	B 17	2932	V 1	2975	J 39	3022	J 5
2924	B 17	2867	B 17	2933	V 1	2976	J 39	3023	J 5
2825	B 17	2868	B 17	2934	K 3	2977	J 39	3024	J 5
2826	B 17	2869	B 17	2935	K 3	2978	J 39	3025	J 5
2827	B 17	2870	B 17	2936	K 3	2979	J 39	3026	J 5
2828	B 17	2871	B 17	2937	K 3	2980	J 39	3027	J 5
2829	B 17	2872	B 17	2938	K 3	2981	J 39	3028	J 5
2830	B 17	2897	V 1	2939	K 3	2982	J 39	3029	J 5
2831	B 17	2898	V 1	2940	K 3	2983	J 39	3030	J 5
2832	B 17	2899	V 1	2941	J 39	2984	J 39	3031	J 5
2833	B 17			2942	J 39	2985	J 39	3032	J 5
2834	B 17	2900	V 1	2943	J 39	2986	J 39	3033	J 5
2835	B 17	2901	V 1	2944	J 39	2987	J 39	3034	J 5
2836	B 17	2902	V 1	2945	J 39	2988	J 39	3035	J 5
2837	B 17	2903	V 1	2946	J 39	2989	J 39	3036	J 5
2838	B 17	2904	V 1	2947	J 39	2990	J 39	3037	J 5
2839	B 17	2905	V 1	2948	J 39	2991	J 39	3038	J 5
2840	B 17	2906	V 1	2949	J 39	2992	J 39	3039	J 5
2841	B 17	2907	V 1	2950	J 39	2993	J 39	3040	J 5
2842	B 17	2908	V 1	2951	J 39	2994	J 39	3041	D 2
2843	B 17	2909	V 1	2952	J 39	2995	J 39	3042	D 2
2844	B 17	2910	V 1	2953	J 39	2996	J 39	3044	D 2
2845	B 17	2911	V 1	2954	O 2	2997	J 39	3045	D 2
2846	B 17	2912	V 1	2955	O 2	2998	J 39	3047	D 2
2847	B 17	2913	V 1	2956	O 2	2999	J 39	3048	D 2
2848	B 17	2914	V 1	2957	O 2			3049	D 2
2849	B 17	2915	V 1	2958	O 2	3000	J 39	3050	D 2
2850	B 17	2916	V 1	2959	O 2	3001	J 1	3051	D 1
2851	B 17	2917	V 1	2960	O 2	3002	J 1	3052	D 1
2852	B 17	2918	V 1	2961	O 2	3003	J 1	3053	D 1
2853	B 17	2919	V 1	2962	J 39	3004	J 1	3054	D 1
2854	B 17	2920	V 1	2963	J 39	3005	J 1	3055	D 1
2855	B 17	2921	V 1	2964	J 39	3006	J 1	3056	D 1
2856	B 17	2922	V 1	2965	J 39	3007	J 1	3057	D 1
2857	B 17	2923	V 1	2966	J 39	3008	J 1	3058	D 1
2858	B 17	2924	V 1	2967	J 39	3009	J 1	3059	D 1
2859	B 17	2925	V 1	2968	J 39	3010	J 1	3060	D 1
2860	B 17	2926	V 1	2969	J 39	3011	J 1	3061	D 1
2861	B 17	2927	V 1	2970	J 39	3012	J 1	3062	D 1
2862	B 17	2928	V 1	2971	J 39	3013	J 1	3063	D 1

3064 D 1	3168 J 50	3251 C 1	3345 J 3	3482 O 2
3065 D 1	3169 J 50	3252 C 2	3350 J 3	3483 O 2
3071 J 2	3170 J 50		3375 J 3	3484 O 2
3072 J 2	3171 J 50		3387 J 3	3485 O 2
3073 J 2	3172 J 50		3388 J 3	3486 O 2
3074 J 2	3173 J 50	3272 C 1	3398 J 3	3487 O 2
3075 J 2	3174 J 50	3273 C 1	3399 J 3	3488 O 2
3076 J 2	3175 J 50	3274 C 1		3489 O 2
3077 J 2	3176 J 50	3275 C 1	3400 D 3	3490 O 2
3078 J 2	3178 J 50	3276 C 1	3401 V 4	3491 O 2
3079 J 2	3179 J 3	3277 C 1	3402 V 4	3492 O 2
3080 J 2	3190 N 1	3278 C 1	3441 K 4	3493 O 2
3081 J 39		3279 C 1	3442 K 4	3494 O 2
3082 J 39	3211 J 50	3280 C 1	3443 K 4	3495 O 2
3083 J 39	3212 J 50	3281 C 1	3444 K 4	3496 O 2
3084 J 39	3213 J 50	3282 C 1	3445 K 4	3497 O 2
3085 J 39	3214 J 50	3283 C 1	3446 K 4	3498 O 2
3086 J 39	3215 J 50	3284 C 1	3456 O 3	3499 O 2
3087 J 39	3216 J 50	3285 C 1	3457 O 3	
3088 J 39	3217 J 50	3286 C 1	3458 O 3	3500 O 2
3089 J 39	3218 J 50	3287 C 1	3459 O 3	3501 O 2
3090 J 39	3219 J 50	3288 C 1	3460 O 3	3521 J 6
3091 J 39	3220 J 50	3289 C 1	3461 O 2	3522 J 6
3092 J 39	3221 J 50	3290 C 1	3462 O 3	3523 J 6
3093 J 39	3222 J 50	3291 C 1	3463 O 3	3524 J 6
3094 J 39	3223 J 50	3293 C 1	3464 O 3	3525 J 6
3095 J 39	3224 J 50	3294 C 1	3465 O 3	3526 J 6
3096 J 39	3225 J 50	3295 C 1	3466 O 3	3527 J 6
3097 J 39	3226 J 50	3296 C 1	3467 O 3	3528 J 6
3098 J 39	3227 J 50	3297 C 1	3468 O 3	3529 J 6
	3228 J 50	3298 C 1	3469 O 3	3530 J 6
3111 J 52	3229 J 50	3299 C 1	3470 O 3	3531 J 6
3155A J 52	3230 J 50		3471 O 3	3532 J 6
3157 J 50	3231 J 50		3472 O 3	3533 J 6
3158 J 50	3232 J 50	3300 C 1	3473 O 3	3534 J 6
3159 J 50	3233 J 50	3301 C 1	3474 O 3	3535 J 6
3160 J 50	3234 J 50	3302 J 3	3475 O 3	3536 J 6
3161 J 50	3235 J 50	3306 J 3	3476 O 3	3537 J 6
3162 J 50	3236 J 50	3313 J 3	3477 O 2	3538 J 6
3163 J 50	3237 J 50	3329 J 3	3478 O 2	3539 J 6
3164 J 50	3238 J 50	3331 J 3	3479 O 2	3540 J 6
3166 J 50	3239 J 50	3332 J 3	3480 O 2	3541 J 6
3167 J 50	3240 J 50	3336 J 3	3481 O 2	3542 J 6

3543	J 6	3586	J 6	3638	J 6	3681	V 2	3840	O 2
3544	J 6	3587	J 6	3639	J 6	3682	V 2	3841	O 2
3545	J 6	3588	J 6	3640	J 6	3683	V 2	3842	O 2
3546	J 6	3589	J 6	3641	V 2	3684	V 2	3843	O 2
3547	J 6	3590	J 6	3642	V 2	3685	V 2	3844	O 2
3548	J 6	3591	J 6	3643	V 2	3686	V 2	3845	O 2
3549	J 6	3592	J 6	3644	V 2	3687	V 2	3846	O 2
3550	J 6	3593	J 6	3645	V 2	3688	V 2	3847	O 2
3551	J 6	3594	J 6	3646	V 2	3689	V 2	3848	O 2
3552	J 6	3595	J 6	3647	V 2	3690	V 2	3849	O 2
3553	J 6	3596	J 6	3648	V 2	3691	V 2	3850	O 2
3554	J 6	3597	J 6	3649	V 2	3692	V 2	3851	O 2
3555	J 6	3598	J 6	3650	V 2	3693	V 2	3852	O 2
3556	J 6	3599	J 6	3651	V 2			3853	O 2
3557	J 6			3652	V 2	3696	A 2/1	3854	O 2
3558	J 6	3600	J 6	3653	V 2			3855	O 2
3559	J 6	3601	J 6	3654	V 2	3813	K 3	3856	O 2
3560	J 6	3602	J 6	3655	V 2	3814	K 3	3857	O 2
3561	J 6	3603	J 6	3656	V 2	3815	K 3		
3562	J 6	3604	J 6	3657	V 2	3816	K 3	3859	J 55
3563	J 6	3605	J 6	3658	V 2	3817	K 3	3908	J 55
3564	J 6	3606	J 6	3659	V 2	3818	K 3	3922	J 52
3565	J 6	3607	J 6	3660	V 2	3819	K 3	3923	J 52
3566	J 6	3608	J 6	3661	V 2	3820	K 3	3925	J 52
3567	J 6	3609	J 6	3662	V 2	3821	K 3	3926	J 52
3568	J 6	3610	J 6	3663	V 2	3822	K 3	3927	J 52
3569	J 6	3621	J 6	3664	V 2	3823	K 3	3929	J 52
3570	J 6	3622	J 6	3665	V 2	3824	K 3	3930	J 52
3571	J 6	3623	J 6	3666	V 2	3825	K 3	3961	J 52
3572	J 6	3624	J 6	3667	V 2	3826	K 3	3962	J 52
3573	J 6	3625	J 6	3668	V 2	3827	K 3	3963	J 52
3574	J 6	3626	J 6	3669	V 2	3828	K 3	3965	J 52
3575	J 6	3627	J 6	3670	V 2	3829	K 3	3966	J 52
3576	J 6	3628	J 6	3671	V 2	3830	K 3	3967	J 52
3577	J 6	3629	J 6	3672	V 2	3831	K 3	3968	J 52
3578	J 6	3630	J 6	3673	V 2	3832	K 3	3969	J 52
3579	J 6	3631	J 6	3674	V 2	3833	O 2	3970	J 52
3580	J 6	3632	J 6	3675	V 2	3834	O 2	3971	J 52
3581	J 6	3633	J 6	3676	V 2	3835	O 2	3972	J 52
3582	J 6	3634	J 6	3677	V 2	3836	O 2	3973	J 52
3583	J 6	3635	J 6	3678	V 2	3837	O 2	3974	J 52
3584	J 6	3636	J 6	3679	V 2	3838	O 2	3975	J 52
3585	J 6	3637	J 6	3680	V 2	3839	O 2	3976	J 52

No.	Code	No.	Code	No.	Code	No.	Code	No.	Code
3977	J 52	4060	J 52	4203	J 52	4246	J 52	4289	J 52
3978	J 52	4071	D 3	4204	J 52	4247	J 52	4290	J 52
3979	J 52	4073	D 3	4205	J 52	4248	J 52		
3980	J 52	4074	D 3	4206	J 52	4249	J 52	4301	D 3
		4075	D 3	4207	J 52	4250	J 52	4302	D 3
4000	K 3	4080	D 3	4208	J 52	4251	J 52	4303	D 3
4001	K 3	4088	J 3	4209	J 52	4252	J 52	4305	D 2
4002	K 3	4090	J 4	4210	J 52	4253	J 52	4306	D 3
4003	K 3	4092	J 3	4211	J 52	4254	J 52	4307	D 3
4004	K 3	4093	J 3	4212	J 52	4255	J 52	4309	D 3
4005	K 3	4094	J 3	4213	J 52	4256	J 52	4310	D 3
4006	K 3	4097	J 3	4214	J 52	4257	J 52	4311	D 3
4007	K 3			4215	J 52	4258	J 52	4312	D 3
4008	K 3	4100	J 3	4216	J 52	4259	J 52	4315	D 3
4009	K 3	4103	J 3	4217	J 52	4260	J 52	4316	D 3
4009A	C 12	4105	J 3	4218	J 52	4261	J 52	4317	D 3
4010	C 12	4106	J 4	4219	J 52	4262	J 52	4318	D 3
4013	C 12	4107	J 4	4220	J 52	4263	J 52	4319	D 3
4014	C 12	4109	J 3	4221	J 52	4264	J 52	4320	D 2
4015	C 12	4113	J 3	4222	J 52	4265	J 52	4321	D 2
4016	C 12	4114	J 3	4223	J 52	4266	J 52	4323	D 2
4018	C 12	4125	J 3	4224	J 52	4267	J 52	4324	D 2
4019	C 12	4126	J 3	4225	J 52	4268	J 52	4326	D 2
4020	C 12	4129	J 3	4226	J 52	4269	J 52	4327	D 2
4035	J 3	4131	J 3	4227	J 52	4270	J 52	4329	D 2
4036	J 3	4133	J 3	4228	J 52	4271	J 52	4330	D 2
4039	J 3	4134	J 3	4229	J 52	4272	J 52	4331	D 2
4040	J 4	4135	J 3	4230	J 52	4273	J 52	4332	D 2
4041	J 4	4137	J 3	4231	J 52	4274	J 52	4333	D 2
4046	J 52	4139	J 3	4232	J 52	4275	J 52	4335	D 2
4047	J 52	4143	J 3	4233	J 52	4276	J 52	4337	D 2
4048	J 52	4146	J 3	4234	J 52	4277	J 52	4338	D 2
4049	J 52	4151	J 3	4235	J 52	4278	J 52	4339	D 3
4050	J 52	4153	J 3	4236	J 52	4279	J 52	4340	D 3
4051	J 52	4160	J 3	4237	J 52	4280	J 52	4343	D 3
4052	J 52	4162	J 3	4238	J 52	4281	J 52	4344	D 3
4053	J 52	4166	J 3	4239	J 52	4282	J 52	4345	D 3
4054	J 52	4171	J 3	4240	J 52	4283	J 52	4346	D 3
4055	J 52	4173	J 3	4241	J 52	4284	J 52	4347	D 3
4056	J 52	4180	D 2	4242	J 52	4285	J 52	4348	D 3
4057	J 52			4243	J 52	4286	J 52	4349	D 3
4058	J 52	4201	J 52	4244	J 52	4287	J 52	4350	D 3
4059	J 52	4202	J 52	4245	J 52	4288	J 52	4351	D 3

D

4352	D 3	4413	C 1	4458	C 1	4502	C 12	4554	N 1
4355	D 3	4414	C 1	4460	C 1	4503	C 12	4555	N 1
4356	D 3	4415	C 1	4461	C 1	4504	C 12	4556	N 1
4357	D 2	4416	C 1	4462	A 4	4505	C 12	4557	N 1
4359	D 2	4417	C 1	4463	A 4	4506	C 12	4558	N 1
4361	D 2	4418	C 1	4464	A 4	4507	C 12	4559	N 1
4364	D 2	4419	C 1	4465	A 4	4508	C 12	4560	N 1
4365	D 2	4420	C 1	4466	A 4	4509	C 12	4561	N 1
4366	D 2	4421	C 1	4467	A 4	4510	C 12	4562	N 1
4368	D 2	4422	C 1	4468	A 4	4511	C 12	4563	N 1
4369	D 2	4423	C 1	4470	A 1	4513	C 12	4564	N 1
4370	D 2	4424	C 1	4471	A 1	4514	C 12	4565	N 1
4371	D 2	4425	C 1	4472	A 1	4517	C 12	4566	N 1
4373	D 2	4427	C 1	4473	A 3	4518	C 12	4567	N 1
4374	D 2	4428	C 1	4474	A 3	4519	C 12	4568	N 1
4377	D 2	4429	C 1	4475	A 1	4520	C 12	4569	N 1
4379	D 2	4431	C 1	4476	A 1	4521	C 12	4570	N 1
4380	D 2	4432	C 1	4477	A 3	4523	C 12	4571	N 1
4381	D 2	4433	C 1	4478	A 3	4524	C 12	4572	N 1
4383	D 2	4434	C 1	4479	A 3	4525	C 12	4573	N 1
4384	D 2	4435	C 1	4480	A 3	4527	C 12	4574	N 1
4385	D 2	4436	C 1	4481	A 1	4528	C 12	4575	N 1
4387	D 2			4482	A 4	4529	C 12	4576	N 1
4388	D 2	4438	C 1	4483	A 4	4530	C 12	4577	N 1
4390	D 2	4439	C 1	4484	A 4	4531	C 12	4578	N 1
4392	D 2	4440	C 1	4485	A 4	4534	C 12	4579	N 1
4393	D 3	4441	C 1	4486	A 4	4536	C 12	4580	N 1
4394	D 2	4442	C 1	4487	A 4	4537	C 12	4581	N 1
4395	D 2	4443	C 1	4488	A 4	4538	C 12	4582	N 1
4398	D 2	4444	C 1	4489	A 4	4539	C 12	4583	N 1
4399	D 2	4445	C 1	4490	A 4	4540	C 12	4584	N 1
4400	C 1	4446	C 1	4491	A 4	4541	C 12	4585	N 1
4401	C 1	4447	C 1	4492	A 4	4542	C 12	4586	N 1
4402	C 1	4448	C 1	4493	A 4	4543	C 12	4587	N 1
4403	C 1	4449	C 1	4494	A 4	4544	C 12	4588	N 1
4404	C 1	4450	C 1	4495	A 4	4545	C 12	4589	N 1
4405	C 1	4451	C 1	4496	A 4	4546	C 12	4590	N 1
4406	C 1	4452	C 1	4497	A 4	4547	C 12	4591	N 1
4408	C 1	4453	C 1	4498	A 4	4548	C 12	4592	N 1
4409	C 1	4454	C 1	4499	A 4	4549	C 12	4593	N 1
4410	C 1	4455	C 1			4551	N 1	4594	N 1
4411	C 1	4456	C 1	4500	A 4	4552	N 1	4595	N 1
4412	C 1	4457	C 1	4501	C 12	4553	N 1	4596	N 1

A 2/I Class

A 4 Class

4597	N 1	4653	K 2	4696	K 2	4754	N 2	4797	V 2
4598	N 1	4654	K 2	4697	K 2	4755	N 2	4798	V 2
4599	N 1	4655	K 2	4698	K 2	4756	N 2	4799	V 2
		4656	K 2	4699	K 2	4757	N 2		
4600	N 1	4657	K 2			4758	N 2		
4601	N 1	4658	K 2	4700	K 2	4759	N 2	4800	V 2
4602	N 1	4659	K 2	4701	K 2	4760	N 2	4801	V 2
4603	N 1	4660	K 2	4702	K 2	4761	N 2	4802	V 2
4604	N 1	4661	K 2	4703	K 2	4762	N 2	4803	V 2
4605	N 1	4662	K 2	4704	K 2	4763	N 2	4804	V 2
4606	N 2	4663	K 2	4721	N 2	4764	N 2	4805	V 2
4607	N 2	4664	K 2	4722	N 2	4765	N 2	4806	V 2
4608	N 2	4665	K 2	4723	N 2	4766	N 2	4807	V 2
4609	N 2	4666	K 2	4724	N 2	4767	N 2	4808	V 2
4610	N 2	4667	K 2	4725	N 2	4768	N 2	4809	V 2
4611	N 2	4668	K 2	4726	N 2	4769	N 2	4810	V 2
4612	N 2	4669	K 2	4727	N 2	4770	N 2	4811	V 2
4613	N 2	4670	K 2	4728	N 2	4771	V 2	4812	V 2
4614	N 2	4671	K 2	4729	N 2	4772	V 2	4813	V 2
4615	N 2	4672	K 2	4730	N 2	4773	V 2	4814	V 2
4630	K 2	4673	K 2	4731	N 2	4774	V 2	4815	V 2
4631	K 2	4674	K 2	4732	N 2	4775	V 2	4816	V 2
4632	K 2	4675	K 2	4733	N 2	4776	V 2	4817	V 2
4633	K 2	4676	K 2	4734	N 2	4777	V 2	4818	V 2
4634	K 2	4677	K 2	4735	N 2	4778	V 2	4819	V 2
4635	K 2	4678	K 2	4736	N 2	4779	V 2	4820	V 2
4636	K 2	4679	K 2	4737	N 2	4780	V 2	4821	V 2
4637	K 2	4680	K 2	4738	N 2	4781	V 2	4822	V 2
4638	K 2	4681	K 2	4739	N 2	4782	V 2	4823	V 2
4639	K 2	4682	K 2	4740	N 2	4783	V 2	4824	V 2
4640	K 2	4683	K 2	4741	N 2	4784	V 2	4825	V 2
4641	K 2	4684	K 2	4742	N 2	4785	V 2	4826	V 2
4642	K 2	4685	K 2	4743	N 2	4786	V 2	4827	V 2
4643	K 2	4686	K 2	4744	N 2	4787	V 2	4828	V 2
4644	K 2	4687	K 2	4745	N 2	4788	V 2	4829	V 2
4645	K 2	4688	K 2	4746	N 2	4789	V 2	4830	V 2
4646	K 2	4689	K 2	4747	N 2	4790	V 2	4831	V 2
4647	K 2	4690	K 2	4748	N 2	4791	V 2	4832	V 2
4648	K 2	4691	K 2	4749	N 2	4792	V 2	4833	V 2
4649	K 2	4692	K 2	4750	N 2	4793	V 2	4834	V 2
4650	K 2	4693	K 2	4751	N 2	4794	V 2	4835	V 2
4651	K 2	4694	K 2	4752	N 2	4795	V 2	4836	V 2
4652	K 2	4695	K 2	4753	N 2	4796	V 2	4837	V 2

4838 V 2	4881 V 2	5016 J 11	5069 O 4	5118 J 10
4839 V 2	4882 V 2	5018 C 13	5070 Q 1	5119 J 10
4840 V 2	4883 V 2	5020 C 13	5072 B 7	5120 J 10
4841 V 2	4884 V 2	5021 N 5	5073 B 7	5121 J 10
4842 V 2	4885 V 2	5022 O 4	5074 J 10	5122 J 10
4843 V 2	4886 V 2	5023 A 5	5075 J 10	5123 J 10
4844 V 2	4887 V 2	5024 A 5	5076 J 10	5124 J 10
4845 V 2	4888 V 2	5025 N 5	5077 J 10	5125 J 10
4846 V 2	4889 V 2	5026 O 4	5078 B 7	5126 J 10
4847 V 2	4890 V 2	5027 C 13	5080 J 10	5127 N 5
4848 V 2	4891 V 2	5028 C 13	5081 J 10	5128 A 5
4849 V 2	4892 V 2	5029 C 13	5082 J 10	5129 A 5
4850 V 2	4893 V 2	5030 A 5	5083 J 10	5130 J 10
4851 V 2	4894 V 2	5031 B 7	5085 Q 4	5131 J 10
4852 V 2	4895 V 2	5032 B 7	5087 Q 1	5132 J 10
4853 V 2	4896 V 2	5033 B 7	5088 A 5	5133 O 4
4854 V 2	4897 V 2	5034 B 7	5089 J 63	5134 J 10
4855 V 2	4898 V 2	5035 B 7	5090 J 10	5136 Q 4
4856 V 2	4899 V 2	5036 B 7	5092 Q 4	5137 Q 4
4857 V 2		5037 B 7	5093 O 4	5138 Q 4
4858 V 2	4900 A 4	5038 B 7	5094 J 10	5141 J 10
4859 V 2	4901 A 4	5039 Q 4	5095 J 10	5142 Q 4
4860 V 2	4902 A 4	5044 Q 1	5096 J 10	5146 Q 4
4861 V 2	4903 A 4	5045 A 5	5097 J 10	5147 Q 4
4862 V 2	4990 J 55	5046 A 5	5098 J 10	5152 Q 4
4863 V 2	4991 Y 1	5047 C 13	5099 J 10	5153 Q 4
4864 V 2	4992 Y 1	5048 Q 1		5154 A 5
4865 V 2	4993 Y 1	5050 C 13	5100 J 10	5155 O 4
4866 V 2		5051 N 5	5101 J 10	5156 A 5
4867 V 2	5001 O 4	5052 B 6	5102 O 4	5157 J 63
4868 V 2	5002 C 13	5053 B 6	5103 J 10	5158 A 5
4869 V 2	5003 A 5	5054 N 5	5104 D 9	5159 Q 4
4870 V 2	5004 B 8	5055 C 13	5105 D 9	5160 Q 4
4871 V 2	5005 O 4	5056 Q 4	5106 D 9	5161 Q 4
4872 V 2	5006 A 5	5057 Q 4	5107 D 9	5162 Q 4
4873 V 2	5007 A 5	5058 Q 1	5108 D 9	5163 Q 4
4874 V 2	5008 O 4	5059 Q 4	5109 D 9	5164 Q 4
4875 V 2	5009 C 13	5060 J 63	5111 D 9	5165 A 5
4876 V 2	5010 O 4	5061 J 63	5112 D 9	5166 A 5
4877 V 2	5011 O 4	5064 Q 4	5114 C 13	5167 A 5
4878 V 2	5012 O 4	5065 Q 4	5115 C 13	5168 A 5
4879 V 2	5013 O 4	5067 Q 4	5116 J 10	5169 A 5
4880 V 2	5015 O 4	5068 Q 4	5117 J 10	5170 A 5

5171	C 13	5215	J 11	5259	C 5	5306	J 11	5350	O 4
5172	J 10	5216	J 11	5260	C 4	5307	J 11	5351	O 4
5173	N 5	5217	J 11	5261	C 4	5308	J 11	5352	O 4
5174	J 10	5218	J 11	5262	C 4	5309	J 11	5353	O 4
5175	J 10	5219	J 11	5263	C 4	5310	C 13	5355	O 4
5176	J 10	5220	J 11	5264	C 4	5311	J 11	5357	C 13
5177	J 11	5221	J 11	5265	C 4	5312	J 11	5358	C 4
5178	C 13	5222	J 11	5267	C 4	5313	J 11	5359	C 13
5179	C 13	5223	J 11	5270	D 6	5314	J 11	5360	C 4
5180	B 5	5224	J 11	5272	L 1	5315	J 11	5361	C 4
5181	B 5	5225	J 11	5273	L 1	5316	J 11	5362	C 4
5182	B 5	5226	J 11	5274	L 1	5317	J 11	5363	C 4
5183	B 5	5227	J 11	5275	L 1	5318	J 11	5364	C 5
5184	B 5	5228	J 11	5276	L 1	5319	J 11	5365	C 5
5185	B 5	5229	J 11	5277	J 63	5320	J 11	5366	L 1
5186	B 5	5230	J 11	5279	B 8	5321	J 63	5367	L 1
5187	B 5	5231	J 11	5280	B 8	5322	J 11	5368	L 1
5188	C 13	5232	J 11	5281	J 11	5323	J 11	5369	L 1
5189	N 5	5233	J 11	5282	J 11	5324	J 11	5370	L 1
5190	C 13	5234	J 11	5283	J 11	5325	J 11	5371	A 5
5191	C 13	5235	J 11	5284	J 11	5326	J 11	5372	A 5
5192	C 4	5236	J 11	5285	J 11	5327	J 11	5373	A 5
5193	C 13	5237	J 11	5286	J 11	5328	J 11	5374	A 5
5194	C 4	5238	J 11	5287	J 11	5329	J 11	5377	O 4
5195	B 18	5239	J 11	5288	J 11	5330	J 11	5378	O 4
5196	B 18	5240	J 11	5289	J 11	5331	O 4	5379	O 4
5197	J 11	5241	J 11	5290	J 11	5332	O 4	5380	O 4
5198	J 11	5242	J 11	5291	J 11	5333	O 4	5381	O 4
5199	C 13	5243	J 11	5292	J 11	5334	O 4	5384	O 4
		5244	J 11	5293	J 11	5335	O 4	5385	O 4
5200	N 5	5245	J 11	5294	J 11	5336	L 1	5386	O 4
5201	J 11	5246	J 11	5295	J 11	5337	L 1	5387	O 4
5202	J 11	5247	J 11	5296	J 11	5338	L 1	5388	O 4
5203	J 11	5248	J 11	5297	J 11	5339	L 1	5389	O 4
5204	J 11	5249	J 11	5298	J 11	5340	L 1	5390	O 4
5205	J 11	5250	J 11	5299	J 11	5341	L 1	5391	O 4
5206	J 11	5252	J 11			5342	L 1	5393	O 4
5207	J 11	5253	J 11	5300	J 11	5343	L 1	5394	O 4
5208	J 11	5254	J 11	5301	J 11	5344	L 1	5395	O 4
5209	J 11	5255	J 11	5302	J 11	5345	L 1	5396	O 4
5210	J 11	5256	J 11	5303	J 11	5347	O 4	5397	O 4
5211	J 11	5257	J 11	5304	J 11	5348	O 4	5398	O 4
5214	J 11	5258	C 5	5305	J 11	5349	O 4	5399	O 4

400	O 4	5450	A 5	5508	D 11	5582	F 1	5750	N 5
403	O 4	5451	A 5	5509	D 11	5584	F 1	5751	N 5
404	O 4	5452	A 5	5510	D 11	5598	F 1	5752	N 5
405	O 4	5453	C 13	5511	D 11			5753	N 5
406	O 4	5454	C 13	5513	N 4			5755	N 5
407	O 4	5455	C 13	5514	N 4	5605	N 4	5757	N 5
408	O 4	5456	C 13	5515	N 5	5606	N 4	5759	N 5
409	N 5	5457	C 13	5516	N 5	5611	N 4	5760	N 5
411	A 5	5458	B 7	5517	N 5	5614	N 4	5761	N 5
412	O 4	5459	B 7	5518	N 5	5620	N 4	5762	N 5
414	O 4	5460	B 7	5519	N 5	5622	N 4	5763	N 5
415	O 4	5461	B 7	5520	N 5	5623	N 4	5764	N 5
416	B 6	5462	B 7	5522	N 5	5625	N 4	5765	N 5
417	O 4	5463	B 7	5523	N 5	5628	N 4	5766	N 5
418	O 4	5464	B 7	5524	N 5	5629	N 4	5767	N 5
419	O 4	5465	B 7	5525	N 5	5632	N 4	5768	N 5
422	O 4	5466	B 7	5526	N 5	5633	N 4	5769	N 5
423	B 2	5467	B 7	5527	N 5	5635	N 4	5770	N 5
424	B 2	5468	B 7	5528	N 5	5636	N 4	5771	N 5
425	B 2	5469	B 7	5529	N 5	5637	N 4	5772	N 5
26	B 2	5470	B 7	5530	N 5	5643	J 10	5773	N 5
27	B 2	5471	B 7	5532	N 5	5673	J 10	5775	N 5
28	B 2	5472	B 7	5533	N 5	5675	J 10		
29	D 10	5473	B 7	5534	N 5	5680	J 10		
30	D 10	5474	B 7	5535	N 5			5776	F 2
31	D 10	5475	B 7	5536	N 5			5777	F 2
32	D 10	5476	B 7	5537	N 5	5713	N 4	5778	F 2
33	D 10	5477	B 7	5538	J 63	5716	N 4	5779	F 2
34	D 10	5478	B 7	5539	N 5	5718	N 4	5780	F 2
35	D 10	5479	B 7	5540	N 5	5720	N 4	5781	F 2
36	D 10	5480	B 7	5541	N 5	5721	N 4	5782	F 2
37	D 10	5481	B 7	5542	N 5	5724	N 4	5783	F 2
38	D 10	5482	B 7	5543	N 5	5725	N 4	5784	F 2
39	B 8	5483	B 7	5544	N 5			5785	F 2
40	B 8	5484	B 7	5545	N 5				
41	B 8			5546	N 5	5730	F 1	5787	J 10
42	B 8	5501	D 11	5547	N 5	5732	F 1	5788	J 10
43	B 8	5502	D 11	5548	N 5	5744	N 5	5789	J 10
44	B 8	5503	D 11	5574	F 1	5745	N 5	5792	J 10
45	B 8	5504	D 11	5575	F 1	5746	N 5	5793	J 10
46	B 8	5505	D 11	5577	F 1	5747	N 5	5794	J 10
48	A 5	5506	D 11			5748	N 5	5795	J 10
49	A 5	5507	D 11	5581	F 1	5749	N 5	5797	J 10

31

5798	J 10	5885	J 62	5933	N 5	5989	J 11	6033	D 9
5799	J 10	5889	J 62	5934	N 5	5990	J 11	6034	D 9
		5890	J 62	5935	N 5	5991	J 11	6035	D 9
5802	J 10	5894	N 5	5936	N 5	5992	J 11	6036	D 9
5803	J 10	5895	N 5	5937	N 5	5993	J 11	6037	D 9
5805	J 10	5896	N 5	5938	N 5	5994	J 11	6038	D 9
5807	J 10	5897	N 5	5939	N 5	5995	J 11	6039	D 9
5808	J 10	5898	N 5	5940	N 5	5996	J 11	6040	D 9
5809	J 10	5899	N 5	5941	N 5	5997	J 11	6041	D 9
5811	J 10			5942	N 5	5998	J 11	6043	J 11
5812	J 10	5900	N 5	5943	N 5	5999	J 11	6044	J 11
5815	J 10	5901	N 5	5944	N 5			6045	J 11
5818	J 10	5902	N 5	5945	N 5	6000	J 11	6046	J 11
5819	J 10	5903	N 5	5946	N 5	6001	J 11	6047	J 11
5820	J 10	5904	N 5	5947	J 11	6002	J 11	6048	J 11
5821	J 10	5905	N 5	5948	J 11	6003	J 11	6049	J 11
5823	J 10	5906	N 5	5949	J 11	6004	J 11	6050	J 11
5824	J 10	5907	N 5	5950	J 11	6005	J 11	6051	J 11
5827	J 10	5908	N 5	5951	J 11	6006	J 11	6052	Q 4
5828	J 10	5909	N 5	5952	J 11	6007	J 11	6054	Q 4
5831	J 10	5910	N 5	5953	J 11	6008	J 11	6055	C 13
5832	J 10	5911	N 5	5954	J 11	6009	J 11	6056	C 13
5835	J 10	5912	N 5	5955	J 11	6010	J 11	6057	C 13
5836	J 10	5913	N 5	5959	Q 1	6011	J 11	6058	C 13
5837	J 10	5914	N 5	5961	Q 1	6012	J 11	6059	C 13
5838	J 10	5915	N 5	5962	Q 4			6060	C 13
5839	J 10	5916	N 5	5966	O 4	6013	D 9	6061	C 13
5841	J 10	5917	N 5	5973	J 11	6014	D 9	6062	C 13
5846	J 10	5918	N 5	5974	J 11	6015	D 9	6063	C 13
5847	J 10	5919	N 5	5975	J 11	6016	D 9	6064	C 13
5848	J 10	5920	N 5	5976	J 11	6017	D 9	6065	C 13
5849	J 10	5921	N 5	5977	J 11	6018	D 9	6066	C 13
5850	J 10	5922	N 5	5978	J 11	6019	D 9	6067	B 5
5851	J 10	5923	N 5	5979	J 11	6021	D 9	6068	B 5
		5924	N 5	5980	J 11	6023	D 9	6069	B 5
		5925	N 5	5981	J 11	6024	D 9	6071	B 5
5853	D 6	5926	N 5	5982	J 11	6025	D 9	6072	B 5
5855	D 6	5927	N 5	5983	J 11	6026	D 9	6076	Q 4
5859	D 6	5928	N 5	5984	J 11	6027	D 9	6077	Q 1
5865	D 6	5929	N 5	5985	J 11	6029	D 9	6078	J 11
5871	D 6	5930	N 5	5986	J 11	6030	D 9	6079	J 11
5874	D 6	5931	N 5	5987	J 11	6031	D 9	6080	J 11
5883	J 62	5932	N 5	5988	J 11	6032	D 9	6081	J 11

082	J 11	6126	C 14	6190	O 4	6243	O 4	6292	O 4
083	C 4	6127	C 14	6191	O 4	6244	O 1	6293	O 4
084	C 4	6128	C 14	6192	O 4	6245	O 4	6294	O 4
085	C 4	6129	C 14	6193	O 4	6246	O 4	6295	O 4
086	C 4	6130	C 14	6194	O 4	6248	O 4	6296	O 4
087	C 4	6131	C 14	6195	O 4	6249	O 4	6298	O 4
088	C 4	6132	Q 4	6198	O 4	6250	O 4	6299	O 4
089	C 4.	6133	Q 4	6199	O 4	6252	O 4		
091	C 4	6134	Q 4			6253	O 4	6300	O 4
092	C 4	6135	Q 4			6254	O 4	6302	O 4
093	C 4	6136	Q 4	6200	O 4	6255	O 4	6303	O 4
094	C 4	6139	Q 1	6201	O 4	6256	O 4	6304	O 4
096	B 4	6140	Q 4	6203	O 4	6257	O 4	6305	O 4
097	B 4	6148	M 1	6205	O 4	6258	O 4	6306	O 4
098	B 4	6150	M 1	6206	O 4	6259	O 4	6307	O 4
099	B 4	6151	M 1	6207	O 4	6261	O 4	6308	O 4
100	B 4	6153	M 1	6208	O 4	6262	O 4	6309	O 4
101	B 4	6154	M 2	6209	O 4	6263	O 4	6310	O 4
102	B 4	6155	M 2	6210	O 4	6264	O 4	6311	O 4
103	B 4	6156	M 2	6211	O 4	6265	O 4	6313	O 4
104	B 4	6158	L 2	6213	O 4	6267	O 4	6314	O 4
105	B 9	6160	L 2	6214	O 4	6268	O 4	6316	O 4
106	B 9	6162	L 2	6215	O 4	6269	O 4	6318	O 4
107	B 9	6163	L 2	6216	O 4	6270	O 4	6319	O 4
108	B 9	6164	B 3	6218	O 4	6271	O 4	6320	O 4
109	B 9	6165	B 3	6219	O 4	6272	O 4	6321	O 4
110	B 9	6166	B 3	6220	O 4	6274	O 4	6323	O 4
111	B 9	6167	B 3	6221	O 4	6275	O 4	6324	O 4
112	B 9	6168	B 3	6222	O 4	6276	O 4	6325	O 4
113	B 9	6169	B 3	6223	O 4	6277	O 4	6326	O 4
114	B 9	6170	S 1	6224	O 4	6278	O 4	6328	O 4
115	J 11	6171	S 1	6226	O 4	6280	O 4	6329	O 4
116	J 11	6172	S 1	6227	O 4	6281	O 4	6331	O 4
117	J 11	6173	S 1	6228	O 4	6282	O 4	6333	O 4
118	J 11	6176	Q 4	6229	O 4	6283	O 4	6334	O 1
119	J 11	6177	Q 4	6231	O 4	6284	O 4	6336	O 4
120	C 14	6179	Q 4	6232	O 4	6285	O 4	6337	O 4
121	C 14	6180	O 4	6234	O 4	6286	O 4	6338	O 4
122	C 14	6184	O 4	6236	O 4	6287	O 4	6341	O 4
123	C 14	6186	O 4	6237	O 4	6288	O 4	6342	O 4
124	C 14	6187	O 4	6240	O 4	6289	O 4	6343	O 4
125	C 14	6188	O 4	6241	O 4	6290	O 4	6344	O 4
		6189	O 4	6242	O 4	6291	O 4	6347	O 4

6349	O 4	6398	D 11	6529	O 4	6586	O 4	6642	O 4
6350	O 4	6399	D 11	6531	O 4	6588	O 4		
6351	O 4			6532	O 4	6589	O 4	6701	Elect.
6352	O 4			6533	O 4	6590	O 4		Bo–Bo
6353	O 4	6400	D 11	6534	O 4	6591	O 4	6807	D 42
6354	O 4	6401	D 11	6535	O 4	6592	O 4	6817	D 42
6356	O 4	6408	J 60	6536	O 4	6594	O 4	6819	D 41
6357	O 4	6409	J 60	6538	O 4	6595	O 1	6820	D 41
6358	O 4	6410	J 60	6539	O 4	6596	O 4	6821	D 41
6359	O 4	6411	J 60	6540	O 4	6598	O 4	6822	D 41
6360	O 4	6415	H 2	6542	O 4	6601	O 4	6823	D 41
6361	O 4	6416	H 2	6543	O 4	6604	O 4	6824	D 41
6363	O 4	6417	H 2	6544	O 4	6606	O 4	6825	D 40
6364	O 4	6418	H 2	6545	O 4	6608	O 4	6826	D 40
6365	O 4	6420	H 2	6546	O 4	6609	O 4	6827	D 40
6366	O 4	6422	H 2	6548	O 4	6611	O 4	6828	D 40
6367	O 4	6495	O 4	6550	O 4	6612	O 4	6829	D 40
6370	O 4	6496	O 4	6552	O 4	6614	O 4	6830	Z 5
6371	O 4	6498	O 4	6553	O 5	6615	O 4	6831	Z 5
6372	O 4			6554	O 4	6616	O 4	6832	Z 5
6374	O 4			6555	O 4	6617	O 4	6833	D 40
6375	O 4	6500	O 4	6556	O 4	6618	O 4	6834	D 40
6376	O 4	6501	O 4	6558	O 4	6619	O 4	6835	D 40
6378	D 11	6502	O 4	6559	O 4	6620	O 4	6836	D 40
6379	D 11	6503	O 4	6561	O 4	6621	O 4	6843	Z 4
6380	D 11	6505	O 4	6562	O 4	6622	O 4	6844	Z 4
6381	D 11	6506	O 4	6564	O 4	6624	O 4	6845	D 40
6382	D 11	6507	O 4	6566	O 4	6625	O 4	6846	D 40
6383	D 11	6510	O 4	6567	O 4	6626	O 4	6847	D 40
6384	D 11	6511	O 4	6568	O 4	6627	O 4	6848	D 40
6385	D 11	6512	O 4	6571	O 4	6629	O 4	6849	D 40
6386	D 11	6513	O 4	6572	O 4	6630	O 4	6850	D 40
6387	D 11	6515	O 4	6573	O 4	6631	O 4	6852	D 40
6388	D 11	6516	O 4	6574	O 4	6632	O 4	6854	D 40
6389	D 11	6518	O 4	6575	O 4	6633	O 4	6878	D 41
6390	D 11	6519	O 4	6576	O 4	6634	O 4	6879	D 41
6391	D 11	6521	O 4	6577	O 4	6635	O 4	6880	D 41
6392	D 11	6522	O 4	6578	O 4	6636	O 4	6881	D 41
6393	D 11	6523	O 4	6579	O 4	6637	O 4	6882	D 41
6394	D 11	6524	O 4	6581	O 4	6638	O 4	6883	D 41
6395	D 11	6525	O 4	6582	O 4	6639	O 4	6887	G 10
6396	D 11	6526	O 4	6583	O 4	6640	O 4	6893	D 41
6397	D 11	6528	O 4	6584	O 4	6641	O 4	6894	D 41

6895	D 41	7004	F 6	7032	J 68	7062	F 6	7091	F 5
6896	D 41	7005	F 6	7033	J 68	7063	F 6	7094	F 5
6897	D 41	7006	F 6	7034	J 68	7064	F 6	7095	F 5
6898	D 41	7007	F 6	7035	J 68	7065	F 6	7096	F 5
6899	D 41	7008	F 6	7036	J 68	7066	F 6		
		7009	F 6	7037	J 68	7067	F 6		
6900	D 41	7010	F 6	7038	J 68	7068	F 6	7100	F 5
6901	D 41	7011	J 67	7039	J 68	7069	F 6	7103	F 5
6902	D 41	7012	J 67	7040	J 68	7070	F 6	7104	F 5
6903	D 41	7013	J 67	7042	J 68	7071	F 4	7108	F 5
6904	D 41	7014	J 67	7043	J 68	7072	F 4	7109	F 5
6905	D 41	7015	J 67	7044	J 68	7074	F 4	7110	F 5
6906	D 41	7016	J 67	7045	J 68	7075	F 4	7111	F 4
6907	D 41	7018	J 67	7046	J 68	7076	F 4	7125	J 70
6908	D 41	7019	J 67	7047	J 67	7077	F 4	7126	J 70
6909	D 41	7021	J 68	7048	J 68	7078	F 4	7127	J 70
6910	D 41	7022	J 68	7049	J 68	7079	F 4	7128	J 70
6911	D 41	7023	J 68	7050	J 68			7129	J 70
6912	D 41	7024	J 68	7051	J 69	7082	J 67	7130	J 70
6913	D 40	7025	J 68	7052	J 69	7083	J 69	7131	J 70
6914	D 40	7026	J 68	7053	J 69	7084	J 69	7133	Y 6
6915	D 40	7027	J 68	7055	J 69	7085	J 69	7134	Y 6
		7028	J 68	7057	J 69	7086	J 67	7135	J 70
7001	F 6	7029	J 68	7059	J 69	7087	J 69	7136	J 70
7002	F 6	7030	J 68	7060	J 69	7089	J 69	7137	J 70
7003	F 6	7031	J 68	7061	F 6	7090	J 69		

NOTES

7139	J 70	7203	J 67	7298	J 66	7357	J 69	7403	J 67
7141	F 5	7204	J 67			7358	J 69	7405	J 67
7142	F 5	7206	J 67	7304	J 66	7359	J 67	7408	E 4
7143	F 5	7207	J 67	7305	J 69	7360	J 67	7409	E 4
7144	F 5	7208	J 67	7307	J 66	7361	J 69	7414	E 4
7145	F 5	7210	Y 4	7309	J 66	7363	J 67	7416	E 4
7147	F 5	7214	F 4	7310	J 66	7365	J 69	7426	B 12
7155	J 65	7219	F 4	7311	J 66	7366	J 67	7437	B 12
7157	J 65	7222	F 4	7313	J 66	7367	J 69	7449	B 12
7160	J 69	7226	Y 4	7319	J 66	7368	J 69	7463	E 4
7161	J 67	7227	Y 4	7320	J 66	7369	J 69	7466	E 4
7162	J 67	7228	Y 4	7321	J 66	7370	J 69	7467	B 12
7163	J 67	7229	Y 4	7322	J 66	7371	J 69	7470	B 12
7164	J 67	7230	Y 5	7323	J 66	7372	J 69	7472	B 12
7165	J 69	7232	F 4	7324	J 66	7373	J 69	7476	B 12
7166	J 69	7233	F 4	7327	J 67	7374	J 69	7477	E 4
7169	J 67	7236	F 4	7328	J 69	7375	J 69	7478	E 4
7170	F 5	7244	F 4	7329	J 67	7376	J 69	7479	B 12
7171	F 4	7247	J 65	7330	J 67	7377	J 67	7482	B 12
7172	F 4	7250	J 65	7331	J 67	7378	J 69	7488	B 12
7173	F 4	7253	J 65	7332	J 69	7379	J 69	7491	B 12
7174	F 4	7256	J 67	7334	J 67	7380	J 69	7492	E 4
7175	F 4	7257	J 67	7335	J 69	7381	J 69	7494	E 4
		7258	J 67	7336	J 67	7382	J 67	7497	E 4
7177	F 4	7260	J 67	7337	J 69	7383	J 69		
7178	F 4	7261	J 67	7338	J 69	7384	J 67	7503	E 4
7179	F 5	7262	J 67	7339	J 67	7385	J 69	7506	E 4
7180	F 4	7263	J 67	7340	J 69	7386	J 69		
7184	F 4	7264	J 67	7341	J 69	7387	J 69	7508	J 15
7185	F 4	7265	J 69	7342	J 69	7389	J 69	7509	J 15
7186	F 4	7266	J 69	7343	J 69	7390	J 69	7510	J 15
7187	F 4	7267	J 69	7345	J 69	7391	J 69	7511	J 15
7188	F 5	7268	J 69	7346	J 69	7392	J 69	7512	J 15
7189	F 4	7269	J 69	7347	J 69	7393	J 69	7514	J 15
7190	J 67	7270	J 69	7348	J 69	7394	J 69	7515	J 15
7191	J 69	7271	J 69	7349	J 69	7395	J 69	7516	J 15
7192	J 67	7273	J 69	7350	J 69	7396	J 67	7517	J 15
7193	J 67	7281	J 66	7351	J 69	7397	J 69	7520	J 15
7194	J 69	7288	J 66	7352	J 67	7398	J 67	7523	J 15
7195	J 69	7289	J 66	7353	J 69	7399	J 67	7526	J 15
7196	J 69	7290	J 66	7354	J 69			7527	J 15
7198	J 69	7293	J 66	7355	J 69	7400	J 67	7530	J 15
7200	J 67	7296	J 66	7356	J 69	7401	J 67	7540	J 15

36

7542	J 15	7640	J 15	7825	J 15	7902	J 15	7992	N 7
7543	J 15	7641	J 15	7828	J 15	7904	J 15	7993	N 7
7544	J 15	7642	J 15	7830	J 15	7906	J 15	7994	N 7
7545	J 15	7643	J 15	7833	J 15	7907	J 15	7995	N 7
7546	J 15	7644	J 15	7834	J 15	7908	J 15	7996	N 7
7547	J 15	7645	J 15	7836	J 15	7910	J 15	7997	N 7
7548	J 15	7646	J 15	7837	J 15	7911	J 15	7998	N 7
7549	J 15	7647	J 15	7840	J 15	7913	J 15	7999	N 7
7550	J 15	7648	J 15	7843	J 15	7914	J 15	8000	
7551	J 15	7649	J 15	7846	J 15	7915	J 15	8001	
7552	J 15	7692	D 16	7847	J 15	7918	J 15	8002	
7553	J 15	7695	D 16	7848	J 15	7920	J 15	8003	
7554	J 15			7849	J 15	7921	J 15	8004	
7555	J 15	7707	D 16	7850	J 15	7922	J 15	8005	
7556	J 15	7708	D 16	7852	J 15	7924	J 15	8006	
7557	J 15	7712	D 16	7853	J 15	7925	J 15	8007	
7558	J 15	7727	D 16	7854	J 15	7926	J 15	8008	
7559	J 15	7728	D 16	7855	J 15	7927	J 15	8009	
7560	J 15	7740	D 16	7857	J 15	7928	J 15	8010	
7561	J 15	7764	D 16	7860	J 15	7929	J 15	8011	
7562	J 15	7770	D 16	7865	J 15	7931	J 15	8040	F 3
7563	J 15	7772	Y 1	7866	J 15	7932	J 15	8041	F 3
7564	J 15	7774	Y 1	7869	J 15	7934	J 15	8042	F 3
7565	J 15	7775	Y 10	7871	J 15	7937	J 15	8043	F 3
7566	J 15	7776	Y 10	7872	J 15	7940	J 15	8044	F 3
7567	J 15	7780	F 5	7874	J 15	7941	J 15	8045	F 3
7568	J 15	7781	F 5	7875	J 15	7942	J 15	8046	F 3
7569	J 15	7782	F 5	7876	J 15	7943	J 15	8047	F 3
7570	J 15	7783	F 5	7877	J 15	7945	J 15	8048	F 3
7571	J 15	7784	F 5	7878	J 15	7978	N 7	8049	F 3
7573	F 4	7785	F 5	7880	J 15	7979	N 7	8060	F 3
7574	F 4	7786	F 5	7881	J 15	7980	N 7	8061	F 3
7578	F 4	7787	F 5	7883	J 15	7981	N 7	8062	F 3
7579	F 4	7788	F 5	7886	J 15	7982	N 7	8063	F 3
7581	F 4	7789	F 6	7887	J 15	7983	N 7	8064	F 3
7584	F 4	7790	F 6	7888	J 15	7984	N 7	8066	F 3
7586	F 4	7791	E 4	7892	J 15	7985	N 7	8067	F 3
7588	F 4	7794	E 4	7893	J 15	7986	N 7	8068	F 3
7589	F 5	7797	E 4	7894	J 15	7987	N 7	8070	F 3
7590	F 5	7802	E 4	7895	J 15	7988	N 7	8071	F 3
		7805	E 4	7897	J 15	7989	N 7	8072	F 3
7597	F 7	7813	J 15	7898	J 15	7990	N 7	8075	F 3
7598	F 7	7821	J 15	7901	J 15	7991	N 7	8077	F 3

8078	F 3	8168	J 17	8209	J 17	8252	J 19	8304	B 1
8079	F 3	8169	J 17	8210	J 17	8253	J 19	8305	B 1
8081	F 3	8170	J 17	8211	J 17	8254	J 19	8306	B 1
8082	F 3	8171	J 17	8212	J 17	8260	J 19	8307	B 1
8085	F 3	8172	J 17	8213	J 17	8261	J 19	8308	B 1
8088	F 3	8173	J 17	8214	J 17	8262	J 19	8309	B 1
8089	F 3	8174	J 17	8215	J 17	8263	J 19	8310	B 1
8092	F 3	8175	J 17	8216	J 17	8264	J 19		
8093	F 3	8176	J 17	8217	J 17	8265	J 19	8401	Y 1
8094	F 3	8177	J 17	8218	J 17	8266	J 19		
8095	F 3	8178	J 17	8219	J 17	8267	J 19	8430	Y 11
8096	F 3	8179	J 17	8220	J 17	8268	J 19	8431	Y 11
8097	F 3	8180	J 17	8221	J 17	8269	J 19		
8099	F 3	8181	J 17	8222	J 17	8270	J 20	8500	B 12
		8182	J 17	8223	J 17	8271	J 20	8501	B 12
8140	J 19	8183	J 17	8224	J 17	8272	J 20	8502	B 12
8141	J 19	8184	J 17	8225	J 17	8273	J 20	8503	B 12
8142	J 19	8185	J 17	8226	J 17	8274	J 20	8504	B 12
8143	J 19	8186	J 17	8227	J 17	8275	J 20	8505	B 12
8144	J 19	8187	J 17	8228	J 17	8276	J 20	8507	B 12
8145	J 19	8188	J 17	8229	J 17	8277	J 20	8508	B 12
8146	J 19	8189	J 17	8230	J 17	8278	J 20	8509	B 12
8147	J 19	8190	J 17	8231	J 17	8279	J 20	8510	B 12
8148	J 19	8191	J 17	8232	J 17	8280	J 20	8511	B 12
8149	J 19	8192	J 17	8233	J 17	8281	J 20	8513	B 12
8150	J 17	8193	J 17	8234	J 17	8282	J 20	8514	B 12
8151	J 17	8194	J 17	8235	J 17	8283	J 20	8515	B 12
8152	J 17	8195	J 17	8236	J 17	8284	J 20	8516	B 12
8153	J 17	8196	J 17	8237	J 17	8285	J 20	8517	B 12
8154	J 17	8197	J 17	8238	J 17	8286	J 20	8518	B 12
8155	J 17	8198	J 17	8239	J 17	8287	J 20	8519	B 12
8156	J 17	8199	J 17	8240	J 19	8288	J 20	8520	B 12
8157	J 17			8241	J 19	8289	J 20	8521	B 12
8158	J 17			8242	J 19	8290	J 20	8522	B 12
8159	J 17	8200	J 17	8243	J 19	8291	J 20	8524	B 12
8160	J 17	8201	J 17	8244	J 19	8292	J 20	8525	B 12
8161	J 17	8202	J 17	8245	J 19	8293	J 20	8526	B 12
8162	J 17	8203	J 17	8246	J 19	8294	J 20	8527	B 12
8163	J 17	8204	J 17	8247	J 19			8528	B 12
8164	J 17	8205	J 17	8248	J 19			8529	B 12
8165	J 17	8206	J 17	8249	J 19	8301	B 1	8530	B 12
8166	J 17	8207	J 17	8250	J 19	8302	B 1	8531	B 12
8167	J 17	8208	J 17	8251	J 19	8303	B 1		

8532	B 12	8782	D 16	8826	D 16	8875	D 16	9020	N 15
8533	B 12	8783	D 16	8827	D 16	8876	D 16	9022	N 15
8534	B 12	8784	D 16	8828	D 16	8877	D 15	9023	N 15
8536	B 12	8785	D 16	8829	D 16	8878	D 16	9025	C 15
8537	B 12	8786	D 16	8830	D 16	8879	D 16	9026	C 15
8538	B 12	8787	D 16	8831	D 16	8880	D 16	9029	N 15
8539	B 12	8788	D 16	8832	D 16	8881	D 15	9031	N 15
8540	B 12	8789	D 16	8833	D 16	8882	D 16	9032	Y 9
8541	B 12	8790	D 16	8834	D 16	8883	D 16	9033	J 37
8542	B 12	8791	D 16.	8835	D 16	8884	D 16	9034	D 34
8543	B 12	8792	D 16	8836	D 16	8885	D 16	9035	D 34
8544	B 12	8793	D 16	8839	D 16	8886	D 16	9038	J 35
8545	B 12	8794	D 16	8840	D 16	8887	D 16	9039	C 15
8546	B 12	8795	D 16	8841	D 16	8888	D 16	9040	Y 9
8547	B 12	8796	D 16	8843	D 16	8889	D 15	9041	C 15
8548	B 12	8797	D 16	8844	D 16	8890	D 15	9042	Y 9
8549	B 12	8798	D 16.	8845	D 16	8891	D 15	9043	C 15
8550	B 12	8799	D 16	8846	D 16	8892	D 15	9044	J 37
8551	B 12			8847	D 16	8893	D 15	9045	J 36
8552	B 12	8800	D 16	8848	D 16	8895	D 15	9046	J 37
8554	B 12	8801	D 16	8849	D 16	8896	D 15	9047	N 15
8555	B 12	8802	D 16	8850	D 16	8897	D 15	9048	C 15
8557	B 12	8803	D 16	8851	D 16	8898	D 15	9049	N 15
8559	B 12	8804	D 16	8852	D 16	8899	D 16	9050	Y 9
8560	B 12	8805	D 16	8853	D 16			9051	C 15
8561	B 12	8806	D 16	8854	D 16	9001	C 15	9052	N 15
8563	B 12	8807	D 16	8855	D 16	9002	C 15	9053	C 15
8564	B 12	8808	D 16	8856	D 16	9003	C 15	9054	N 15
8566	B 12	8809	D 16	8859	D 16	9004	C 15	9055	N 15
8567	B 12	8810	D 16.	8860	D 16	9005	C 15	9056	J 35
8569	B 12	8811	D 16	8861	D 16	9006	C 15	9057	J 35
8570	B 12	8812	D 16	8862	D 16	9007	N 15	9058	J 35
8571	B 12	8813	D 16	8863	D 16	9008	J 37	9059	J 35
8572	B 12	8814	D 16	8864	D 16	9009	Y 9	9060	N 15
8573	B 12	8815	D 16	8865	D 16	9010	Y 9	9061	N 15
8575	B 12	8816	D 16	8866	D 16	9011	Y 9	9062	J 37
8576	B 12	8817	D 16	8867	D 15	9012	C 15	9063	Y 9
8578	B 12	8818	D 16	8868	D 16	9013	J 37	9064	C 15
8579	B 12	8819	D 16	8869	D 16	9014	Y 9	9065	N 15
8580	B 12	8820	D 16	8871	D 16	9015	C 15	9066	J 88
		8821	D 16	8872	D 16	9016	C 15	9067	N 15
8780	D 16	8823	D 16	8873	D 16	9017	Y 9	9068	J 36
8781	D 16	8824	D 16	8874	D 16	9019	N 15	9069	N 15

9070	N 15	9123	J 37	9182	J 36	9234	J 88	9287	D 34
9071	N 15	9124	J 35	9183	J 36	9235	J 88	9288	J 88
9072	J 37	9125	N 15	9185	J 35	9236	J 88	9289	J 88
9073	J 37	9126	J 35	9186	J 35	9237	J 88	9290	J 88
9074	N 15	9127	J 35	9187	J 35	9238	J 88	9291	D 34
9075	N 15	9128	J 37	9188	J 35	9240	N 15	9292	J 37
9076	N 15	9129	J 35	9189	J 35	9241	D 34	9295	J 37
9077	N 15	9130	J 88	9190	J 35	9242	D 34	9296	J 37
9078	N 15	9131	C 15	9191	J 35	9243	D 29	9297	J 37
9079	N 15	9132	J 88	9192	J 35	9244	D 29	9298	D 34
9084	J 37	9133	C 15	9193	J 35	9245	D 29	9299	J 37
9086	J 35	9134	C 15	9194	J 35	9246	N 15		
9087	J 88	9135	C 15	9195	J 35	9247	J 36	9300	J 37
9088	J 37	9136	J 37	9196	J 35	9248	J 36	9301	J 37
9089	J 37	9139	J 37	9197	J 35	9250	J 36	9302	J 37
9096	N 15	9141	C 15	9198	J 35	9251	N 15	9303	J 37
9097	N 15	9142	N 15	9199	J 35	9252	N 15	9304	J 37
9098	J 37	9143	J 37			9253	J 35	9305	J 37
9099	N 15	9144	Y 9	9200	J 35	9254	J 35	9306	J 37
		9146	Y 9	9201	J 35	9255	J 37	9307	D 34
		9147	N 15	9202	J 35	9256	D 34	9308	Y 9
9100	D 34	9149	D 34	9203	J 35	9257	N 15	9309	C 15
9101	J 37	9151	J 37	9204	J 35	9258	D 34	9310	Y 9
9102	C 15	9152	J 88	9205	J 35	9259	N 15	9313	J 37
9103	J 37	9153	D 34	9206	J 35	9260	J 37	9314	J 37
9104	J 37	9154	N 15	9207	J 35	9261	J 37	9315	J 37
9105	J 37	9155	C 15	9208	J 35	9263	J 37	9329	J 35
9106	N 15	9157	J 37	9209	N 15	9264	N 15	9330	J 35
9107	N 15	9158	J 37	9210	N 15	9265	C 15	9331	D 33
9108	N 15	9161	J 37	9215	D 31	9266	D 34	9332	D 33
9109	J 37	9162	J 37	9219	N 15	9267	C 15	9333	D 33
9110	J 37	9164	C 15	9220	J 35	9270	D 34	9335	J 35
9111	J 37	9165	N 15	9221	D 34	9271	J 88	9336	J 35
9113	J 37	9166	N 15	9222	J 37	9272	J 37	9337	J 35
9114	J 88	9167	J 37	9223	N 15	9273	J 37	9338	D 29
9115	J 35	9171	J 37	9224	N 15	9274	J 37	9339	D 29
9116	J 88	9172	J 36	9225	N 15	9276	N 15	9340	D 29
9117	J 88	9174	N 15	9226	J 35	9277	J 88	9347	J 35
9118	J 88	9175	J 37	9227	N 15	9278	D 34	9348	J 35
9119	J 88	9176	J 36	9228	J 35	9279	J 88	9357	J 36
9120	J 35	9177	J 36	9229	N 15	9280	J 36	9358	J 36
9121	J 88	9180	J 36	9230	N 15	9281	D 34	9359	D 29
9122	C 15	9181	J 36	9233	J 88	9282	N 15	9360	D 29

9361	D 29	9405	D 34	9448	C 16	9497	D 30	9625	J 36
9362	D 29	9406	D 34	9449	C 16	9498	D 30	9628	J 36
9363	D 30	9407	D 34	9450	C 16	9499	D 30	9632	J 36
9364	J 35	9408	D 34	9451	C 16			9635	D 31
9365	J 35	9409	D 30	9452	C 16	9500	D 30	9642	D 31
9366	J 35	9410	D 30	9453	N 15	9501	D 30	9643	J 36
9367	J 35	9411	D 30	9454	J 37	9502	D 34	9644	J 36
9368	J 35	9412	D 30	9455	J 37	9503	D 34	9645	J 36
9369	J 35	9413	D 30	9456	J 37	9504	D 34	9646	J 36
9370	J 35	9414	D 30	9457	J 37	9505	D 34	9647	J 36
9371	J 35	9415	D 30	9458	J 37	9506	J 37	9648	J 36
9372	J 35	9416	D 30	9459	J 37	9507	J 37	9649	J 36
9373	J 35	9417	D 30	9460	J 37	9508	J 37	9650	J 36
9374	J 35	9418	D 30	9461	J 37	9511	C 16	9651	J 36
9375	J 35	9419	D 30	9462	J 37	9512	C 16	9652	J 36
9376	J 35	9420	D 30	9463	J 37	9513	C 16	9653	J 36
9377	J 35	9421	D 30	9464	J 37	9514	C 16	9654	J 36
9378	J 35	9422	D 30	9465	J 37	9515	C 16	9655	J 36
9379	J 35	9423	D 30	9466	J 37	9516	C 16	9656	J 36
9380	J 35	9424	D 30	9467	J 37	9517	J 37	9657	J 36
9381	J 35	9425	D 30	9468	J 37	9518	J 37	9658	J 36
9382	D 33	9426	D 30	9469	J 37	9519	N 15	9659	J 36
9383	D 33	9427	D 30	9470	J 37	9520	N 15	9660	J 36
9384	D 33	9428	D 30	9471	J 37	9521	N 15	9663	J 36
9385	D 33	9429	J 37	9472	J 37	9522	N 15	9664	J 36
9386	N 15	9430	J 37	9473	J 37	9523	N 15	9667	J 36
9387	N 15	9431	J 37	9476	J 37	9524	N 15	9668	J 36
9388	N 15	9432	J 37	9477	J 37	9525	N 15	9669	J 36
9389	N 15	9433	J 37	9478	J 37	9526	N 15	9670	J 36
9390	N 15	9434	J 37	9479	J 37	9527	N 15	9673	J 36
9391	N 15	9435	J 37	9480	J 37	9528	N 15	9675	J 36
9392	N 15	9436	J 37	9485	J 37	9529	Y 1	9677	J 36
9393	N 15	9437	J 37	9486	J 37	9546	Y 9	9678	J 36
9396	N 15	9438	C 16	9487	J 37	9547	Y 9	9679	J 36
9397	N 15	9439	C 16	9488	J 37			9680	J 36
9398	N 15	9440	C 16	9489	J 37			9681	J 36
9399	N 15	9441	C 16	9490	D 34	9604	J 36	9682	J 36
		9442	C 16	9491	J 37	9610	Y 9	9683	J 36
9400	D 30	9443	C 16	9492	D 34	9611	J 36	9684	J 36
9401	J 37	9444	C 16	9493	D 34	9612	J 36	9685	J 36
9402	J 37	9445	C 16	9494	D 34	9617	J 36	9686	J 36
9403	J 37	9446	C 16	9495	D 34	9622	J 36	9687	J 36
9404	D 31	9447	C 16	9496	D 34	9623	J 36	9688	J 36

9689	J 36	9748	J 36	9792	J 36	9834	J 83	9892	D 32
9690	J 36	9749	J 36	9793	J 36	9836	J 88	9893	D 32
9691	J 36	9750	J 36	9794	J 36	9837	J 88	9894	D 33
9692	J 36	9751	J 36	9795	J 83	9838	J 88	9895	D 29
		9752	J 36	9796	J 83	9839	J 88	9896	D 29
		9753	J 36	9797	J 83	9840	J 88	9897	D 29
9705	J 36	9754	J 36	9798	J 83	9841	J 88	9898	D 29
9706	J 36	9755	J 36	9799	J 83	9842	J 88	9899	D 29
9707	J 36	9756	J 36			9843	J 88		
9708	J 36	9757	J 36	9800	J 83	9844	J 88	9900	D 29
9709	J 36	9758	J 36	9801	J 83	9845	J 88	9907	N 15
9710	J 36	9759	J 36	9802	J 83	9846	J 88	9908	N 15
9711	J 36	9760	J 36	9803	J 83	9847	J 88	9909	N 15
9712	J 36	9761	J 36	9804	J 83	9848	J 35	9910	N 15
9713	J 36	9762	J 36	9805	J 83	9849	J 35	9911	N 15
9714	J 36	9763	J 36	9806	J 83	9850	J 35	9912	N 15
9715	J 36	9764	J 36	9807	J 83	9851	J 35	9913	N 15
9716	J 36	9765	D 31	9808	J 83	9852	J 35	9914	N 15
9717	J 36	9767	D 31	9809	J 83	9853	J 35	9915	N 15
9718	J 36	9768	D 31	9810	J 83	9854	J 35	9916	N 15
9719	J 36	9769	D 31	9811	J 83	9855	J 35	9917	N 15
9720	J 36	9770	D 31	9812	J 83	9856	J 35	9918	N 15
9721	J 36	9771	J 36	9813	J 83	9857	J 35	9919	N 15
9722	J 36	9772	J 36	9814	J 83	9858	N 14	9920	N 15
9723	J 36	9773	J 36	9815	J 83	9859	N 14	9921	N 15
9724	J 36	9774	J 36	9816	J 83	9860	N 14	9922	N 15
9725	J 36	9775	J 36	9817	J 83	9861	N 14	9923	N 15
9726	J 36	9776	J 36	9818	J 83	9862	N 14	9924	N 15
9727	J 36	9777	J 36	9819	J 83	9863	N 14	9925	N 15
9728	J 36	9778	J 36	9820	J 83	9864	D 33	9926	N 15
9729	D 31	9779	J 36	9821	J 83	9865	D 33		
9731	D 31	9780	J 36	9822	J 83	9866	D 33	10000	W 1
9732	D 31	9781	J 36	9823	J 83	9867	D 33		
9733	D 31	9782	J 36	9824	J 83	9882	D 32	10083	Y 9
9734	D 31	9783	J 36	9825	J 83	9883	D 32	10084	Y 9
9739	D 31	9784	J 36	9826	J 83	9884	D 32	10088	Y 9
9740	D 31	9785	J 36	9827	J 83	9885	D 32	10089	Y 9
9742	J 36	9786	J 36	9828	J 83	9886	D 32	10090	Y 9
9743	J 36	9787	J 36	9829	J 83	9887	D 32	10091	Y 9
9744	J 36	9788	J 36	9830	J 83	9888	D 32	10092	Y 9
9745	J 36	9789	J 36	9831	J 83	9889	D 32	10093	Y 9
9746	J 36	9790	J 36	9832	J 83	9890	D 32	10094	Y 9
9747	J 36	9791	J 36	9833	J 83	9891	D 32	10095	Y 9

B 12 Class

0096	Y 9	09	C 17	083	J 3	090	J 4	099	J 93
0097	Y 9	015	J 93	084	J 4	091	J 4		
0098	Y 9	016	J 93	085	J 4	092	J 4		
		050	D 53	086	J 3	094	J 93	B	J 92
0100	Y 9	077	D 53	087	J 4	095	J 93	C	J 92
0101	Y 9	081	J 3	088	J 3	096	J 93	D	J 92
0102	Y 9	082	J 4	089	J 4	098	J 93		

J 38 Class

A 3 Class

D 49 Class

B 17 Class (Streamlined)

44

NAMED ENGINES
A1 Class " Pacific "

43	Melton	2565	Merry Hampton
46	Donovan	2567	Sir Visto
47	Doncaster	2569	Gladiateur
48	Galtee More	2570	Tranquil
50	Blink Bonny	2572	St. Gatien
55	Centenary	4470	Great Northern
56	Ormonde	4472	Flying Scotsman
57	Blair Atholl	4475	Flying Fox
60	Pretty Polly	4476	Royal Lancer
61	Minoru	4479	Robert the Devil
62	Isinglass	4481	St. Simon
64	Knight of the Thistle		

A3 Class " Pacific "

00	Windsor Lad	2579	Dick Turpin
01	Colombo	2580	Shotover
02	Hyperion	2581	Neil Gow
03	Firdaussi	2582	Sir Hugo
04	Sandwich	2595	Trigo
05	Cameronian	2596	Manna
06	Salmon Trout	2597	Gainsborough
07	Singapore	2598	Blenheim
08	Brown Jack	2599	Book Law
44	Lemberg	2743	Felstead
45	Diamond Jubilee	2744	Grand Parade
49	Persimmon	2745	Captain Cuttle
51	Prince Palatine	2746	Fairway
52	Sansovino	2747	Coronach
53	Prince of Wales	2748	Colorado
54	Woolwinder	2749	Flamingo
58	Tracery	2750	Papyrus
59	The Tetrarch	2751	Humorist
63	Tagalie	2752	Spion Kop
66	Ladas	2795	Call Boy
68	Sceptre	2796	Spearmint
71	Sunstar	2797	Cicero
73	Harvester	4471	Sir Frederick Banbury
74	St. Frusquin	4473	Solario
75	Galopin	4474	Victor Wild
76	The White Knight	4477	Gay Crusader
77	Night Hawk	4478	Hermit
78	Bayardo	4480	Enterprise

45

P.1 Class loco "Flood"

A4 Class Streamlined " Pacific "

509 Silver Link
510 Quicksilver
511 Silver King
512 Silver Fox
462 William Whitelaw
463 Sparrow Hawk
464 Bittern
465 Guillemot
466 Herring Gull
467 Wild Swan
468 Mallard
482 Golden Eagle
483 Kingfisher
484 Falcon
485 Kestrel
486 Merlin
487 Sea Eagle
488 Union of South Africa

4489 Dominion of Canada
4490 Empire of India
4491 Commonwealth of
Australia
4492 Dominion of
New Zealand
4493 Woodcock
4494 Andrew K. McCosh
4495 Golden Fleece
4496 Golden Shuttle
4497 Golden Plover
4498 Sir Nigel Gresley
4499 Sir Murrough Wilson
4500 Sir Ronald Matthews
4900 Gannet
4901 Sir Charles Newton
4902 Seagull
4903 Peregrine

B1 Class

301 Springbok
302 Eland
303 Impala
304 Gazelle
05 Oryx

8306 Bongo
8307 Blackbuck
8308 Klipspringer
8309 Kudu
8310 Hartebeeste

B2 Class

423 Sir Sam Fay
424 City of Lincoln
425 City of Manchester

5426 City of Chester
5428 City of Liverpool

B3 Class

64 Earl Beatty
65 Valour
66 Earl Haig

6168 Lord Stuart of Wortley
6169 Lord Faringdon

B4 Class

6097 Immingham

B8 Class

04 Glenalmond
79 Earl Kitchener of
Khartoum

5439 Sutton Nelthorpe
5446 Earl Roberts of
Kandahar

" Sandringham " Class, B 17

2800	Sandringham	2837	Thorpe Hall
2801	Holkham	2838	Melton Hall
2802	Walsingham	2839	Norwich City
2803	Framlingham	2840	Somerleyton Hall
2804	Elveden	2841	Gayton Hall
2805	Lincolnshire Regiment	2842	Kilverstone Hall
2806	Audley End	2843	Champion Lodge
2807	Blickling	2844	Earlham Hall
2808	Gunton	2845	The Suffolk Regiment
2809	Quidenham	2846	Gilwell Park
2810	Honingham Hall	2847	Helmingham Hall
2811	Raynham Hall	2848	Arsenal
2812	Houghton Hall	2849	Sheffield United
2813	Woodbastwick Hall	2850	Grimsby Town
2814	Castle Hedingham	2851	Derby County
2815	Culford Hall	2852	Darlington
2816	Fallodon	2853	Huddersfield Town
2817	Ford Castle	2854	Sunderland
2818	Wynyard Park	2855	Middlesbrough
2819	Welbeck Abbey	2856	Leeds United
2820	Clumber	2857	Doncaster Rovers
2821	Hatfield House	2858	The Essex Regiment
2822	Alnwick Castle	2859	East Anglian
2823	Lambton Castle	2860	Hull City
2824	Lumley Castle	2861	Sheffield Wednesday
2825	Raby Castle	2862	Manchester United
2826	Brancepeth Castle	2863	Everton
2827	Aske Hall	2864	Liverpool
2828	Harewood House	2865	Leicester City
2829	Naworth Castle	2866	Nottingham Forest
2830	Tottenham Hotspur	2867	Bradford
2831	Serlby Hall	2868	Bradford City
2832	Belvoir Castle	2869	Barnsley
2833	Kimbolton Castle	2870	City of London
2834	Hinchingbrooke	2871	Manchester City
2835	Milton	2872	West Ham United
2836	Harlaxton Manor		

C 5 Class (G.C. Atlantic)

5258	The Rt. Hon. Viscount Cross, G.C.B., G.C.S.I.	5364	Lady Faringdon
5259	King Edward VII	5365	Sir William Poilitt

D9 Class

104 Queen Alexandra	6021 Queen Mary

" Director " Class, D10

429 Prince Henry	5434 The Earl of Kerry
430 Purdon Viccars	5435 Sir Clement Royds
431 Edwin A. Beazley	5436 Sir Berkeley Sheffield
432 Sir Edward Fraser	5437 Prince George
433 Walter Burgh Gair	5438 Worsley-Taylor

" Director " Class, D11

501 Mons	6385 Luckie Mucklebackit
502 Zeebrugge	6386 Lord Glenallan
503 Somme	6387 Lucy Ashton
504 Jutland	6388 Captain Craigengelt
505 Ypres	6389 Haystoun of Bucklaw
506 Butler-Henderson	6390 Hobbie Elliott
507 Gerard Powys Dewhurst	6391 Wizard of the Moor
508 Prince of Wales	6392 Malcolm Graeme
509 Prince Albert	6393 The Fiery Cross
510 Princess Mary	6394 Lord James of Douglas
511 Marne	6395 Ellen Douglas
378 Bailie MacWheeble	6396 Maid of Lorn
379 Baron of Bradwardine	6397 The Lady of the Lake
380 Evan Dhu	6398 Laird of Balmawhapple
381 Flora Maclvor	6399 Allan Bane
382 Colonel Gardiner	6400 Roderick Dhu
383 Jonathan Oldbuck	6401 James Fitzjames
384 Edie Ochiltree	

D16 Class

7770 Claud Hamilton

" Scott " Class, D29

243 Meg Merrilees	9361 Vich Ian Vohr
244 Madge Wildfire	9362 Ravenswood
245 Bailie Nicol Jarvie	9895 Rob Roy
338 Helen MacGregor	9896 Dandie Dinmont
339 Ivanhoe	9897 Redgauntlet
340 Lady of Avenel	9898 Sir Walter Scott
359 Dirk Hatteraick	9899 Jeanie Deans
360 Guy Mannering	9900 The Fair Maid

" Scott " Class, D30

9363 Hal o' the Wynd	9421 Jingling Geordie
9400 The Dougal Cratur	9422 Kenilworth
9409 The Pirate	9423 Quentin Durward
9410 Meg Dods	9424 Lady Rowena
9411 Dominie Sampson	9425 Kettledrummle
9412 Laird o' Monkbarns	9426 Norna
9413 Caleb Balderstone	9427 Lord Glenvarloch
9414 Dugald Dalgetty	9428 Adam Woodcock
9415 Claverhouse	9497 Peter Poundtext
9416 Ellangowan	9498 Father Ambrose
9417 Cuddie Headrigg	9499 Wandering Willie
9418 Dumbiedykes	9500 Black Duncan
9419 The Talisman	9501 Simon Glover
9420 The Abbot	

" Glen " Class, D34

9034 Glen Garvin	9298 Glen Sheil
9035 Glen Gloy	9307 Glen Nevis
9100 Glen Dochart	9405 Glen Spean
9149 Glen Finnan	9406 Glen Croe
9153 Glen Fruin	9407 Glen Beasdale
9221 Glen Orchy	9408 Glen Sloy
9241 Glen Ogle	9490 Glen Dessary
9242 Glen Mamie	9492 Glen Gour
9256 Glen Douglas	9493 Glen Luss
9258 Glen Roy	9494 Glen Loy
9266 Glen Falloch	9495 Glen Mallie
9270 Glen Garry	9496 Glen Moidart
9278 Glen Lyon	9502 Glen Fintaig
9281 Glen Murran	9503 Glen Arklet
9287 Glen Gyle	9504 Glen Aladale
9291 Glen Quoich	9505 Glen Cona

D40 Class

6845 George Davidson	6849 Gordon Highlander
6846 Benachie	6850 Hatton Castle
6847 Sir David Stewart	6852 Glen Grant
6848 Andrew Bain	6854 Southesk

" Shire " Class, D49

234 Yorkshire	309 Banffshire
236 Lancashire	310 Kinross-shire
245 Lincolnshire	311 Peebles-shire
246 Morayshire	318 Cambridgeshire
249 Aberdeenshire	320 Warwickshire
250 Perthshire	322 Huntingdonshire
251 Derbyshire	327 Nottinghamshire
253 Oxfordshire	329 Inverness-shire
256 Hertfordshire	335 Bedfordshire
264 Stirlingshire	2753 Cheshire
265 Lanarkshire	2754 Rutlandshire
266 Forfarshire	2755 Berkshire
270 Argyllshire	2756 Selkirkshire
277 Berwickshire	2757 Dumfries-shire
281 Dumbartonshire	2758 Northumberland
306 Roxburghshire	2759 Cumberland
307 Kincardineshire	2760 Westmorland

" Hunt " Class, D49

201 The Bramham Moor	288 The Percy
205 The Albrighton	292 The Southwold
211 The York and Ainsty	297 The Cottesmore
214 The Atherstone	298 The Pytchley
217 The Belvoir	336 The Quorn
220 The Zetland	352 The Meynell
222 The Berkeley	353 The Derwent
226 The Bilsdale	357 The Fernie
230 The Brocklesby	359 The Fitzwilliam
232 The Badsworth	361 The Garth
235 The Bedale	362 The Goathland
238 The Burton	363 The Grafton
247 The Blankney	364 The Grove
255 The Braes of Derwent	365 The Morpeth
258 The Cattistock	366 The Oakley
269 The Cleveland	368 The Puckeridge
273 The Holderness	370 The Rufford
274 The Craven	374 The Sinnington
279 The Cotswold	375 The South Durham
282 The Hurworth	376 The Staintondale
283 The Middleton	377 The Tynedale

J36 Class

9176 French	9650 Haig
9611 Allenby	9657 Plumer
9612 Ypres	9659 Gough
9643 Arras	9660 Horne
9646 Somme	9673 Maude
9647 Albert	9682 Joffre
9648 Mons	

" Loch " Class, K 2

4674 Loch Arkaig	4697 Loch Quoich
4682 Loch Lochy	4698 Loch Rannoch
4684 Loch Garry	4699 Loch Laidon
4685 Loch Treig	4700 Loch Lomond
4691 Loch Morar	4701 Loch Laggan
4692 Loch Eil	4704 Loch Oich
4693 Loch Sheil	

" Loch " Class, K 4

3441 Loch Long	3444 Lord of the Isles
3442 The Great Marquess	3445 MacCailin Mor
3443 Cameron of Lochiel	3446 MacLeod of MacLeod

K 4 Class

P 2 Class

2001 Cock o' the North
2003 Lord President

2004 Mons Meg

M 2 Class (ex L.P.T.B.)

6154 Lord Aberconway
6155 Robert H. Selbie

6156 Charles Jones
6157 Brill

" Green Arrow " Class, V2

4771 Green Arrow
4780 The Snapper, The East Yorkshire Regiment—The Duke of York's Own
4806 The Green Howards, Alexandra, Princess of Wales's Own Yorkshire Regiment

4818 St. Peter's School, York, A.D. 627

4831 Durham School

4843 King's Own Yorkshire Light Infantry

4844 Coldstreamer

V 4 Class
3401 Bantam Cock

SENTINEL STEAM RAIL CARS
100 h.p. (2-cylinder)

26 Tally-ho
210 High Flyer
212 Eclipse
225 True Blue
226 Ebor
237 Rodney
238 Yorkshire Huzzar
244 True Briton
250 Rob Roy

253 Red Rover
254 Phoenix
263 North Star
265 Neptune
272 Hero
273 Trafalgar
283 Teazle
2135 Integrity

100 h.p. (6-cylinder)

33	Highland Chieftain	2219	New Fly
34	Tweedside	2231	Swift
35	Nettle	2235	Britannia
36	Royal Eagle	2236	British Queen
37	Clydesdale	2242	Cornwallis
38	Pearl	2245	Criterion
312	Retaliator	2257	Defiance
313	Banks of Don	2261	Diligence
314	Queen of Beauty	2267	Recovery
2133	Cleveland	2268	Emerald
2136	Hope	2270	Independent
2139	Hark Forward	2271	Industry
2140	Eagle	2276	North Briton
2144	Traveller	2279	Norfolk
2147	Woodpecker	31073	Quicksilver
2151	Umpire	51909	Waterloo
2198	Times	51912	Rising Sun
2217	Royal Charlotte	51913	Rival
2218	Telegraph		

PRINCIPAL DIMENSIONS OF L.N.E.R. LOCOMOTIVES.

All locomotives have two cylinders unless another number appears in parenthesis in the cylinders column.
An "O" denotes a 2-cylinder engine with outside cylinders.

Class	Type	Designer	Building Date	Weight of Loco. T. C.	Boiler Pressure Lb. per Sq. In.	Cylinders Ins.	Driving Wheels	Tractive Effort Lb.
A-1	4-6-2	Gresley	1922–1925	92 9	180	(3) 20 ×26	6' 8"	29,835
A-2	4-6-2	Gresley Reb. Thompson	1936	101 10	225	(3) 20 ×26	6' 2"	40,318
A-2/1	4-6-2	Thompson	1944	98 0	225	(3) 19 ×26	6' 2"	36,387
A-3	4-6-2	Gresley	1922–1934	96 5	220	(3) 19 ×26	6' 8"	32,909
A-4	4-6-2	Gresley	1935–1938	102 19	250	(3) 18½×26	6' 8"	35,455
A-5	4-6-2 T	Robinson	1911–1923	85 18	180	20 ×26	5' 7"	23,743
A-5	4-6-2 T	Robinson	1925–1926	90 11	180	20 ×26	5' 7"	23,743
A-6	4-6-2 T	W. Worsdell Reb. Raven	1907–1908	78 0	175	19 ×26	5' 1¼"	22,830
A-7	4-6-2 T	Raven	1910–1911	87 10	{ 180 / 160 }	(3) 16½×26	4' 7¼"	{ 29,403 / 26,140 }
A-8	4-6-2 T	Raven Reb. Gresley	1913–1922	86 18	175	(3) 16½×26	5' 9"	22,940
B-1	4-6-0	Thompson	1942–	71 3	225	O 20 ×26	6' 2"	26,878
B-2	4-6-0	Robinson	1912–1913	75 4 75 4	{ 180 }	21¼×26 20 ×26	6' 9"	22,700 19,644
B-3	4-6-0	Robinson and Robinson Reb. Gresley	1917–1920	79 5	180	(4) 16 ×26	6' 9"	25,145
B-3/3	4-6-0	Robinson Reb. Thompson	1917–1920	71 7	225	O 20 ×26	6' 9"	24,556

55

Class	Type	Designer	Building Date	Weight of Loco. T.C.	Boiler Pressure Lb. per Sq. In.	Cylinders Ins.	Driving Wheels	Tractive Effort Lb.
B-4	4-6-0	Robinson	1906	70 · 14	180	O 19 × 26	6' 7"	18,178
B-5	4-6-0	Robinson	1902–1904	71 · 15	180	O 21 × 26	6' 1"	22,206
B-6	4-6-0	Robinson	1918–1921	64 · 3	180	O 19 × 26	5' 8"	19,672
B-7	4-6-0	Robinson	1921–1924	65 · 4	180	O 21 × 26	5' 8"	24,030
B-8	4-6-0	Robinson	1913–1915	72 · 18	180	(4) 16 × 26	5' 7"	25,798
				79 · 10				29,952
B-9	4-6-0	Robinson	1906	74 · 7	180	O 21½ × 26	5' 7"	27,445
				65 · 0		O 20 × 26	5' 4"	23,750
				66 · 1		O 20 × 28		22,438
B-12	4-6-0	S. D. Holden	1912–1920	63 · 0	180	O 19 × 26	6' 6"	27,410
B-12/3	4-6-0	S. D. Holden / Reb. Gresley	1912–1927	69 · 10	180	O 21 × 26	6' 6"	21,969
						O 20 × 28		21,969
B-15	4-6-0	Raven	1911–1913	71 · 2	180	O 20 × 26	6' 1¼"	21,723
B-16	4-6-0	Raven	1919–1924	77 · 14	180	(3) 18½ × 26	5' 8"	30,031
B-16/2	4-6-0	Raven Reb. Gresley	1919–1924	79 · 4	180	(3) 18 × 26	5' 8"	30,031
B-16/3	4-6-0	Raven / Reb. Thompson	1919–1924	78 · 19	180	(3) 18½ × 26	5' 8"	30,031
B-17	4-6-0	Gresley	1928–1937	77 · 5	200	(3) 17½ × 26	6' 8"	25,380
B-18	4-6-0	Robinson	1903–1904	72 · 18	180	O 21 × 26	6' 9"	21,658
C-1	4-4-2	Ivatt	1902–1908	69 · 12	170	O 19 × 24	6' 8"	15,649
		Ivatt-Gresley	1902–1910	69 · 12	170	O 20 × 26	6' 8"	17,340
		Ivatt / Reb. Gresley	1904	69 · 19	170	O 20 × 24	6' 8"	18,785
C-2	4-4-2	Ivatt	1903	60 · 0	170	O 19 × 24	6' 8"	15,649
C-4	4-4-2	Robinson	1903–1906	70 · 17	180	O 20 × 24	6' 6"	17,340
				71 · ?		O 19 × 26	6' 9"	17,729

Class	Type	Designer	Date			Press.	Cyls.	Driving Wheel	Weight
C-6	4-4-2	W. Worsdell	1903–1904	76	4	175	19¾ × 28	6′ 10″	20,350
C-7	4-4-2	Raven	1910	76	4	175	19¾ × 28	6′ 10″	19,350
C-7/2	4-4-2	Raven	1911–1918	79	5	175	16½ × 26	6′ 10″	19,300
	4-4-2	Reb. Gresley	1911—1918	76	2	175	17 × 26	6′ 10″	20,446
C-12	4-4-2 T	Ivatt	1898–1907	62	6	170	18 × 26	5′ 8″	17,900
C-13	4-4-2 T	Robinson	1903–1905	66	13	175	18 × 26	5′ 7″	18,424
C-14	4-4-2 T	Robinson	1907	71	0	160	18 × 26	5′ 7″	17,100
C-15	4-4-2 T	Reid	1911–1913	68	15	175	18 × 26	5′ 9″	17,100
C-16	4-4-2 T	Reid	1915–1921	72	10	165	18 × 26	6′ 9″	18,160
C-17	4-4-2 T	Marriott	1904–1910	68	9	160	17¼ × 24	6′ 0″	19,078
D-1	4-4-0	Ivatt	1911	53	6	170	18½ × 26	6′ 8″	13,491
D-2	4-4-0	Ivatt	1897–1909	47	10	170	17½ × 26	6′ 8″	16,074
D-3	4-4-0	Ivatt / Reb. Gresley	1896–1899	45	14	175	17½ × 26	6′ 8″	14,382
									14,805
									14,805
D-6	4-4-0	Pollitt	1898–1899	49	4	160	18½ × 26	7′ 0″	14,421
D-9	4-4-0	Robinson	1901–1904	55	14	180	19 × 26	6′ 9″	17,729
D-10	4-4-0	Robinson	1913	61	0	180	20 × 26	6′ 9″	19,644
D-11	4-4-0	Robinson	1919–1924	61	3	180	20 × 26	6′ 9″	19,644
D-13	4-4-0	J. Holden	1895–1897	48	6	180	18 × 24	7′ 0″	14,163
D-15	4-4-0	J. Holden	1900–1903	52	4	180	19 × 26	7′ 0″	17,096
D-16	4-4-0	J. Holden & Hill / Reb. Hill	1901–1923	54	18	180	19 × 26	7′ 0″	17,096
D-16/3	4-4-0	J. Holden & Hill / Reb. Gresley	1900–1923	55	18	180	19 × 26	7′ 0″	17,096
D-17	4-4-0	W. Worsdell	1893–1897	50	2	160	19 × 26	7′ 1¼″	15,001
D-20	4-4-0	W. Worsdell	1899–1907	54	2	175	19 × 26	6′ 10″	17,026

* Low pressure cyls.   † High pressure cyls.

57

Class	Type	Designer	Building Date	Weight of Loco. T. C.	Boiler Pressure Lb. per Sq. In.	Cylinders Ins.	Driving Wheels	Tractive Effort Lb.
D-20	4-4-0	W. Worsdell	1899-1906	55 9	175	19 × 26	6′ 10″	17,026
D-21	4-4-0	Reb. Gresley	1908-1909	59 0	175	19 × 26	6′ 10″	17,026
D-29	4-4-0	W. Worsdell	1909-1911	54 4	190	19 × 26	6′ 6″	19,434
D-30/1	4-4-0	Reid	1912	57 6	165	20 × 26	6′ 6″	18,700
D-30/2	4-4-0	Reid	1914-1920	57 16	165	20 × 26	6′ 6″	18,700
D-31	4-4-0	Holmes / Reb. Reid	1890-1899	46 8	175	18¼ × 26	6′ 6″	16,514
D-32	4-4-0	Reid	1906	53 14	180	19 × 26	6′ 0″	19,945
D-33	4-4-0	Reid	1909-1910	54 3	180	19 × 26	6′ 0″	19,945
D-34	4-4-0	Reid	1913-1920	57 4	165	20 × 26	6′ 0″	20,258
D-40	4-4-0	Pickersgill	1899-1915	46 7	165	18 × 26	6′ 1″	16,184
D-40	4-4-0	Heywood	1920-1921	48 13	165	18 × 26	6′ 1″	16,184
D-41	4-4-0	Pickersgill and J. Johnson	1895-1898	45 0	165	18 × 26	6′ 1″	16,184
D-42	4-4-0	Manson	1888	44 0	165	18 × 26	6′ 0½″	16,296
D-49/1	4-4-0	Gresley	1927-1929	66 0	180	17 × 26	6′ 8″	21,556
D-49/2	4-4-0	Gresley	1928-1935	64 10	180	17 × 26	6′ 8″	21,556
D-53	4-4-0	S. W. Johnson / Reb. Nash	1894-1899	44 7	160	18½ × 26	6′ 6½″	15,416
D	4-4-0	Gresley / Reb. Thompson	1934	52 0	180	20 × 26	6′ 8″	19,890
E-4	2-4-0	J. Holden	1891-1902	40 6	160	17½ × 24	5′ 8″	14,700
F-1	2-4-2 T	Parker	1889-1892	60 12	160	18 × 24	5′ 7″	15,784
F-2	2-4-2 T	Pollitt	1898	62 6	160	18 × 24	5′ 7″	17,100
F-3	2-4-2 T	J. Holden	1893-1902	58 12	160	17½ × 24	5′ 8″	14,709
F-4	2-4-2 T	J. Holden	1906-1909	53 19	160	17½ × 24	5′ 4″	15,618
F-5	2-4-2 T	Holden	1903-1909	53 19	180	17½ × 24	5′ 4″	17,571

Class	Type	Designer	Dates			Pressure	Cylinders	Coupled wheels		Weight
G-5	0-4-4 T	W. Worsdell	1894–1901	54	4	160	18 × 24	5'	1¼"	17,200
G-10	0-4-4 T	J. Johnson	1893	53	17	165	17½ × 26	5'	0"	18,612
H-2	4-4-4 T	Jones	1920–1921	78	14	170	19 × 26	5'	9"	19,656
J-1	0-6-0	Ivatt	1908	46	10	175	18 × 26	5'	8"	18,427
J-2	0-6-0	Ivatt	1912	50	12	175	19 × 26	5'	8"	19,945
J-3	0-6-0	P. Stirling & Ivatt · Reb. Gresley	1892–1901	42		175	17½ × 26	5'	2"	19,105
J-4	0-6-0	P. Stirling & Ivatt	1896–1901	41	5	175	17½ × 26	5'	2"	19,105 / 20,210
J-5	0-6-0	Ivatt	1909–1910	47	6	175	18 × 26	5'	2"	19,632
J-6	0-6-0	Ivatt & Gresley	1911–1922	50	10	170	19 × 26	5'	2"	21,875
J-10	0-6-0	Parker & Pollitt	1892–1902	41	6	160	18 × 26	5'	1"	18,781
J-11	0-6-0	Robinson & Robinson · Reb. Thompson	1901–1910	52	2	180	18½ × 26	5'	2"	21,959
J-15	0-6-0	J. Holden	1886–1913	37	2	160	17½ × 24	4'	11"	16,942
J-17	0-6-0	J. Holden	1900–1910	45	8	180	19 × 26	4'	11"	24,340
J-19	0-6-0	Hill	1916–1920	50	7	180	19 × 28	4'	11"	26,212
J-20	0-6-0	Reb. Gresley · Hill	1920–1923	54	15	170	20 × 28	4'	11"	27,430 / 29,044
J-21	0-6-0	T. W. Worsdell · Reb. W. Worsdell	1886–1895	42 / 43	1 / 15	180	20 × 28	5'	1¼"	17,266 / 19,237
J-24	0-6-0	T. W. Worsdell · W. Worsdell	1894–1898	38 / 39	10 / 11	160	18 × 24 / 19 × 24	4'	7¼"	20,840 / 19,141 / 20,219
J-25	0-6-0	W. Worsdell and W. Worsdell · Reb. Raven	1898–1902	39	11	160	18½ × 26	4'	7¼"	21,904
J-26	0-6-0	Reb. Raven · W. Worsdell	1904–1905	46	16	180	18½ × 26	4'	7¼"	24,642

Class	Type	Designer	Building Date	Weight of Loco. T. C.	Boiler Pressure Lb. per Sq. In.	Cylinders Ins.	Driving Wheels	Tractive Effort Lb.
J-27	0-6-0	W. Worsdell	1906-1908	47 0	180	18 × 26	4′ 7¼″	24,642
J-35	0-6-0	Raven	1921-1923	49 10	180	18¼ × 26	5′ 0″	22,082
J-36	0-6-0	Reid / Holmes — Reb. Reid	1906-1912 / 1888-1900	50 15 / 41 19	165	18¼ × 26	5′ 0″	19,691
J-37	0-6-0	Reid	1914-1921	54 14	180	19¼ × 26	5′ 8″	25,211
J-38	0-6-0	Gresley	1926	58 19	180	20 × 26	4′ 8″	28,414
J-39	0-6-0	Gresley	1926-1941	57 17	180	20 × 26	5′ 2″	25,664
J-40	0-6-0	S. W. Johnson	1896-1899	38 16	160	18 × 26	5′ 3″	18,184
J-50/1	0-6-0 T	Gresley	1914	56 6	175	18½ × 26	4′ 8″	23,636
J-50/2	0-6-0 T	Gresley	1914-1924	57 0	175	18½ × 26	4′ 8″	23,636
J-50/3	0-6-0 T	Gresley		58 3	175	18½ × 26	4′ 8″	
J-50/4	0-6-0T	Gresley	1926-1939		175	18½ × 26	4′ 8″	24,636
J-52	0-6-0ST	P. Stirling / Reb. Gresley / Ivatt	1892-1897	51 14	170	18 × 26	4′ 8″	21,737
J-55	0-6-0ST	P. Stirling / Reb. Gresley	1897-1908 / 1891-1892	45 16	175 / 175 / 160	17½ × 26	4′ 8″	22,378 / 21,151 / 19,339
J-60	0-6-0 T	Kitson & Co.	1897	46 16	160	17 × 24	4′ 7″	17,468
J-62	0-6-0ST	Pollitt	1897	30 17	150	13 × 20 (O O)	3′ 6″	10,260
J-63	0-6-0 T	Robinson	1906-1914	37 9	150	13 × 20	3′ 6″	10,260
J-65	0-6-0 T	J. Holden	1889-1893	36 11	160	14 × 20	4′ 0″	11,106
J-66	0-6-0 T	J. Holden	1886-1889	40 6	160	16½ × 22	4′ 0″	16,970
J-67/1	0-6-0 T	J. Holden	1890-1901	40 0	160	16½ × 22	4′ 0″	16,970
J-67/2	0-6-0 T	J. Holden and S. D. Holden	1890-1912	41 8	160	16½ × 22	4′ 0″	16,970
J-68	0-6-0 T	S. D. Holden	1912-1923	42 9	180	16½ × 22	4′ 0″	19,091
J-69	0-6-0 T	J. Holden	1890-1904	42 9	180	16½ × 22	4′ 0″	19,091
J-70	0-6-0 T	J. Holden		27		13 × 15		8,931

Class	Type	Designer	Dates			Pressure	Cylinders	Driving wheels	Tractive effort
J-71	0-6-0 T	T. W. Worsdell...	1886–1895	37	12	140	18 × 22	4′ 7¼″	15,353
J-72	0-6-0 T	W. Worsdell	1898–1925	38	12	140	16¾ × 22	4′ 1¼″	13,300
J-73	0-6-0 T	W. Worsdell	1891–1892	46	15	160	17 × 24	4′ 7¼″	16,700
J-75	0-6-0 T	M. Stirling	1908	47	7	175	19 × 24	4′ 6″	18,788
J-77	0-6-0 T	Fletcher & T. W. Worsdell / Reb. W. Worsdell and Raven	1874–1884	43	0	160	17 × 22 · 18 × 26	4′ 1¼″	17,560 · 21,320 · 23,197
J-83	0-6-0 T	Holmes	1900–1901	45	5	150	17 × 26	4′ 6″	17,744
J-88	0-6-0 T	Holmes	1904–1919	38	14	130	15 × 22	3′ 9″	12,155
J-92	0-6-0-OCT	Contractors	1868	40	8	140	16 × 20	4′ 0″	13,962
J-93	0-6-0 T	S. W. Johnson	1897–1905	37	14	150	20 × 26	3′ 7″	15,181
K-2	2-6-0	Gresley	1912–1921	64	8	180	18½ × 26	5′ 8″	23,400
K-3	2-6-0	Gresley	1921–1937	72	12	180	18½ × 26	5′ 8″	30,031
K-4	2-6-0	Gresley	1937–1938	68	8	200	21 × 26	5′ 2″	36,598
L-1	2-6-4 T	Robinson	1914–1917	97	9	180	20 × 26	5′ 1″	28,759
L-2	2-6-4 T	Hally	1925	87	7	200	19 × 26	5′ 6″	26,085
M-1	0-6-4 T	Thom	1904–1906	77	11	160	19 × 26	4′ 9″	26,036
M-2	0-6-4 T	Jones	1916	71	1	160	20 × 26	5′ 9″	22,394
N-1	0-6-2 T	Ivatt	1907–1912	65	17	175 / 170	18 × 26	5′ 8″	20,498 · 18,427
N-2	0-6-2 T	Gresley	1920–1929	71	9	170	19 × 26	5′ 8″	17,901 · 19,945
N-4	0-6-2 T	Parker	1889–1891	61	9	160	18 × 26	5′ 1″	18,781
N-5/2	0-6-2 T	Parker & Pollitt...	1891–1901	62	7	160	18 × 26	5′ 1″	18,781
N-5/3	0-6-2 T	Pollitt... / Reb. Robinson	1898	64	13	160	18½ × 26	5′ 1″	19,842
N-7	0-6-2 T	Hill & Gresley ...	1914–1928	64	17	180	18 × 24	4′ 10″	20,512
N-8	0-6-2 T	T. W. Worsdell... / Reb. W. Worsdell	1886–1890	56	5	160	18 × 24	5′ 1¼″	17,266

Class	Type	Designer	Building Date	Weight of Loco. T.C.	Boiler Pressure Lb. per Sq. In.	Cylinders Ins.	Driving Wheels	Tractive Effort Lb.
—N-8—	contd.	T. W. Worsdell...	1886–1890	58 14	160	19 × 24	5' 1¼"	19,237
		Reb. Raven						20,840
N-9	0-6-2 T	W. Worsdell	1893–1894	56 10	160	19 × 26	5' 1¼"	20,840
N-10	0-6-2 T	W. Worsdell	1902–1903	57 14	160	19 × 26	4' 7¼"	21,904
N-11	0-6-2 T	Kitson & Co.	1901	58 4	175	18½ × 26	4' 9"	21,976
N-12	0-6-2 T	M. Stirling	1901	58 0	175	18 × 26	4' 6"	23,197
N-13	0-6-2 T	M. Stirling	1913–1914	61 9	175	18 × 26	4' 6"	23,197
N-14	0-6-2 T	Reid	1909	62 19	175	18 × 26	4' 6"	23,205
N-15	0-6-2 T	Reid	1910–1923	60 18	175	18 × 26	4' 6"	23,205
O-1	2-8-0	Gresley	1913–1919	76 4	180	21 × 28	4' 8"	33,736
O-1	2-8-0	Robinson	1921–1921	73 6	225	20 × 26	4' 8"	35,518
O-2	2-8-0	Reb. Thompson	1918	76 8	180	(3) 18 × 26	4' 8"	34,523
O-2	2-8-0	Gresley	1921–1943	78 13	180	(3) 18½ × 26	4' 8"	36,470
O-4/1 /2&/6 /4/5 &/7	2-8-0	Robinson	1911–1921	73 4	180	21 × 26	4' 8"	31,236
O-4/4	2-8-0	Reb. Gresley	1911–1921	74 13	180	21 × 26	4' 8"	31,236
	2-8-0	Robinson	1918–1919	73 16	180	21 × 26	4' 8"	31,236
P-1	2-8-2	Gresley	1925	91 14	220	(3) 19 × 26	5' 2"	42,466
P-2	2-8-2	Gresley	1934–1936	107 3	220	21 × 26	6' 2"	43,462
Q-1	0-8-0 T	Robinson	1902–1911	69 18	180	19 × 26	4' 8"	25,644
		Reb. Thompson	1902–1911	73 13				
Q-4	0-8-0	Robinson	1902–1911	63 0	180	19 × 26	4' 8"	25,644
Q-5	0-8-0	W. Worsdell	1901–1911	64 1	175	21 × 26	4' 7¼"	31,326
	0-8-0			58 8		20 × 26		28,000
Q-6	0-8-0	Raven	1913–1921	65 18		20 × 26	4' 7¼"	28,800

Table continued (column headings are cut off at the top edge of the page):

Class	Wheel arr. / Type	Builder / Designer	Date			Pressure	Cylinders	Driving wheel	Weight
S-1/2	0-8-4 T	Robinson	1908	104	9	180	(3) 18 × 26	4' 8"	34,523
S-1/3	0-8-4 T	Reb. Gresley	1932	104	5	180	(3) 18 × 26	4' 8"	34,523
T-1	4-8-0 T	Raven	1909–1925	85	8	175	(3) 18 × 26	4' 7¼"	34,080
U-1	2-8-8-2 T	Gresley	1925	178	1	180	(6) 18½ × 26	4' 8"	72,940
V-1	2-6-2 T	Gresley	1930–1939	86	16	180	(3) 16 × 26	5' 8"	22,464
V-2	2-6-2	Gresley	1936–1943	93	2	220	(3) 18½ × 26	6' 2"	33,730
V-3	2-6-2 T	Gresley	1935–1940	86	16	200	(3) 16 × 26	5' 8"	24,960
V-4	2-6-2	Gresley	1941	70	8	250	(3) 15 × 26	5' 8"	27,420
W-1	4-6-4	Gresley*	1929	107	17	250	(3) 20 × 26	6' 8"	41,437
Y-1	0-4-0 T	Sentinel Co.	1925–1933	19	16	275	6¾ × 9	2' 6"	7,260
Y-3	0-4-0 T	Sentinel Co.	1927–1931	20	16	275	6¾ × 9	2' 6"	8,872
Y-4	0-4-0 T	Hill	1913–1921	38	1	180	O 17 × 20	3' 10"	12,600
Y-5	0-4-0ST	J. Holden	1903	21	4	140	O 12 × 20	3' 7"	15,962
Y-6	0-4-0 T	J. Holden	1897	21	5	140	O 11 × 15	3' 1"	19,224
Y-7	0-4-0 T	T. W. Worsdell	1897–1923	22	14	140	11 × 15	3' 6¼"	7,970
Y-8	0-4-0 T	T. W. Worsdell	1890	15	10	140	O 14 × 20	3' 0"	5,837
Y-9	0-4-0 T	Holmes	1882–1899	27	16	130	11 × 20	3' 8"	11,041
Y-10	0-4-0ST	Sentinel Co.	1930	23	19	275	O 6¾ × 9	3' 2"	5,999
Z-4	0-4-2 T	Manning-Wardle	1915	25	17	160	O 13 × 20	3' 6"	10,945
Z-5	0-4-2 T	Manning-Wardle	1915	30	18	160	O 14 × 20	4' 0"	11,107

63

NOTES.—O — Outside cylinders (2).   T — Tank.   ST — Saddle Tank.   C — Crane engines.

* Originally designed as 4-6-4 compound engine with water tube boiler, and subsequently rebuilt as 3-cylinder simple engine with a Stephenson-type boiler.

ELECTRIC PASSENGER

Class	Type	Designer	Date Built	Weight of Loco. T. C.		Voltage	Tractive Effort Lb.
				T.	C.		
Express ...	4-6-4	Raven	1922	110	1	1,500 DC.	28,000

ELECTRIC FREIGHT

Class	Type	Designer	Date Built	Weight of Loco. T. C.		Voltage	Tractive Effort Lb.
				T.	C.		
Shunting ...	0-4-4-0	Brush & Thompson-Houston	1905	56	0	600 DC.	25,000
Shildon ...	0-4-4-0	Raven	1914	74	8	1,500 DC.	28,000
Mixed Traffic ...	0-4-4-0	Gresley	1940	87	18	1,500 DC.	45,000

PETROL FREIGHT

Class	Engine	Type	Designer	Date Built	Weight of Loco. T. C.		Horse Power
					T.	C.	
Y-11	Petrol	0-4-0	Motor, Rail & Tram Car Co. ...	1921	8	0	40